Reclaiming our Land

Rob Gibson

First Published in 2020 by Rob Gibson
In assocation with
Highland Heritage Educational Trust (HHET)
ISBN: 978-1-5272-8181-3

Design & Typesetting by Lumphanan Press
www.lumphananpress.co.uk

Printed & Bound by Ingram Spark, UK

Contents

Acknowledgements

Many people encouraged me to complete this book. Some are mentioned in the text and deserve much thanks. David Worthington, Ian Robertson, Mairi McFadyen, Mike MacKenzie, Magnus Davidson, Duncan McLean, Malcolm Kerr, Cllr Heather Anderson, Kirsteen Shields, Angus MacDonald MSP and others stand out. Thanks to my editors, Carrie Hutchinson and Duncan Lockerbie of Lumphanan Press

Illustrations are cited where known. If any source is misidentified, I apologise. I have tried to be as accurate as possible.

Above all thanks to my sparring partner in life, Eleanor Scott for her patience and cross-examination of my arguments. To her this book is dedicated with love

Recalling our land history
A timeline

Early Middle Ages, 6th century to 11th century

Pre-feudal society had various types of land holding. Leading territorial thanes were renamed earls under King Malcolm 1. Exclusive hunting forests for monarchs and barons were created. Ideas of service to superiors developed as homage and fealty. Hereditary offices were created at all levels. Lands were to be divided by forfeiture of enemies. Feudal ideas from Low Countries and Normandy were imported.

1123–50

King David 1 invited the Norman knights into Scotland with offers of land under a military feudal system. The feudal system placed all people into rank order from God, down through the king to earls, barons, knights, commoners and serfs.

16th century

Feudal superiorities and the growing role of great landowners or territorial magnates tended to replace services according to rank with annual feudal dues, land use and sale conditions. From the 1520s the corrupt Roman Catholic Church which owned half of Scotland was targeted to replace clerics with lay abbots and other administrators. Clan chiefs and local landowners placed their sons in posts to appropriate fertile church lands which became their private property.

1532
Court of Session was created to regulate land matters.

1557
Lords of the Congregation ensured that church property went to the largest land holders using the Protestant Reformation turmoil. Primogeniture and succession was enshirned in law.

1599
King James VI demanded Highland lairds proved ownership of land by title deeds.

1608
The first of many Commonty Acquisition Acts started raids by lairds on open lands to exclude common access.

1608–09
StatuteS of Iona passed. Highland and Island chiefs forced into feudal system and sons educated in the Lowlands.

1617
Land Registration Act set up the Register of Sasines (not compulsory till 1690) and the Prescription Act legalised land holdings taken into noble hands.

1685
The Entail Act was passed. It ensured indebted landowners could not be dispossessed.

1707
Treaty of Union of England and Scotland recognises landowners' rights.

1746
The Abolition of Hereditary Jurisdiction saw justice administered through sheriffs appointed by the Crown.

1792
Bliadhna nan Caorach – the Year of the Sheep – a huge illegal sheep drive from the Oykell to Beauly was thwarted by militia.

1812–30
In this period there were many evictions of Sutherland straths in the hope of replacing the native people with sheep. Other areas followed as ancient clan chiefs lost their lands through increasing debt burdens.

1832
The Day Trespass Act sought to exclude poaching of game and deer.

1845–50
The potato blight hit Western Europe. Ireland was the most affected, a result of deliberate UK policies. Scottish sufferers were saved from starvation by Free Church and Central Relief.

1848
The Chartists agitated for more land for the people. Ignored. Queen Victoria and Prince Albert leased Balmoral Castle (they bought it in 1852) starting the 'rage for sport', aped by old and new landowners.

1872
After sustained agitation by radicals, the UK parliament agreed to Lord Derby's demand for a statistically-sound return of land holdings. Scottish Returns delivered in February 1874 showed that of 18 million acres 92.3% was owned by 1,809 lairds, 69% by 345 lairds and, of 2,500,000 million Scots, only 132,230 Scots owned any land. This showed that Scotland had the most concentrated ownership of land in Europe.

1879
Henry George published Progress and Poverty, an argument for a single (land) tax. Disappointed in Ireland he turned his attention to Scotland in 1883.

1880

Irish Home Rule agitation was linked to the security of tenure for small farmers which stemmed from the 2nd Irish Land Act. This offered fair rents, fixity of tenure and free sale of farms. But the Irish Land League, founded in 1879, continued agitation against evictions.

1881

An agricultural depression. Cheap food imports, bad weather, evictions for arrears of rent increase sometimes led to violent responses in both Ireland and Scotland. Lord MacDonald's tenants on Ben Lee near Portree became a flashpoint.

April 1882

Peaceful protest turned violent at the Braes as Sheriff officers sought to arrest ring leaders. Running fights to free those arrested led to press reports of a Crofters' War. Attention to grievances motivated urban radicals and Gaelic revivalists. Michael Davitt visited Skye shortly after the Braes clash to whip up support for land reform and made links to the Irish cause. Sympathetic MPs called for enquiry. A case for land nationalisation was published by AR Wallace which competed with the community land value theory.

1883

The 1st Agricultural Holdings (Scotland) Act gave tenants greater security of tenure and rights to compensation for improvements. Gladstone's 2nd government launched a Royal Commission into the condition of tenants (crofters) in the Highlands and Islands led by Lord Napier. HLLRA (Highland Land Law Reform Association) of London incorporated the Inverness, Glasgow and Edinburgh bodies and encouraged branch formation in every community. Its officers primed local people to give evidence to Napier at 61 meetings and, for the first time, 775 persons did so in Gaelic.

1884

Henry George toured the country and set up the Scottish Land

Restoration League to promote the single tax and fight elections. Napier published his evidence and report.

1885

Voting franchise was extended to include male crofters. The Crofters' Party win four county seats and one group of burghs in the Highlands. The abortive Crofting Bill was launched by Gladstone's government.

1886

A new Bill, based on the 1880 Irish Land Act, met most crofters wishes. Fair rents were to be decided by a Crofters Commission, and there was to be compensation for improvements and hereditary tenancies of crofts. But the restoration of the land lost to sheep farms was not included, so the agitation continued as the economic conditions deteriorated. The incoming Tory government was determined to crack down on law breaking. In November starving Lewis crofters conducted the Great Deer Raid in Pairc but its leaders were acquitted of rioting.

1887–88

More land raiding on Lewis, Assynt and elsewhere. Troops and the navy were sent in to keep peace.

1892

Liberals again rule and set up 'Red Deer' Royal Commission for the Highlands and Islands targeting land for reclamation and croft extension. The commission reported in 1895, but it had no powers to apply for money for land purchase.

1897

The Tory government created the Scottish Congested Districts Board on Irish lines to promote peasant proprietorship. Some small land purchases were made, but the Scottish land hunger was unabated.

1904

CDB buys Glendale Estate and sells land to 147 crofters on 50-year mortgages in 1908

1906

The Liberal Government was intent on major land reform. Lloyd George planned a land valuation study in order to charge increment value duty.

1911

George's land study begun after the House of Lords powers were curbed. The Scottish report was delivered in 1915. But the tax scheme was blocked by a Tory majority in 1920.

1912

The Pentland Act passed. It covered all small holdings across Scotland including crofts under the Board of Agriculture. The first Crofters Commission was abolished.

1913

The National Farmers Union of Scotland (NFUS) was founded to lobby for better farm support.

1919

The Land Settlement Act gave support in kind and cash to abate further land raiding.

1923

The Stornoway Trust was created as Lord Leverhulme relinquished ownership in Lewis.

1929–31

Chancellor Snowden maintained the case for site value rating on the lines of Lloyd George's aborted proposals.

1948
Knoydart land raid as a result of the Labour Government support of big estates.

1949
Security of tenure and succession was strengthened for farm tenants.

1952
A Royal Commission on crofting led to rebirth of the Crofters Commission in 1955. Attempts to register all crofts and proposals to restructure crofting townships was stalled.

1961
A new Bill encouraged subletting with Crofters Commission approval and also ruled out compulsory amalgamation of crofts. Depopulation was still rampant from the north-west Highlands and Islands.

1963
The Scottish Law Commission proposed the modernisation of heritable property and the abolition of feu duties.

1965
The incoming Labour Government created the Highlands and Islands Development Board with the intention of tackling population loss and effecting land use change.

1976
Labour took on a previous Tory idea and passed a law which allowed croft purchases at 15 times the annual rental.

1991
A new farm tenancy law again bolstered security of tenure and assignation rules.

1993
Assynt crofters successfully purchased North Lochinver Estate – the first tenant owned estate in Scotland.

1995
The Local Government Reform Act contained the abolition of shooting rates.

1997
The Highlands and Islands Enterprise Land Unit was created by the incoming Labour Government. Eigg gained its freedom after a ten year struggle.

1999
Knoydart freed 51 years after the land raid. The Scottish Parliament is 'reconvened'.

2000
The Feudal System was abolished by the Scottish Parliament, along with the Title Conditions and Tenements Act, these Acts became fully operational in 2004.

2003
The Agricultural Holdings Act created short and limited duration tenancies. The Land Reform (Scotland) Act defined the right to roam, community and crofting right to buy.

2006
The Crofting Reform Act. Minor changes to existing practice further complicated croft laws.

2010
The Crofting Reform Act included various items remaining from the 2006 law.

2011
Following the SNP manifesto commitment the First Minister instigated the Land Reform Review Group.

2012

The Aquaculture & Wild Fisheries Act made salmon fisheries boards open to public scrutiny and included river catchment monthly reports on sea lice numbers.

2012

The Agricultural Holdings Act increased scope for tenant assignations.

2012

The Agricultural Holdings Amendment Order set in motion a remedial action following the Supreme Court ruling on the 2003 provisions to increase security for limited duration farm tenancies.

2014

The Final Report of Land Reform Review Group, 'The Land of Scotland and the Common Good', contains 60 recommendations.

November 2014

Nicola Sturgeon announced radical land reform proposals.

2015

The Community Empowerment Act enhanced urban, crofting and other rural community rights to buy.

2016

The Land Reform Act implemented parts of the Land Reform Review Group proposals and proposals from the Agricultural Holding Legislative Reform Group.

Introduction

Despite having been my plan for some years, retiring as an MSP was still a real wrench. This emotion was eased somewhat by a sense of having reached a destination of sorts on land reform's long and winding road. By the time of my retirement in March 2016 progressive land reform policies were rooted at the heart of government and in the public discourse. These were backed up by a Statement of Rights and Responsibilities and the creation of a Scottish Land Commission which had the overwhelming support of MSPs across all parties but the Conservatives.

As we reached the final stages of the Land Reform (Scotland) Bill in early 2016, I began reflecting on the progress of land reform over the past half century. Since my student days in the late 1960s the pace of change had quickened, stuttered and regained momentum with changes of government, and then it had fundamentally taken off with the popular vote in favour of creating our new Scottish Parliament.

It seemed fitting to find a way to assess the various phases of change in the land reform story which I witnessed and took a part in achieving. This was helpfully focused by a conversation with Mairi McFadyen in the summer of 2017. Before that I had explored the prospects of researching a PhD with the University of the Highlands and Islands History Department. But Mairi urged me to tell the story in my own words, not in some dry academic text which would need translation for public consumption after possibly seven years work. The idea of a thematic study was prompted by her reference to Alastair McIntosh and his interpretation of Rekindling Community[1]. This drew on social action theory from Brazil and liberation theology from Peru that encouraged communities to recognise, as a starting point, the value of their shared history. Alastair summarised the steps as follows:

> Re-membering, that which has been dis-membered; re-visioning, how the future could be; and re-claiming, what is needed to bring it about.

My instinct was to fit the course of my own experiences of the land reform journey into remembering, revisioning and reclaiming our land. This in no way discounts the various legal interventions from the 1880s to the 1960s to secure land for crofting and farming and to modernise the ancient recording of land ownership. In 1872, the UK Government ordered a Return of Land Ownership. It was confirmed to be a highly concentrated pattern which placed Scotland at an extreme data point on any survey of land ownership and control across Europe.

Much has been written of land history and policy. Subjects like the Highland and Lowland Clearances have produced impassioned work. Various scholars and would-be land reform activists have assessed early interventions by governments on ownership, ecology and regulation. In this account I have chosen as a starting point when the UK Labour Government created the Highlands and Islands Development Board (HIDB) in 1965. This coincided with the beginning of my own awareness of the need for Highland regeneration as I walked our hills and glens as a youth. I will describe my personal experiences from student campaigns to policy engagement and finally to the task of being an elected MSP who scrutinised and helped to develop our current land laws. I will also look back on the key moments that aided the foundation of the eventual flourishing of land reform laws in the new Scottish Parliament – when real strides could be made to reclaim or land.

---

1. Alastair McIntosh, *Rekindling Community: Connecting People, Environment and Spirituality*, Schumacher Briefings, Green Books, 2008, inspiration from Paulo Freire and Gustavo Gutiérrez, pp.77–80

Access to land had never been fully achieved previously, despite land raids and well-meaning land resettlement schemes, there was a pervasive sense that farms, estates and country parks were off limits. Ultimately, the HIDB lacked the power and resources to make real change to the injustices that it observed and this went unresolved through the tenure of two Labour Governments sandwiching a Conservative one. As James Grassie, a journalist by training and sometime information officer for the HIDB wrote:

> It was not a battle it [HIDB] had lost, but the war. The injustices inflicted by some landowners on the communities depending on them – and which had been identified by the board itself – would be allowed to continue.[2]

Any hope of real land reform was off the UK Government's agenda for 17 more years but the stirrings of change and plans for a better, more collective, approach were being hatched in those desiccated years of legislative drought.

---

2. James Grassie, *Highland Experiment: The Story of the Highlands and Islands Development Board*, Aberdeen University Press, 1983

1. Only the air is free
My political awakening

I don't like the spirit. It's too dangerous in these unsettled times. Once [you] let the masses get into their heads that landed property is a thing to play tricks with, you take the pin out of the whole system.[3]
 – *John Macnab* by John Buchan

In Scotland few of us own the land we live on and only the air is free to breathe. Centuries of land injustices have led to clashes contested in the fields, streets, communities and courts. The roots of this issue are embedded in laws largely made by, with and for the landowning elite. The legal conditions attached to landholdings have been subject to much amendment, governments of various hues adding layer upon layer of complexity to the laws of our land.

As a teenager, the launch of the HIDB in 1965, which coincided with the rise of the SNP (Scottish National Party), opened my eyes to new ways of understanding and tackling this injustice. My political awakening and enthusiastic support for independence began to take shape: I joined the campaign for crofting rights and wider land reform. In September 1970, I journeyed to Glendale, a place of lasting resonance in this continuing struggle, and there joined the Federation of Student Nationalists' (FSN) Skye Crofting Scheme. Our objectives were the resettlement of the country and the creation of a new sustainable life for many more people – aspirations which the HIDB was committed to promote.

Family visits to Dalfaber, by Aviemore, in the '60s opened my eyes

---

3. John Buchan, *John Macnab*, Houghton Mifflin, 1925

to the predicament of the tenants, when Seafield Estates sought to sell MacInnes' good grazing land from under him in order to build a timeshare resort. Witnessing this convinced me that secure local tenure of basic natural resources was the key to the repopulation of the Highlands. I came to believe then, as I do now, that radical land reform would be needed to tackle the most glaring problems of concentrated land ownership and devastated landscapes.

One such landscape was the Isle of Arran. Arran had become the destination of many of our families' holidays, thanks to my uncle and aunt moving there. In 1967, Arran was in the grip of a population crisis. The local Council of Social Services commissioned an academic critique in the hope of finding a solution.[4] But this simply opened up debate on the island's economic options for tourism, afforestation, sport shooting and so on. Given Arran's projected depopulation, I was surprised that the island had not been included in the HIDB remit. However, this was because the HIDB had been restricted to assisting only the crofting counties (Argyll, Inverness, Ross and Cromarty, Sutherland, Caithness, Orkney and Shetland) in its founding legislation. This piqued my interest. Why was Arran, with many of the same issues, excluded from the list of crofting counties? I discovered that through the influence of the great landowners on their compliant MPs during the 1880s, upland Aberdeenshire, Banff, Nairn and Perthshire were also excluded. With the crofting laws of 1955 and 1961, the Tory Governments segregated the Highlands and Islands from the rest of Scotland again with a reinstated Crofting Commission which had been absorbed by the 1911 Small Landholders Act that placed all tenant farming under the Scottish Board of Agriculture. HIDB inherited that blinkered outlook in 1965.

When hillwalking in my later teens, I noticed the many ruined houses sinking into the heather. Why were they abandoned and empty? This question spurred me search further into Highland history – school books had given me little clue beyond the Jacobite uprisings and the disaster at Culloden. While studying Modern History at the

---

4. Margaret C Storrie and CI Jackson, *Arran 1980–81:2,021?*, Arran Council for Social Service in association with the Scottish Council of Social Service, 1967

University of Dundee from 1968 to 1972, I became aware of the 1886 Crofters Holding Act and met fellow students who were interested in Highland regeneration. Late 19th century British politics which opened my eyes to the land struggles in Ireland and how they affected the balance of power at Westminster. Irish politicians Charles Stewart Parnell and Michael Davitt took opposing stances in those crucial times. The former aimed for an Irish Parliament led by landlords shorn of much of their estates, while the latter wanted all landlords removed from the island. That tension played itself out until the Irish Free State set up its Land Commission to distribute land. My reading introduced me to academic historians such as Margaret Adam, Rosalind Mitchison, Philip Gaskell and TC Smout[5] who were challenged in a string of febrile debates in the 1960s about Highland estate 'improvements' (as they called the upheavals and displacement of people or 'clearances'). The rise of social history in the 1960s revealed long-hidden evidence 'beyond the factor's window' that threatened long-accepted narratives. The works of John Prebble, Ian Grimble, Iain Fraser Grigor, James Hunter, Willie Orr and others gave voice to the crofters and cottars by delving into police records, poetry and song.[6] In particular, the controversial journalistic work of Prebble, a radical Englishman whose boyhood had been spent on the Canadian prairies, informed and fuelled up my indignation about the Highland situation. Learning about and discussing Culloden, the Highland Clearances and Glencoe was an antidote to academe's denial that these events were essential to understanding the Highlands of today.

In 1969 and 1970 the *Scottish Geographical Magazine* published maps by Roger Millman of the marches of Highland estates.[7] Intended to reform recreational policy development, these maps revealed patterns

---

5. 'The Sutherland Story: Fact and Fiction', in *Sar Gaidheal: Essays in Honour of Ruaridh MacKay*, An Comunn Gaidhealach, 1986

6. James Hunter, *The Making of the Crofting Community*, John Donald, 1976; Iain Fraser Grigor, *Mightier than a Lord*, Acair, 1979

7. Roger Millman, 'The Marches of Highland Estates' & 'The Landed Properties of Northern Scotland' *Scottish Geographical Magazine*, December 1969 & January 1970, Vol.85 Issue 3 & Vol.86 Issue 3

of land ownership little different from those identified in surveys made by Liberal Governments in 1872 and 1911. Millman's maps geographically demonstrated the huge constraints and challenges faced by anyone seeking alternative models of land ownership.

Our student radicalism was not unusual in the 1960s and '70s. A group of student journalists led by Brian Wilson, then editor of *Annasach*, Dundee University's student newspaper, aspired to challenge the docile local papers of the West Coast. Brian, later to become a Labour MP and minister, took up the mantle of Bob Cuddihy, whose *Islander* newspaper was first published on Arran in 1967, and founded a new radical paper. Brian wanted to expand this across Argyll. He fund-raised tirelessly, mounting running concerts in his hometown of Dunoon with bands including The Corries and Marmalade (as well as my own student folk band Avizandum, on one occasion). On completing his postgraduate journalism course at Cardiff, Brian set up the *West Highland Free Press* based at Kyleakin in Skye in 1972 with the slogan, An Tir, An Cànan, 'S na Daoine (The Land, The Language and The People).

Only two years before, one September day, I drove from Brechin to north-west Skye. I was to meet fellow students in the Skye Crofting Scheme. In that summer recess, between my second and third year at Dundee, I learned of Scotland's land history, and current land uses, from industrial Lanarkshire to the Mearns, thence to Skye and Islay.

In the days before internships and international development experiences, summer work for students could be varied but often boring. Not for me that year. My first temporary work was in Dalzell Steelworks, during their summer maintenance period. Behind piles of steel tubes, I read *A Scots Quair* by Lewis Grassic Gibbon. The themes were riveting: hard graft on small farms and the trauma of the Great War forced the main characters into town life but with a lasting attachment to nature. Considering my next work slot, grouse beating in the Mearns, Gibbon was a kind of primer to the feudal world of the grouse moor – in my case, on the Hill of Wirren, a 2,000-foot lump of hill overlooking Strathmore. Know your place was the lesson for student grouse beaters. After three weeks of energetic walking over heather-clad hillsides the car drive to Skye was epic; I passed through Tayside, Laggan, Spean Bridge, Invergarry, Glen Shiel, Kyle. It was my first visit to the Misty Isle since a family holiday there in 1956. But, I soon found my friends from the FSN bothying in the mothballed school room in Colbost. The Skye Crofting Scheme was in its third year as an active collaboration with local crofters. As a kind of summer school, it introduced us to practical agriculture in the Glendale area. We would do some harvesting work or clear out a drain and a crofter's wife would feed us. In the evening we could sing Scots songs in the Dunvegan hotels till 10pm, closing time, or if stovies were served we'd dance till 11pm. Two months before my arrival, on 25 July 1970, a memorial to the Glendale Martyrs had been unveiled. On the stone plinth its plaque read:

To commemorate
the achievements of
the Glendale Land Leaguers
1882-1886
Locus where 600 crofters challenged the government forces
Imprisoned
John MacPherson Glendale Martyr
Rev. D. MacCallum, Donald Macleod
John Morrison

The cairn sits to this day beside the B884 as the road climbs to the pass leading from Colbost to Fasach in the glen. It recalls the Glendale men who struck the first blow against landlord tyranny in what *The Scotsman* dubbed 'The Crofters' War'. This story was researched by James Hunter for his PhD and published in 1976 reviewing these critical events. For the first time ordinary Highlanders were heard in their native Gaelic and received a sympathetic hearing from a faraway London Government.

While on the Crofting Scheme we were befriended by Peter MacAskill. Peter had turned his croft house, The Three Chimneys, into a B&B and restaurant in 1969. He was a key source of local history, feeding my early interest with on-the-spot stories. He was a determined local man who returned from the south to make a go of life in his native place for his own growing family.

We invited more students, and others, to come and learn the history of the crofters' revolt and sang in pubs to boot. In 1971 we invited the recently elected SNP MP for the Western Isles, Donald Stewart, to address a public meeting in Dunvegan we were having. We were exploring some of the similarities of Skye to his native Lewis, namely an interest in a healthy economy. Stewart agreed to visit us en route to a by-election campaign in the Stirling and Falkirk burghs. At this time, the future for crofting was uncertain and the likely effects of entry to the European Common Market loomed.

A year later, on a rainy September evening in 1972, the FSN students at the Glendale Crofting Scheme set off to support a crofter's protest at Strollamus near Broadford. There, Horace Martin, a new landlord with 2,000 acres of 'poor' crofts between Dunan and Luib, was embroiled in court cases and confrontation. Our contribution was to organise concerts to raise cash for the Strollamus Crofters Defence Fund. I wrote a short account, *The Promised Land*, that spread the story abroad which was published in 1974 by the Strollamus Crofters Defence Committee. The Strollamus saga drifted on for years, which was a lesson for me on the seemingly intractable complexity of crofting law and community injustices. We Skye Crofting Scheme volunteers were a politically committed band. The following summer, in 1973, Malcolm Kerr, Graeme Purves, Barbara Hine, Brian Macgriogair and Kenneth Gibb contributed to a report on the scheme ranging over its philosophical base, a review of land use in Glendale and the scheme in action. Believe it or not, the report was part of an environmental competition run by Coca Cola. This marked ten years in the development of our 'practical summer school' run by nationalist students in north-west Scotland. Some of the authors of this report went on to play leading parts in land use and land reform over the years as student aspirations became informed and critical contributions to land reform debates were made.

In the background to our Crofting Scheme life, political change in Scotland was brewing. A Liberal surge against the Tories was building in the 1960s. Urban voters now added their protests to the rural, with the feeling that Scotland was being left behind while 'Scotland's Oil' was discovered and exploited by multinational companies with scant regard for local people. The rising SNP vote prompted Tory and Labour politicians to offer some form of devolution of powers. After much delay from the Royal Commission under Lord Kilbrandon, support for Scottish and Welsh Assemblies became Labour policy in 1974 – in a nearly hung parliament they had to find a way to stem the rising tide of SNP MPs. Some Labour MPs had already published land ownership ideas. In a pamphlet made from the content of their minority report to the Scottish Affairs Select Committee, MPs Jim Sillars, Alex Eadie and Harry Ewing made the case for public ownership in December 1972. However, under the Tory administration, the sanctity of private property prevailed.

In Edinburgh, in April 1973, I attended the 'What Kind of Scotland' conference organised by the *Scottish International Review*. It attracted a range of radical opinion-makers from across Scotland. One of the highlights was a revolutionary theatre production which fuelled the fervour for land reform. The highly regarded performance of John McGrath's ceilidh play *The Cheviot, the Stag and the Black, Black Oil*,[8] and its subsequent tour of small Highland halls, combined the stories that Prebble portrayed with dramatic sketches of the latest threats to Highland life. It neatly represented popular opinion for social justice and played to rapturous applause at the SNP Conference at Oban in the spring of 1973. The BBC screened a version soon after as the debate about land reform blossomed.

This wide-ranging debate on land reform was accompanied by a demand for a Scottish Assembly – the SNP increased its Westminster representation to 11 MPs in October 1974. During that time, I helped form an SNP policy group for land reform, led by party chairman Billy Wolfe and eloquent Glasgow solicitor and three-times Ross-shire parliamentary candidate Willie McRae. We were joined by farmers and foresters up and down the country, not forgetting young urban activists who pressed for a radical land policy to tap into widespread perceptions of injustice and dispossession. The SNP has a democratic heart: when our land group presented plans for wider discussion in the party's National Assembly and on to National Council, we received overwhelming approval. Our policy proposals called for the establishment of a Land Use Commission with local participation and many other guidelines

---

8. SNP Annual Conference, 1974, Res. 29

for land policy development which I explore in later chapters.[9] Suffice to say, revisioning the rural landscape became a recurrent theme as the devolution debate rolled on.

With high hopes of a Scottish Assembly becoming a reality, the SNP adopted a set of detailed policies on land, agriculture, forestry and crofting in 1977. These pointed the way for Scots to tackle land ownership and use. The SNP were not surpassed in ambition for over 20 years and the actual arrival of the new Scottish Parliament in 1999. Their ideas did have certain points of agreement with the Labour position. For example, they both proposed that a Land Commission should purchase under-achieving estates, set up a two-tier structure for local input and offer to diversify land ownership and use. Both parties were eschewing the previous approach, which made better behaviour voluntary, in the hopes of encouraging it to happen naturally; both parties deemed intervention in the capitalist system a necessity if Scots were to thrive. Labour, in government again from 1974 to 1979, did try to address the needs for access to land for development. They aimed to encourage the community to control land development and restore the increase in land values. However, its Land Commission proposals, encompassed in an Act of 1967, was repealed by the incoming Tories in 1970.

A Tory proposal to offer a right to buy for crofters at 15 times the annual rent fell with the Tory Government early in 1974. Labour adapted the proposal and passed it in the 1976 Crofting Reform (Scotland) Act with considerable opposition from leading activists Brian Wilson and Margaret MacPherson. Wilson and MacPherson would have preferred the all-tenancy condition to continue despite the obvious sale of crofts for rent and other detrimental issues affecting the health of the crofting sector. As it transpired, few crofts were bought outright in the following 20 years because the capital for croft development loans for tenanted properties could not be won from the banks.

Tom Nairn's ground-breaking book *The Break-Up of Britain* inspired

---

9.   Jim Sillars, 'Scotland's land... case for public ownership...' Minority Report to Scottish Affairs Select Committee, 1972

us when it appeared in 1977.[10] My well-thumbed copy was bought with a book token on leaving Invergordon Academy. I wrote a short review for the new magazine *Crann Tara*. Nairn suggested that the SNP should have been out campaigning to make the Assembly a certainty instead of poring over policy details. He was sympathetic to land reform but saw the constitutional change required as paramount at that time.

Westminster, in the meantime, ground down the devolution process, accepted the notorious 40% rule and deliberately botched the 1979 referendum. Soon a motion of no confidence brought down Labour and ushered in Margaret Thatcher and the certainty of deep cold storage for land reform. The advent of the Thatcher era put paid to the optimism of the 1970s but it spurred on a series of local actions to remember past struggles and envision a better future. It would be more than a decade before James Hunter would be tasked by the HIDB to scope out a Scottish Crofters Union to co-ordinate that very work.

---

10.   Tom Nairn, *The Break-Up of Britain: Crisis and Neo-nationalism*, Verso, 1977, 2nd edition 1981; my review in *Crann Tara*, Winter 1977, Issue 1

2. Hostile Tory land
Thatcher and the 1980s

Ach 's e sealladh leòinte is gann
Tha an seo aig ceann thall an linn
Talaimh àlainn nan daoine
Fhathast an làmhan duine no dithis.
But it is a wounding and a hollow sight
here as we reach the end of the century
the beautiful soil of the people
still in the hands of the few.
 – *Alba*, Runrig

They laid the foundations that we might build thereon.
 – Inscription on the Land League Cairn
    at Gartymore, Helmsdale

The shock of Tory Government, following the Scottish and Welsh Assembly referendums debacle, cast a pall over land reform activists like myself. People emigrated rather than face Thatcherism, but others looked to their roots to find hope and the seeds of change for land reform. Tangible reminders of past land struggles and the hopes for revision were being built by scattered communities in the north. History was being used to bolster resistance to the new Tory assault on the very concept of society.

One of these reminders was Skye's Battle of the Braes plinth, built with voluntary donations and thanks to the persistence of Aviemore County Councillor Sandy Lindsay. In 1980, I joined friends and supporters at the site where the Braes folk had confronted the sheriff and police almost a century before. The Battle of the Braes committee had asked local resident Sorley MacLean, the leading Gaelic poet of the century, to write the inscription. The plinth recalled the Braes folk's link to the wider Skye revolt, such as the Glendale action, then dubbed The Crofters' War. The bilingual inscription by Sorley reads:

Faisg air a'charn seo,
air a 19mh latha deug de'n ghiblean 1882,
chriochnaich, an cath a chuir muinntir a'Bhraighe
air sgath tuath na gaidhealtachd.

Near this cairn
on the 19th of April 1882,
ended the Battle fought by the people of Braes
on behalf of the crofters of Gaeldom.

In that same year at Gartymore, local crofters commemorated the foundation of the Highland Land League by locally-born Angus Sutherland. They built a cairn that was suitably inscribed with the biblical text 'They laid the foundations that we might build thereon.' Winnie Ewing MEP and Kay Matheson, one of the four students who retrieved the Stone of Destiny in 1950, joined Geoff MacLeod, an Inverness solicitor who was the Crofers Commission chairman, to celebrate that spark of organised resistance in Sutherland against landlord power. Sutherland's Highland Land League had spread far and wide, built community by community. We were undaunted by the torrential downpour on the day as the celebrations were led off with 'Mo Mhallachd aig na Caoraich Mhòr' ('My Curses on the Big Sheep') sung in Gaelic by Joseph MacKay. Composed by the Bard of the Clearances, Ewen Robertson, the song dismisses the 1st Duke of Sutherland with the phrase: 'Gum b' ann an Iutharn 'n robh do shàil, 'S gum b'fheàrr leam Iùdas làmh rium', translated by Durness journalist Willie Morrison as, 'Were I with you in Hell to meet, I'd sooner stand wi' Judas.' Those present applauded with gusto.

Such acts of remembrance as those at Braes and Gartymore were inspired by the work of Iain Grimble and John Prebble in the '60s and '70s to expose the horrors of the Highland Clearances. Grimble's trilogy on the Clan MacKay lands sheds light on their tragic downfall.

These two writers pioneered the present-day popular understanding of these terrible events and perpetuated the memory of poet and writer Donald Macleod for his crucial work as one who had ensured that the views of the victims were recorded for posterity.

Joseph Mackay's choice of song at Gartymore made a direct link between clearance and resistance. A pillar of resistance for Ewen Robertson was one of two important memorials which were erected in connection with the Strathnaver Clearances at the instigation of Grimble, who had lived in Bettyhill for several years. The second monument is central to the exposure of the true Sutherland story. It contains a plaque set in a stone plinth on the roadside on the B871 on the west bank of the River Naver opposite the forestry plantation which, until recently, obscured the cleared village of Rossal. It reads:

In memory of Donald Macleod Stonemason who witnessed the destruction of Rossal in 1814 and wrote 'Gloomy Memories'

Highland Heritage

In the '80s, a group of history-minded SNP Highland activists, including myself, began to spread the message of past struggles. Building on policy ideas forged in the 1970s, we were determined to incite resistance to the Thatcherite climate of UK politics. A successful rally at Croick Church in Strathcarron, Ardgay, where the diamond-shaped, east-facing window-pane is scratched with contemporary comments on the nearby Glen Calvie clearance of May 1845. Those attending, on that sunny afternoon, agreed that there should be support for our mission to recall the local history which few were taught in schools. The location chosen for the rally was connected to the cleared people of Glen Calvie had sheltered at the churchyard in 1845. The Highland Regional Council had previously been urged on by Councillor Sandy Lindsay to improve the parking area there to encourage people to visit the site. The rally set in motion some restoration work to the fabric of the Telford-designed church. Ironically, the refugees from Glen Calvie in 1845 would not enter the building, as they, and their minister Gustavus Aird, had joined the Free Church two years before.

In November 1981 Highland Heritage (HH), of which I was a founding member, became a formal organisation to promote an alternative view to the tourist brochure take on castles, tartan and heather. Taking the motto, 'Keeping the people's history in the public eye', we produced a leaflet entitled *The Highland Clearances Trail*. This listed places to visit where the glens had been stripped of their people over the previous 200 years and where the crofters fought back. It included some present-day flash points for good measure. We offered it free of charge to the Inverness Tourist Office but we were rebuffed with this comment:

> Although the leaflet is not of a party-political nature, it is clearly controversial and inappropriate for distribution from our information centres.

Stuart Lindsay, the then Highland correspondent of *The Glasgow Herald*, filed a story headlined 'Highland Tourist Offices Ban Leaflet Explaining Clearances' and, in an editorial, the paper enquired if the leaflet was 'unsuitable for tourists.'[11] The ensuing furore and embarrassing publicity were noted by the HIDB later in 1981. HH, now a charity, was offered a small sum by HIDB to produce a publicity poster for the 'unsuitable' leaflet. Subsequently, I compiled five editions of a pamphlet which expanded on *The Highland Clearances Trail* with additional information on many more sites to visit. It referenced the Croick, Gartymore, Glendale and Braes monuments to the Land League and books to read on those events. Over the next 20 years around 10,000 copies of this pamphlet were sold, many in tourist information offices, book shops and museums. My words were viewed by some as an early advocation for 'green tourism' by encouraging visitors to see the locations where these tragic events occurred.

Who owns Scotland? A trigger for opposition debate

Both the Scottish Council of the Labour Party and the SNP at this time were active in campaigns concerning the size of estates and the origins of their owners. This had been prompted by a report published late in the Labour regime from 1974–79 which revealed the rising number

---

11. Stuart Lindsay, 'Highland Tourist Offices Ban Leaflet Explaining Clearances', *The Glasgow Herald*, 19 November 1981

of overseas purchasers of Scottish land. Led by Lord Northfield it reasoned that a comprehensive land register was required to kick-start the modernisation of the ancient Register of Sasines created in 1617.

Labour continued to back nationalisation of land, but with the local control of assets to be removed from the big estates. John McEwen, a retired forester from Perthshire, had been a staunch Clause IV Labour member, but he found it shameful that no government agency had provided a comprehensive land register to that date. In 1977, he began to survey the owners of Perthshire estates and soon widened his scope across other areas. Later that year he published his estimate of who owned Scotland following the painstaking study of Dr Millman's maps of 1969-70 and his own research. A second edition with some corrections of his estimated size of estates and ownership came out in 1981. Writing in the new forward, playwright John McGrath noted:

> As we go into the eighties with the landowners of Scotland encouraged in their arrogance by their triumphant friends in Westminster, the need for this book becomes, if anything, even greater than when it was first published.[12]

The SNP were also active at this time but were in the midst of three years of turmoil. The internal 79 Group was promoting a 'Scottish Socialist Republic.' As an active member of the group, I contributed articles to *79 Group News*, such as one where I developed the SNP's 1977 land policy containing a two-tier Land Commission. I wrote:

> Our people need land for basic economic and housing requirements and to serve this, a sort of land holders contract, containing both rights and duties, is needed. Under such conditions the large accretions which sterilise land today would publicly fit the test at local or national Land Commission hearings. The use to which the land is put, and not the value of the site, should be the criterion for development.[13]

12. John McEwen, *Who Owns Scotland*, E.U.S.P.A., 1977 & Polygon, 1981
13. Rob Gibson, *79 Group News*, October 1981, p.4

Even after SNP internal groups were banned in 1982, the party continued to advocate strong measures of land reform on the lines laid out in 1977 as Tory opposition continued to change Scotland. Following the demise of the 79 Group and suspension of its leaders, a non-party Scottish Socialist Society was formed to draw together left-wing thinkers and activists from across the spectrum. George Kerevan from Labour was one new adherent of this society.

The Dalnavert Co-operative

A little remembered, but important, process began in 1982. Highland Regional Cllr Sandy Lindsay and Dr Iain Glen, HH members and former 79 Group members, joined six others to take the bold step of buying some forestry land for sale at Dalnavert on the River Spey near Feshiebridge. Iain and his family had moved north because of his work on mental health at Craig Dunain Hospital near Inverness. They had purchased a historic house at Dalnavert which was associated with Sir John A. MacDonald, the first prime minister of Canada, and the house was surrounded by pine clad slopes and a lush water meadow. Despite the vocal lairds who were opposed to the purchase, Iain's co-operative of eight partners managed to buy the forestry land and began to build homes to work the land. Their story is still developing, and is well told by Euan MacAlpine. This is one of the earliest examples of alternative not-for-profit land ownership.[14]

The sale of Knoydart

The fragile community of Knoydart, in its mountainous, West Coast setting, was facing uncertainty in 1982. Major Nigel Chamberlayne-MacDonald, the laird of Knoydart's 52,000 acres, was proposing to sell his land. While it had been on offer for over a year, it only hit the headlines in November 1982 and the papers revealed that the Ministry of Defence (MoD) was an interested party. The MoD were seeking a new training area, indeed an area extensively used by them in World War 2. This revelation galvanised a disparate campaign of resistance

---

14. Euan MacAlpine, Dalnavert Community Co-operative Limited', Caledonia, www.caledonia.org.uk/socialland/dalnaver.htm

into existence. It was started by the majority of Knoydart residents and led by Frederick Rohde of Li on the north of the peninsula, but it soon included the Highland Regional Council (HRC), the HIDB, the Chris Brasher Trust and the National Trust for Scotland (NTS). It also attracted attention from local MP Russell Johnston, as well as the Scottish Council of the Labour Party and the SNP.

Accessible only by sea or a 15-mile hike from the nearest road, the Rough Bounds of Knoydart had previously been in national headlines over the abortive land raid of 1948, the tragic story of the Clearances after the failure of the Jacobite Rising and the subsequent bankruptcy of Alexander Macdonell of Glengarry in 1852. After these events a series of absentee lairds had treated Knoydart as a private shooting and fishing domain. One laird after another failed or tired or died and as the Chamberlayne-Macdonald factor, Sandy Macdonald, told *The Glasgow Herald* on 6 December 1982:

> the problem is that the kind of fortunes which created places like Knoydart no longer exist.[15]

None were able to persuade the MoD off the Knoydart land. But the local people, who were vocally opposed to a military takeover, continued to work with Highland Regional SNP councillors, Sandy Lindsay and Jimmy Munro, and local Lochaber councillor Tom Kirkwood to stymie the MoD's plans.

In December 1982, as convener of the SNP's Land and Crofting Policy Committee, I sought and gained the support of the SNP's National Executive Committee to oppose the purchase of Knoydart by the MoD. This offered support to the local communities in their strenuous opposition to the sale of the estate to the MoD. Our statement was:

> We urge the Highland Regional Council to oppose and change of land use in Knoydart for military purposes; we call on the Secretary of State for Scotland to bring forward

---

15. Stuart Lindsay, 'Knoydart passions roused at prospect of MoD laird', *The Glasgow Herald*, 6 December 1982

proposals for land settlement to promote the peaceful use of Knoydart with appropriate environmental safeguards.[16]

For several months a range of proposals by conservationists and the HIDB were debated and the Secretary of State for Defence, John Nott, was questioned in the House of Commons. The NTS took an interest in buying the land but baulked at the £1.9 million price. The SNP and Labour took the view that a mix of small land developments instead of the MoD would give a nod to wilderness protection that various conservation interests squabbled over. While the HIDB chairman, Sir Robert Cowan, and MP Russell Johnston supported the MoD approach claiming it would save the Fort William to Mallaig rail line and bring jobs.

However, in January 1983, the MoD announced that there were too many difficulties in the purchase of the land – the new Secretary of State for Defence, Michael Heseltine, had been forced to abandon the bid amidst debates on austerity and defence cuts. There was delight in Knoydart and beyond. Thereafter the HRC, HIDB, NTS, the Countryside Commission and Scottish Office looked at the idea of a public agency consortium to run the peninsula. But they concluded, only a couple of months later, that it could not be made to work. The NTS was only willing to buy if HRC and HIDB paid the annual running costs and the Countryside Commission were the only group prepared to chip in. Chris Brasher, the eminent mountaineer, offered a plan for a conservation trust buyout, but this also fell through. This, however, sowed the seeds of a later purchase by the John Muir Trust of the highest peaks of Knoydart some years later.

Knoydart, and its underlying problems, highlighted the issues caused by the ownership of huge tracts of land as private feudal domains. It also revealed the inability of agencies and local government to gain the necessary traction to effect modern community-based development. This conundrum hung over land ownership till a breakthrough by crofters in Assynt in 1993 which opened the door to community empowerment.

---

16. SNP press notice dated 15 December 1982, in the author's possession

We'll leave the last word to Sandy Macdonald:

> I feel there must be a future for estates like Knoydart. The pity is that it is up for sale now, because the place is nearer breaking even than it ever has been in its history.[17]

Debating land reform in the deep freeze Thatcher era

As a member of the 79 Group of SNP radicals it was logistically difficult for me to meet other nationalists in the early '80s, other than local activists in Easter Ross where I was based. Weekly phone calls in the coldest winter for years, however, offered considerable debate. I, and the SNP, started to develop a more nuanced socialist outlook on land reform than the Labour Party's default land nationalisation. As I discussed Peter Kropotkin's *Fields, Factories and Workshops* with local SNP activist Andrew Currie in my home, I began to see community empowerment as a key concept to land reform.

In March 1985, a conference was held in Glasgow under the banner of the Socialist Society created, in part, by former 79 Group members. A range of papers were delivered under the title *The Land for the People*. The organisers felt that

> the issue of land is absolutely central to the possibility of political progress in the future and was acutely aware that, historically and politically, the Scottish people have been disinherited from their own country, and that the impact of this has been huge and catastrophic.

A comparison by Irene Evans and Joy Hendry in 1985 of the land policies of Scottish political parties, under the title *Land for the People*, displayed a wide variance of approaches and ideologies which underpinned some later policy positions. In sum, the Labour and SNP policies were the most worked-out, while the newly fledged Green Party's policy was quite distinctive. The Green Party declared that

---

17. Stuart Lindsay, 'Knoydart passions roused at prospect of MoD laird', *The Glasgow Herald*, 6 December 1982

The prerequisite for ecological reforms is … a fundamental change in our system of land tenure.

Founded on the principles of Henry George and his single tax, the modern Green Party and Scottish Green Party founded in 1989 have championed Land Value Tax (LVT) as the cornerstone of such change.[18] The Liberal Democrats' and Conservative Party's policies said very little on land reform at all.[19]

So, six years into the Thatcher era and hopes of early change were minimal. But, the energy for policy formation of the 1970s had gained momentum and the campaign for a Scottish Assembly morphed into the Scottish Constitutional Convention. The 1990s spurred widespread hopes for the return of a Labour Government in London in 1997. One that would seem to meet the 'settled will of the Scottish people', in John Smith's famous words; one that was committed to establishing a Scottish Parliament where land reform could be tackled properly.

Marking the Crofting Act centenary

1986, the centennial anniversary of the Crofters' War, saw several re-assessments of its history. Fresh light was thrown onto these seminal events for modern Scottish land politics, least of all the crofters' part in the foundation of the Scottish Labour Party in 1888 by elements which included Highland land reformers and Home Rulers. From the renewed attention on these events there was an inevitable backlash from the establishment. In an interview with Dr James Hunter in the new *Sunday Standard* newspaper, 3 May 1981, recently appointed Historiographer Royal for Scotland, Professor Gordon Donaldson, declared:

> I am 68 now and until recently I had hardly heard of the Highland Clearances. The thing has been blown up out of all proportion.

---

18.   Irene Evans and Joy Hendry (eds.), *Land for the People: Scottish Socialist Society*, publisher unknown, 1985
19.   ibid.

Two years later Lord Strathnaver, heir to the Sutherland estates which had shrunk from a million acres in the 1860s to 90,000 acres today, was attending an international clan gathering in Canada. He told the astonished reporter of the *Toronto Globe and Mail* on 16 July 1983 that, 'The Sutherland Clearances did not occur.' The paper commented that this was like one of Hitler's generals saying that the Holocaust had not taken place. However, Lord Strathnaver's mother, the Countess of Sutherland, went some way to admitting the family's guilt when she told the *Sunday Post* on 9 October 1983 that

> the improvements [to the estate] involved the clearance of 5,000 people from their ancestral dwellings in the glens and it was bitterly resented... often there was too much cruelty.

There was also no sympathy for the centenary from the Post Office. The London-based chairman, Sir Ronald Dearing, refused to issue a commemorative stamp for the 1886 Crofters' Holdings Act, citing Professor Donaldson, as the measure was far too controversial. Ian Barr, then Chairman of the Scottish Postal Board, who had not been consulted by Dearing, belatedly arranged for a series of six commemorative cards.

Despite HH's three-year campaign, it fell to the philatelically-minded laird of the Summer Isles, Kenneth Frampton, to commission the commemorative stamps. He approached Dingwall designer, Seoris McGillivray, to create the vignettes of crofting life. These were to be sold from Frampton's island stamp business. The postage stamp campaign had the near unanimous support of Highland MPs, councils, the NFU, the Scottish Crofters Union and various leading Scottish historians. But, still the Post Office had failed to recognise the case summed up in Dr James Hunter's words:

> In 1886, 1911 and 1919 crofters gained security of tenure, judiciously determined rents, compensation for improvements, more land and a steadily increasing amount of economic and financial assistance. These were tremendous

victories. Between 1881, when the land war began in Skye, and the 1920s, when a massive land settlement programme had been virtually completed, the whole trend of early nineteenth century crofting history was reversed.[20]

In the centenary year, an ambitious stage presentation, *The Crofting Act*, was commissioned and produced by Eden Court Theatre in Inverness. Amongst several writers engaged in its production was George Gunn, a Caithness poet and playwright, whose forebears came from Helmsdale and thence from Kildonan. His plot was an imaginary attempt to blow up the Duke of Sutherland's statue on Ben Bhraggie. But, while a watered-down version of the original script was performed, the director undoubtedly cut back the trenchant message before *The Crofting Act* went on a successful tour round the north. A highlight of Gunn's one-act drama is an exchange between two of the would-be demolition squad. One says,

> The way I see it is the longer the likes of thon man at the top of thon column up there is allowed to stay there the worse it'll get, too. There's those who are erectors an' there's those who are the worshippers at the shrines. Well, I want to change all that, to hell with their false gospels! D'ye know what I mean?[21]

My research, *Crofter Power in Easter Ross*, was published by HH in 1986 to coincide with the Crofting Act centenary. The work for this had been triggered by a reference to Donald MacRae, the Alness Martyr, in a book review for Willie Orr's *Deer Forests, Landlords and Crofters*. MacRae, a Land League organiser in Easter Ross, had been sacked on a trumped-up charge by the Roskeen school board in 1886. He was then head-hunted to teach Balallan children on the Isle of Lewis in 1887.[22] I

20. Hunter, *The Making of the Crofting Community*, 1976
21. George Gunn, *The Crofting Act*, a copy of the script was donated by the playwright, in the author's possession
22. Rob Gibson, *Crofter Power in Easter Ross: Land League at Work, 1884–88*,

was able to compare the ensuing reaction of MacRae's political opponents via two rival local newspapers: the *Ross-shire Journal*, established by the laird of Novar; and the crofter-supporting *Invergordon Times*. At a weekend conference held at Balallan in September 2012, to commemorate the Great Deer Raid on Pairc planned and led by MacRae, I took great pleasure in contributing to a history of MacRae's earlier experiences in Alness.

Cultural Scotland stirred

The 1980s were eventful years in the cultural resistance to Thatcher. Runrig's songs *Alba* and *Protect and Survive* sum up the mood of seeking a Scottish Parliament and non-nuclear policies. While, The Proclaimers sang *Letter from America*, bemoaning enforced emigration and industrial decline but encouraging defiance and struggle. In the same spirit as these bands many new folk music festivals sprang up across the country.

For my part I joined the new committee of the Highland Traditional Music Festival in Dingwall to help organise our first festival in June 1981. Two years later I took over the reins and led the team till 2002 when it became too expensive to continue on a small scale. We enjoyed inspiring music, some of it very political. Along with Rita Hunter, past organiser of Fèis Rois, I reviewed our taped archives of over 20 years of the Dingwall festival for Eberhard Bort's celebration of the tradition in 2011.[23] And in 2010, for the same publisher, I explored the Highland's political songs since Hamish Henderson wrote *The Ballad of the Men of Knoydart* in 1948.[24]

Political temperatures soared as Thatcherism declined into the fiasco over the poll tax. But land issues continued to inspire protest songs. Andy Mitchell wrote *Indiana*, a tale of returning emigrants to the USA determined to return to live in Scotland. It received wide air plays and sales thanks to Andy Irvine, who heard the song performed

Highland Heritage Educational Trust, 1986 and revised 2012

23. Eberhard Bort (ed.), *'Tis 60 Years Since: The 1951 Edinburgh People's Festival Ceilidh and the Scottish Folk Revival*, Grace Note Publications, 2011

24. Eberhard Bort (ed.), *Borne on the Carrying Stream: The Legacy of Hamish Henderson*, Grace Note Publications, 2010

by Mitchell in Ullapool, and included it in Patrick Street's first record. Dougie MacLean's albums *Real Estate* in 1988 and *Indigenous* in 1991 contained explicit examples of uncomprehending incomers and feudal relics. The songs *Homeland – Duthaich Mo Chridhe* and *Rank and Roses* stand out especially.

Capercaillie, the rising West Highland Gaelic song and traditional music group, issued their record *Delirium* in 1991. It included a warning of the new Clearances in *Waiting for the Wheel to Turn* and *Four Stone Walls* that attacked the lack of housing for local people. Written by the group's accordion and keyboard player, Donald Shaw, whose work has produced a modern sunburst of Scottish music, it reminded us that feelings for the land still ran deep. Also in 1991, Derek Dick, aka Fish, formerly lead singer of the pop group Marillion, produced a CD entitled *Internal Exile*. The title track told of the human cost of industrial destruction and emigration and has eerie resonances with the age of Brexit.

These musicians captured the defiant mood of the Thatcher dog days, and those other successor John Major, when land reform was swept from politics at Westminster – but not from the wishes of many Scots.

Moidart & Knoydart – Lessons learned

Back in the 1940s two new Moidart crofters embarked on independent living, Wendy Wood and Margaret Leigh. They were middle-aged women of very different outlooks who had come to Moidart to become crofters of vacant holdings on the Glenuig Estate. Wendy Wood and her husband Mac had arrived in 1939 at Allt Ruadh; Margaret Leigh arrived in the nearby Smirisary township in 1941. Both women wrote books about their 'back to the land' lives. Neither mentioned the other directly and their conclusions over the future of Gaelic, crofting and Scotland diverge radically. They lived, for several years, less than a mile apart, yet the only thing they held in common was their determination to show that crofting was a viable way of life.[25]

In the 1940s it seemed that townships like Smirisary, two and a half

25. Margaret Leigh, *Spade Among the Rushes*, Birlinn, 2011; Wendy Wood, *Mac's Croft*, Frederick Muller, 1946

miles west of Glenuig via a cart track and rough path, were dying. Indeed, the whole lands of Moidart and Knoydart had been emptied of its people over the previous two centuries by brutal clearances following the last Jacobite Rising. The arrival of the great sheep flocks, potato famine and economic decline followed by two World Wars compounded the outflow of people. In the 1940s, young men went away to fight, while the older folk, living a traditional life, knew that the bright lights of Fort William, Glasgow or even Capetown could easily break the chain of generations if no new work was available to attract the younger generation to return to. The crofter's struggles to keep the land viable during wartime austerity opened our eyes to the pioneering prospects of living on small holdings that commercial farmers viewed as fit only for sheep ranches. Compare this with the breakthrough of repopulation today where new settlers have the major advantages of modern life: better transport, broadband, renewable energy and proper support from government. As we shall see this repopulation has delivered over 500,000 acres, or 2.9% of Scotland into local hands.

A word about the backgrounds of the educated and articulate Wood and Leigh. Born in south-east England in 1892 and brought up in South Africa, Wendy Wood was an artist and writer who took up the cause of Scottish independence in 1927. She led a firebrand life among the few who supported peaceful Scottish self-rule. Her political exploits were extra-parliamentary and included burning Union flags and so on. This was a time when fascism was rising in Germany and Italy, which was always used as a stick to beat militant Scottish patriots. But her crofting sojourn was certainly a far cry from fascist behaviour. In his collected memories of folklore in Moidart, Calum Iain Maclean noted a typical Wendy Wood protest on Loch Shiel:

> A launch named Loch Ailort plies daily on the loch, up from Acharacle and down again in the evening. The launch belongs to David McBrayne & Co. and quite recently replaced the old Clanranald, owned by a local concern. Here too the cancer of mammoth companies is eating into the very heart of local endeavour. McBrayne's new boat rejoiced in the very English name, Rosalind, until

some brave spirit, Wendy Wood, if I remember rightly, obliterated the offending name and painted Clanranald on it instead. Messrs. McBrayne & co. very wisely had the boat rechristened Loch Ailort. Local opinion accepted the compromise.[26]

Margaret Leigh was born in London in 1894. Her family were academics and she followed the family tradition to Oxford. Her individualist streak sent her off to farm in Cornwall, but then she rode on horseback to Scotland and took up farming single-handedly before World War 2. She took the wee croft at Smirisary with the help of sympathetic local landowner Graham Croall. After that she entered an Inverness convent in the 1950s. With few family ties, she started to write of her experiences while farming at Fernaig, Wester Ross. Her later work, *Spade Among the Rushes*, her acute observations of crofting life in war time are combined with an acerbic critique of the indigenous people. The chapter addressed *The Highland Problem: A Few More Stones on the Cairn*, opens with a warning:

> If any of my Highland friends have read with pleasure so far, so I advise them to skip this chapter, for it may offend. The few things I have to say need saying and I shall try to disarm criticism by apologising beforehand for any corns I may tread on.[27]

Leigh saw the problem of depopulation as moral not economic – a stark indictment of the Celts. She saw the coastal communities in decay and yet she argued:

> Whatever may be the choice and the future of the Highland people, the challenge of the highlands remains, and will never lack a response, though perhaps not from the

---

26. Calum Iain MacLean, *The Highlands*, Club Leabhar, 1975, first published in 1959
27. Leigh, *Spade Among the Rushes*, 2011, p.177

race that once gave it. The glens will not be empty, but it may not be Gaels who fill them. A pity. But if they go, it will be of their own will. Those who come in their place will be men who can respond to an environment which, though always exacting, is never beyond a reasonable man's courage and resource.[28]

She goes on to remind readers how Icelanders, Faroese and northern Norwegians talked of settlement not evacuation. Yet Leigh takes no account of the estate system that strangled access to most of the available land in Scotland. She states that all sorts of government support cannot win if human will and character fail. She concludes:

To make all things, even the highest, too easy, to hand out bribes and doles, to rob life of individuality, stimulus and adventure is the final vice of democracy, and its viscous snail-trail winds all over the Highlands.

I first read this chapter while sitting on a sunny beach in Brittany in the 1980s. I can't place the exact year, but I remember how it grated on my sense of Moidart and its people. On reflection, I know Leigh's days were those of depopulation and that there were considerably changed expectations among the young after their demob in 1945; and they weren't encouraging for crofting, because small communities were even more vulnerable to distant decisions. This was soon emphasised by the abortive outcome of the land raid in nearby Knoydart in November 1948.

This chapter has been largely ignored by analysts of the condition of the West Highlands and indeed Leigh's conclusions target the perceived loss of self-belief among the Gaels without real cross-examination of the historic context. And this context was what propelled this self-proclaimed individualist, and 'a convinced regionalist', to target 'the extremer type of nationalist' (perhaps alluding to Wendy Wood) as resettlement of previously Gaelic speakers by non-Gaels was the subject of a lively debate at that time in An Comunn Gàidhealach.[29]

---

28. Ibid., p.183
29. John A Burnett, *The Making of the Modern Scottish Highlands, 1939–1965: Withstanding the 'Colossus of Advancing Materialism'*, Four Courts Press, 2011

Wendy Wood concludes *Mac's Croft* on an altogether more engaging note. She describes travelling with her husband to Glenfinnan for the 200th anniversary of the raising of Bonnie Prince Charlie's standard there, 24 August 1745. Jacobite sympathisers from near and far came to remember and celebrate. Many of these people may have been concerned about the future of their land after the cataclysm of World War 2 and the depletion of the local population. A staunchly Catholic and Jacobite area had much to fear for the future. But, Wood took a positive view of renewed life in Moidart in her own inimitable way.

Leigh, for her part, showed some shrewd shafts of insight. She also exhibited the blinkers that put progress down to individual will. And certainly, the experience of faraway governments gave little cause for confidence in those days. Nationalisation of transport led to the MacBrayne takeover on Loch Shiel. And central government concerns for mass food production saw no place for crofting, other than tolerating those still clinging to older ways. During the same period Frank Fraser Darling researched and reported on the crofting way of life in sympathy with nature in his *West Highland Survey*. It was ignored by the Scottish Office for ten years in that crucial post-war period when croft amalgamation was policy.[30]

I first visited Glenuig in the 1980s as a participant of the Glenuig music festival to celebrate the vibrant music scene there. This was a time when people were encouraged to live and repair estate houses, in the days of the Llewellyn family who were related to the Croalls. The Glenuig music festival ran for a decade as a key fundraiser for the local population to build a new community hall. They succeeded. Of the longstanding resident families of Glenuig, I never got to know Ronald Macdonald, 'The Whaler,' mentioned by Leigh and Wood. He had skippered the store boat to Loch Ailort before the opening of the new road in 1963. However his three sons Angus, Alan and Iain, the piping brothers, and daughter Sandra are friends to this day.

Ronald Taylor, who by the time I met him in the 1970s, worked for Inverness-shire County Council as a bridge inspector and clerk

---

30. Frank Fraser Darling, *West Highland Survey: An Essay in Human Ecology*, Oxford University Press, 1955

of works. He was an active SNP man who also helped me launch my own political campaign in 1974 for which I'm very grateful. But he also provided another insight into Glenuig life at the end of World War 2 as, in 1945 he was taking care of Wood's croft. He had been in some scrapes with the law over nationalist protests in Lanarkshire in his youth and, due to this, he was sent to live in faraway Smirisary. He recalled that the artist who created the lovely woodcuts of crofting life for Leigh's book would visit Wood's croft for a good feed – Leigh applied strict rationing rules in the her croft. Rationing for the UK was only lifted in part in 1951. Ronnie was also the organising secretary of Clann Albainn, a pressure group set up with some lordly support at the outset to resettle returning servicemen in the Highlands in the 1940s. In that light, the pre-planned, well-publicised and ultimately unsuccessful Knoydart land raid of November 1948 received Ronnie's full support.

From the kilt-wearing Ronnie, I learned the story of Smirisary and Knoydart where an important theme links Leigh, Wood and the Knoydart raiders. Each shared an age-old belief that a secure land holding is the basis for family life. Even more so, if a whole community is determined to take control of their land. The evidence from Moidart showed it to be a far-off hope in the 1950s as crofting populations continued to dwindle due to individual's choices and adverse government policy which ignored the reality of these out-of-the-way parts of Highland Scotland. While events in the 1980s encompassed unveiling memorials, it also brought some political development for land reform ideas. The underlying expectations for change, which while unlikely during the Thatcher regime, showed the wellsprings of cultural awakening and returning self-confidence which had been so badly dented by the aborted 1979 referendum. The pace would quicken on all fronts in the 1990s.

3. The '90s
Land reform recalled and revised

In winning the land, Assynt crofters have struck a historic blow for people on the land throughout the Highlands.
– Allan MacRae, Stoer Primary School, 8 December 1992

The 1990s was a breakthrough decade for land reform hopes across Scotland. The status quo was challenged in the academic realm, through the John McEwen Memorial Lectures, and through physical protest, such as by Ian Thomson in Perthshire. On the Whitbread estate, crofters asserted their legal right to their land and Assynt was reclaimed by its people. In the brand new Scottish legislature, serious considerations were given to how best to tackle such a divisive subject, now that is was free from the landowners' direct influence in the House of Lords. TV coverage of the Assynt crofters' nail-biting and protracted bid to buy their crofts townships and common grazings as one unit captured a public mood. Palpable demands for change after 12 long years of Tory government was stimulated by the success in North Assynt. Other communities such as the Isle of Eigg and Knoydart gained control of their land before the decade was out.

The symbolism of recalling past injustices such as the quixotic tilt at the removal of the statue of the 1st Duke of Sutherland, the Clearing Duke, bolstered public awareness that land reform was unfinished business. The dogged work of researchers and campaigners projected new prospects for land reform in the series of John McEwen Memorial Lectures that preceded real political change.

The Kinlochewe ruling

In 1970 the Whitbread estate was the largest in Ross and Cromarty, at

71,000 acres. It was shocking to hear of the removal of an old couple from their tied house on that estate. This pitiless act prompted a Mr and Mrs Macdonald, who lived and worked on Skye, to offer a portion of their croft at Kinlochewe to the evicted couple near to their former dwelling. The Macdonalds would make a house site available and give the couple security. So saying, a snag occurred to them: under the 1976 Crofting Reform Act, any material change, such as offering part of the croft to another party, would allow the landlord to clawback half the development value of the croft. And, the last thing the Macdonalds wanted was to reward the Whitbread laird for the consequences of his callous eviction.

At the time I worked with Mrs Macdonald, a fellow guidance teacher at Portree High School in a Highland-wide careers programme, and heard how she and her husband planned to decroft part of their land to help the old couple. I had also previously worked with solicitor Donald Ferguson, a staunch supporter of mine in various campaigns. As a Portree solicitor with crofting law expertise, Ferguson was engaged by the Macdonalds. He began to pore over the text of the 1976 Act regarding paybacks to landlords for ongoing developments such as decrofting land for house building. After much work, he spied a possible loophole in the wording and engaged an advocate (Roseanna Cunningham, also a long-time political associate of mine) to put the case to the outer house of the Court of Session in early 1992. Described correctly as Whitbread v Macdonald, or colloquially as the Kinlochewe Ruling or Judgement, Ferguson's argument was upheld – Roseanna had succeed in gaining the support of two of the three judges. The Court of Session agreed that if a crofter requested that the landlord transfer ownership of land to a third party (or nominee), that transfer would not trigger a clawback liability.

However, unintended consequences arose from this legal precedent. The Kinlochewe ruling began to be used by speculators to gain greater profit. For example, they would sell house sites from crofts needlessly without the landlord's clawback. Thus, a widespread call arose for closing the loophole again and land reform was once again halted.

Assynt reclaimed

Progress was widely reported, and welcomed, later in 1992 when the Assynt Crofters' Trust was successful in buying 20,000 acres of north Assynt from a liquidated speculator, in a deal finally brokered early in 1993. While the precedent of the Kinlochewe Ruling was not needed in the community buyout of Assynt, it had given Assynt crofters a back-stop if they had failed as a group to purchase their land. For individuals could have sought to buy their crofts and, crucially, an apportionment of their common grazings. The details of that story have been well told in John MacAskill's authoritative book *We Have Won the Land*.[31] This nail-biting saga, engrossed TV audiences far and wide and raised new hopes of reclaiming Scottish land for the resident working people. Moreover, prolonged campaigns by residents of Eigg in 1997 and Knoydart in 1999 to buy their land led to community buyouts becoming Scottish Parliament policy with the Land Reform Act of 2003.

In the wake of the Assynt triumph, in November 1994, political commentator Tom Nairn summarised the link between constitutional change and land reform in a critique in *The Scotsman*. He captured the essence of the underlying mood:

> The reason the land question arouses such deep feelings in the Lowlands as well as in Gaeldom is that it symbolises impotence so perfectly. The largest of Scotland's private domains, Buccleuch Estates, is four times the size of the European Union's smallest state, Luxemburg. Now, the blights Scotland suffers from are, of course, not all rural, or connected with land ownership. But they are connected with an absent democracy, for which this monstrous scale of land alienation is an appropriate emblem.[32]

---

31. John MacAskill, *We Have Won The Land: The Story of the Purchase by the Assynt Crofters' Trust of the North Lochinver Estate*, Acair, 1999
32. Rob Gibson, *Toppling the Duke: Outrage on Ben Bhraggie*, Highland Heritage Educational Trust, 1996, p.9

John McEwen Memorial Lectures 1993–99

The role of the University of Aberdeen in educating many prominent land reform theorists and activists is remarkable. The departments of History, Economics, Agriculture and Forestry have each contributed alumni whose place in modern Scottish land reform has been invaluable. The names of Dr James Hunter, Robin Callander, Andy Wightman MSP and Professor Bryan MacGregor come readily to mind.

James Hunter's PhD thesis was published in 1976 as *The Making of the Crofting Community*. It took the Land League era of the 1880s as the genesis of the fight back of the common people for land reform. Its popularity is such that it has remained in print to this day.

Robin Callander dedicated his book, *A Pattern of Land Ownership in Scotland*, published in 1987, to the land reform activist John McEwen on his 100th birthday. In it Callander focuses on the Aberdeenshire story from his home at Finzean on Deeside where he helped to bring the two major landowners together with the residents to manage the old commonty land of native pine forest.[33] John McEwen, however, sadly died on 22 September 1992, two days short of his 105th birthday. Yet, to honour this single-minded land reform pioneer, an opportunity arose in the mind of Robin Callander. Stimulated by his research and that of Hunter and Wightman, Callander formed the Friends of John McEwen and instigated a series of John McEwen Memorial Lectures.

The first lecture, in 1993, and was made by Professor Bryan Mac-Gregor, who had been a sometime student activist with the FSN in the Skye Crofting Scheme; in his professional life, he had been the MacRobert Professor of Land Economics at the University of Aberdeen since 1990. His talk made undeniable the link between ownership and use. His lecture set a precedent for challenging speeches in coming years. Jim Hunter took the theme in 1995, 'Towards a Land Reform Agenda for a Scots Parliament'. In 1996 John Bryden addressed 'Land Tenure & Rural Development in Scotland'. Professor David McCrone explored 'Land, Democracy & Culture in Scotland' at the 1997 event. In September 1998, 'Land Reform in the 21st Century' was the theme of the incoming Labour Scottish Secretary, the Rt. Hon Donald Dewar

---

33. Robin Fraser Callander, *A Pattern of Landownership in Scotland*, Haughend Publications, 1987

MP. The sixth and final lecture was presented by Andy Wightman in 1999 entitled 'Land Reform: Politics, Power & the Public Interest'.[34] The work of these men, and others involved in the John McEwen Memorial Lectures in the 1990s, was pivotal in linking land ownership, land use and the nexus of power which was held in the hands of around 450 landowners – combined, these landowners held half of rural Scotland.

Earlier in the decade, Andy Wightman had been one of the organisers of the Reforesting Scotland Norway Study Tour in 1993. The tour represented a stellar range of participants and consultants, including Robin Callander, whose part in the evolving land debates of the following 20 years proved to be invaluable.[35] Callander's influence on Wightman, as a mentor and co-worker for land reform, encouraged the forestry student to undertake the most modern and rigorous non-governmental study of *Who Owns Scotland* to 1995.[36] Following the welcome for *Who Owns Scotland* (1996), the Scottish Wildlife and Countryside Link commissioned Wightman to contribute to the debate about preserving the wild places of Scotland, of which mountains are central. He produced *Scotland's Mountains: An Agenda for Sustainable Development* in 1996. In it he concluded, in his recommendations as a Scottish agenda for sustainable mountain development, that:

> We have the opportunity to transform Scotland's mountain country into an area capable of standing scrutiny against international environmental standards, and one which can also provide a high-quality environment for economic development, wildlife and unrivalled recreation. All that is needed is political will.[37]

And there was a struggle for the political will of Scotland in the '90s. An atmosphere of heightened expectations hung in the air ahead of the

34. The John McEwen Memorial Lectures 1993–99, The Friends of John McEwen

35. Reforesting Scotland, 1994

36. Andy Wightman, *Who Owns Scotland*, Canongate, 1996

37. Andy Wightman, *Scotland's Mountains: An Agenda for Sustainable Development*, SWCL, 1996

expected Labour victory in the 1997 General Election – and the promise of a powerful Scottish Parliament stimulated various political responses. SNP leader Alex Salmond MP was anxious to have a say in the potential policy drive of a Scots Parliament. During 1994 he proposed to the SNP's National Executive Committee that an independent 'Scottish Land Commission', like the work of an official Royal Commission, should be formed. With the Committee's approval, Salmond appointed Professor Allan MacInnes with three commissioners – Dot Jessieman, Ron Greer and Douglas MacMillan – to take evidence from around Scotland. They duly reported in November 1997 in 'Public Policy Towards Land in Scotland'.[38]

In this MacInnes envisaged involving local communities to be a key part to decisions about the uses of Scottish land – not full-blown land reform as such. The theme of elected Locality Land Councils to empower communities in that task was praised by MP Donald Dewar in his McEwen Memorial Lecture in 1998. Dewar also claimed that many of SNP and Labour's ideas were complimentary because

> we need solutions which give local communities the means as well as the scope to contribute actively to decisions about local land issues.[39]

He had entrusted the development of policy under Lord Sewell in the Scottish Office. And, in 1998, a classic programme of land reform was published. Again, Robin Callander contributed a crystal clear argument for a major measure of land reform in May 1999 in the soon to be resumed Scottish Parliament.[40]

Remembrance, outrage and Highland Heritage

Highland Heritage's work during the 1990s included increasing the size and content of *The Clearances Trail* guide and two campaigns relating

---

38. Allan MacInnes et al., 'Public Policy Towards Land in Scotland', SNP, 1996
39. Donald Dewar, 'Land Reform for the 21st Century, John McEwan Memorial Lecture, 1998
40. Robin Callander, *How Scotland is Owned*, Canongate, 1998

to the Sutherland Clearances. In 1993 another HH project was achieved with the assistance of the HRC. The trial and acquittal of Patrick Sellar in 1816 'by a jury of his peers' for atrocities committed in Strathnaver was marked by a plaque attached to the steeple of the court building in Church Street, Inverness where the trial had been conducted. The memorial was built with the permission from Inverness Provost, Alan Sellar – who was no relation to Patrick, but it made for good publicity. The plaque also highlighted the subsequent disgrace and dismissal of the unfortunate Sheriff Robert McKid, who had courageously brought Sellar to trial following the Strathnaver burnings in 1814. The tribute ends in Gaelic: 'Se firinn is ceartas a sheasas' ('Truth and justice will prevail').

Without a doubt, the most widespread controversy raised by a HH campaign came in October 1994. Two stalwarts, former Councillor Sandy Lindsay and retired engineer Peter Findlay, lodged an outline planning application for the removal of the nine-metre-high statue of the first Duke of Sutherland (known locally as the Mannie) from his 20-metre-high red sandstone plinth on the 400-metre-high Ben Bhraggie. The statue overlooks, and some say dominates, the East Sutherland town of Golspie. It can be seen for miles around.

Lindsay and Findlay wished to see the white stone statue relocated to the gardens of the Sutherland family's palatial castle at Dunrobin. The suggestion provoked debate as far away as New Zealand and Canada. The Highland Council rejected the statue's removal while agreeing, in principle, to the erection of an interpretive notice board at the main carpark in Golspie. I chronicled the story of the campaign in my book *Toppling the Duke: Outrage on Ben Bhraggie*.[41] The Mannie as his grace is known thereabouts, is undoubtedly a landmark. But to this day it serves to prompt discussion of the first Duke and Duchess and their 'improvements' that relocated between 5,000–10,000 people to stony ground by the coasts while the rich pastures of central Sutherland were chewed up and overgrazed by Cheviot sheep to the long-term detriment of our local biodiversity.

Dennis MacLeod, a Helmsdale-born mining engineer who had

recently returned to Scotland from Canada, suggested an alternative. Don't try to remove the statue, create a new one. He offered to erect another statue at Helmsdale to the victims of the Clearances. Through his generosity – he was a descendent of one of those cleared from Kildonan in 1816 – the Emigrants Statue sculpted by Gerald Laing was unveiled in July 2007. Dennis subsequently also gave a substantial sum to endow the Chair of History at the fledgling University of the Highlands and Islands based in Dornoch. And, its first professor appointed was none other than Dr James Hunter.

Highland Heritage and friends had once again proved that highlighting the historical land struggles helped boost local morale in remote communities which had been drained of so many people by the 1950s. Recollecting and remembering these events which had fashioned the Highlands were also an important part of the developing programmes of land reform being drawn up by political parties in the '90s.

A one-man protest

One day in May 1996, Ian Thomson, a serial protester against environmental wrongs in Scotland, set up camp in a derelict farm cottage. Boreland Farm cottage had been abandoned along with many others on the 15,000 acres of Blackford Farms Estate in Perthshire which was owned by the wealthy Al-Tajir family of the United Arab Emirates via registration in Liechtenstein.[42]

Thomson, who had previously protested at Dounreay and over the Skye Bridge tolls, was attempting to point out that so many ruined cottages could be occupied by new residents if taken by compulsory purchase. He cited the Land Settlement Act of 1919 in seeking a land grant for the Boreland Cottage and a machinery grant from the Tory Government if available. His polite letter to Michael Forsyth the Secretary of State for Scotland was to no avail, as Thomson had expected.

During the month of May he received offers of tatties to plant in the cottage's garden ground and received support from Roseanna Cunningham, now an SNP MP. She had been elected the previous year

---

42. *The Scotsman*, 2 May 1996

in a sensational by-election caused by the death of Tory MP Nicholas
Fairbairn. She was a strong advocate of land reform and on a visit to
Boreland with a tattie for Ian Thomson's patch stated:

> I am sure that I am not alone in saying a quiet 'good to
> you' when I hear of Ian Thomson's modern day land raid.[43]

She went on,

> It matters little where a particular millionaire happens
> to come from or where they currently live. What matters
> is how the land is used. That is the point Ian Thomson
> is making so visibly. In the 3 1/2 acres he has claimed for
> himself, he has brought fire back to a cold hearth and is
> starting to cultivate the land that has lain unused for too
> long.[44]

Offers of help and support came from far and wide. And I visited
Ian during that month to offer my support as the SNP land reform
spokesperson.

The estate adopted a low profile, but on 7 June in Perth Sheriff Hugh
Neilson heard from Blackford Farms that Ian's occupation of the farm
was a political protest. Neilson described Thomson 'in common par-
lance' as a squatter without rights to occupy the cottage and garden.
The sheriff gave the protester 13 days to remove himself. In a second
action the estate also sought to interdict Thomson from unlawfully entering any part of its land in the future.[45] The Al-Tajir family, who also
owned the nearby Highland Spring water bottling plant in Blackford,
did not seek bad publicity, but their management plan for this huge
farming estate was highlighted as a result of Thomson's protest. Calls
for affordable rural housing and land redistribution were prominent
during this land raid, a method that had served crofters and cottars

43. *Press & Journal*, 10 May 1996
44. ibid.
45. *Press & Journal*, 8 June 1996

well early in the century. But that was not to hold under an increasingly embattled '90s Tory administration.

Since the 1919 Land Settlement Act, which has been celebrated as one of the biggest contributors to the repopulation of the Highlands and Islands, various governments of different leanings have rebuffed land reform. The Labour Government of 1945 rejected the land settlement plans in Knoydart and the Tories rejected all sorts of land reform, anything that would cost the public purse. So, it is needless to say that the Boreland Cottage episode got a short shrift, shorter than it deserved.

Land reform debates and protests along with actual community buyouts were about to underpin the early work of the newly elected UK Labour Government. It would take debate and protest to actual policy making in the first Scottish Parliament with appropriate powers for 282 years. It would bring the art of the possible to making Scottish land reform laws.

4. Knoydart

The land raid that wasn't in vain

Much has been said, written or sung of the land raid by seven Knoydart men who attempted to settle their families there in November 1948. Their return from active service in World War 2 was to a land made unfit for heroes, by a laird with Nazi sympathies. The 1919 Land Settlement Act had failed this community, which had suffered crippling depopulation. In defiance of the law, the Knoydart Seven first tried the old Highland tactic of land raiding but, they soon went down the legal route to try beat their hated landlord, Lord Brocket. Sympathy with their plight cut no ice with the Labour Government, which, unwilling to create 'unprofitable' new crofts, backed the big estate. The Knoydart Seven may have failed, but their struggle inspired others to subsequent success. Hamish Henderson's lyrics kindled support for the seven that still sings out to us today: 'The lamp we've lit in Knoydart will never now go out.'[46]

Deference towards lairds had been somewhat dented by the levelling process of World War 2 and the 'We're all in it together' rallying cry. Service personnel in new education classes had debated the Beveridge Report of 1942, which addressed the five great evils in society: squalor, ignorance, want, idleness and disease. People were questioning the deep divisions of poverty and wealth that were so prevalent before 1939

---

46. Hamish Henderson, 'Ballad of the Men of Knoydart'

and a big swing to Labour in the 1945 general election confirmed that popular appetite for change.

The Inverness-shire MP from 1922 to 1950 was Sir Murdoch Mac-Donald. Sitting as a National Liberal since the 1930s, his majority in 1945 fell to its lowest in 1945. The combined votes of Labour's Neil Maclean and the Liberal Party's John MacCormick totalled 57%. Both opposition parties had gained votes that signalled rising expectations from demobbed troops.

Power to the Highlands, a government information film released in 1943, featured a conversation between five men in a railway carriage. One soldier talked of returning home, another aimed for the colonies, a civilian shepherd expressed his backing for the big estates, a sailor decried the forced removal of the Highland people and a man who qualified as an engineer was set to return to the Highlands to help construct the new hydro schemes. (A later scene had American soldiers meet the shepherd and explain how the Tennessee Valley Authority had transformed their depopulated land by hydro power.[47]) No doubt the servicemen who returned to Knoydart after the war would have engaged in similar discussions, but the reality of working on a remote West Highland estate for its infamous landlord offered nothing in the way of secure prospects or wider horizons.

Pre-war, the multi-millionaire brewer had been a leading light of the Anglo-German fellowship. He had even attended Hitler's birthday celebrations in 1938. Brocket had remained under government surveillance thereafter but his estate, which had been commandeered to boost sheep production, was still returned to his care after VE Day. Brocket's preference for exclusive shooting and angling rights resulted in a reduction in jobs on the estate and his unconcealed pro-Nazi sentiments reinforced fears for the future among those who had fought against fascist tyranny.

The talk among seven of the Knoydart ex-service men – Henry MacAskill, Archie MacDonald, Jack MacHardy, Duncan McPhail, Donald and Sandy Macphee and William Quinn – was of new land

---

47. UK Government information film used in part of the Channel 4 film *Edgeland*, 1986

holdings and the arrival of a keen new parish priest, Colin Macpherson, who sympathised with their plight, was a great help to their schemes. John Prebble commented that,

> Father Colin Macpherson spoke for the raiders, publicly and at the Court of Enquiry. Knoydart has been fortunate in its Catholic priests. Twice in the last century they defended their parishioners, and one went with them into Canadian exile.[48]

On the men's behalf Macpherson posted a resettlement plan to the Department of Agriculture in 1946 for over 40 new holdings. In response, civil servants instead proposed 19 new holdings. The estate ignored this interference.[49] Frustration began to build and with Father Macpherson's backing, the landless locals decided to stage a land raid as a well-publicised stunt. The Seven Men each staked claims and cleared the land around Inverie on Tuesday 9 November 1948. They did so, as they put it, 'for life itself'.[50]

In the following days, the national press splashed photographs and headlines about the raid across their pages. Brocket was aware of the raiders, but studiously ignored them. He left Knoydart and sought an interim interdict from Edinburgh, which was immediately granted by the 'obliging' Lord Strachan in the Court of Session.[51] Some Knoydart people also disapproved of the land raid. They were keeping their heads down to keep their jobs.

After the raiders received their notices to desist, supporters arranged a meeting in Mallaig. Incensed by Brocket's statement to the press that the peninsula was unsuitable for a big community as it rained a lot, they set up a defence fund and appointed Ewen Robertson as secretary/

---

48. John Prebble, *John Prebble's Scotland*, Secker & Warburg, 1984
49. Colin Macpherson's croft plans mentioned in *Scottish Daily Express*, 1946
50. *Scottish Daily Mail*, November 1948
51. Iain Fraser Grigor, 'The Seven Men of Knoydart' in Billy Kay (ed.), *The Complete Odyssey: Voices from Scotland's Recent Past*, Polygon, 1980, Grigor emphasised 'obliging'

treasurer.[52] Soon, offers of help and cash were arriving by post and telegram daily. Large and small sums were promised to fight the interim interdict. On 10 November 1948, George Houston, the organiser of the Scottish Union of Students employment bureau, offered volunteers to help with the spade work at Inverie.[53]

Father MacPherson also took the raiders' message far and wide. In Glasgow, the week following the raid, he chaired the first of several public meetings. (Brocket would thereafter blacken Macpherson's name in retaliation.) JM Buchanan of Clann Albainn wrote on 7 December 1948 to Ewen Robertson: he enclosed a cheque for £5 and 4 shillings, proceeds from a Glasgow rally of support on 19 November.[54] Clann Albainn was also trying to resettle returning soldiers in new homes. Its impressive letterhead at that date included well-known Scots such as their Honorary President the Countess of Erroll and among their 14 vice-presidents were Neil Gunn and Nigel Tranter.

Lochaber Labour Party, strong in the aluminium smelter town of Fort William, also backed the raiders. As of 22 November 1948, it alerted all branches to support the seven workers of Knoydart. It urged the greater Labour Party and trade unions to do the same, saying, 'the step they have taken will move forward towards Nationalisation of the Land'.[55] On 12 December 1948, an all-party demonstration by the Knoydart Defence Campaign was held in St Andrews (Berkeley) Hall, Glasgow. Oliver Brown, the campaign's honorary secretary and treasurer, sent cash to the assistance fund.[56]

Hamish Henderson was at that rally. He was employed at that time by the Workers Educational Association in Northern Ireland. Hamish, a distinguished former soldier, poet, folklorist and socialist, was inspired on his overnight passage back to Belfast to write the 'Ballad of the Seven Men of Knoydart'. Henderson set his highly satirical words

---

52. Knoydart Defence Fund started 10 November 1948 – letter in Henderson file (HF)
53. Letter – G Houston, SUOS, HF, 10 November 1948
54. Letter – Clann Albainn, HF, 7 December 1948
55. Letter – H MacGregor to E Robertson, HF, 22 November 1948
56. Letter – O Brown to E Robertson, HF, rec. 12 January 1949

at Brocket's expense to the tune of *Johnston's Motor Car*. Timothy Neat, Hamish's biographer, discovered that the song was banned by the BBC.[57] While the song was too nationalistic for the Communists and too socialist for the SNP and Labour, it became a folk song in no time nonetheless. For many of my generation, the version by Hamish Imlach in the 1960s introduced us to the land raid, to 'show the world that Highlanders have a right to Scottish land'. But, before the end of 1948, the Labour Government set out to quell the popular support for the Knoydart raiders. They engaged a Perthshire farmer, John Cameron, formerly on the Land Court, to conduct an enquiry. This enquiry met in Mallaig in an all-day session on 22 December 1948.[58]

The raiders had by then provisionally accepted the interdict and ceased land reclamation. With the help of Father Macpherson, some represented by solicitor John Shaw of Donald Shaw & Co. of Edinburgh[59], they prepared their case to present to Cameron. Meanwhile Brocket engaged an advocate to press the estate view. This was Charles JD Shaw, later to become the distinguished judge, Lord Kilbrandon, famous author of the Royal Commission on the Constitution in 1974.[60] Press coverage from the time suggests that, at the hearing, the management of Knoydart Estate was under searching examination. Bad sheep management was admitted by the estate's team, but energetic improvements were said to be in hand. A possible solution to the land dispute was proposed by Charles Shaw near the end of the meeting and was reported in the *Scottish Daily Express*:

> I would be happy to see how a compromise could be arrived at between the different interests. I think it should be reached.[61]

57. Timothy Neat, *Hamish Henderson: A Biography. Volume 1 – The Making of the Poet*, Polygon, 2007
58. Denis Rixson, *Knoydart: A History*, Birlinn, 1999
59. Letter – D Shaw to E Robertson, 26 November 1948
60. Charles JD Shaw QC for Lord Brocket
61. Charles JD Shaw, *Scottish Daily Express*, 23 December 1948

John Shaw then wrote to Lord Brocket to see what he thought.

However, the Secretary of State for Scotland, Arthur Woodburn MP, had other ideas and John Cameron's enquiry gave him the perfect excuse. Woodburn followed his government's doctrinaire policy of producing large quantities of food on large farms, be there arable or pasture. And Knoydart was ideal sheep ranching land. So, he ignored the 1912 Smallholders Act and the 1919 Land Settlement Act – each of which could have been applied to new holdings in Knoydart. The extent of his disinterest in the families who lived on Knoydart is summed up in the allegation that on his annual tour of the Highlands and Islands, on board a fishing protection vessel, Woodburn did not deign to set foot on Knoydart and simply viewed the coast through his binoculars from Loch Nevis.[62] As a result of Woodburn's influence, Cameron reported in late March 1949 that he saw only one sheep farm as the best plan for Knoydart. The idea of new holdings could not be sustained, he said. Outraged, the Knoydart Seven, with the help of Father Macpherson and John Shaw, composed a memorial to Arthur Woodburn and in it refuted the Cameron findings point by point. It is a model document for land settlement, even by 2020 standards, but it was to no avail.[63]

The official enquiry divided Highland opinion. Attempts to get around the interim interdict and negotiate with Brocket continued. Costs were met from the defence fund and donations poured in, such as five shillings from a Mull 'Wellwisher' and ten pounds and ten shillings from a ceilidh organised by a Mr Scott Moncrieff on the Isle of Eigg.[64] By mid-1949, the defence fund had accrued three times its expenditure to date. Brocket's legal team probed the health of that fund to gauge the likelihood of further court challenges ahead of a final hearing on the interdict. Legal discussions dragged on. Debate in the newspapers flared. Could crofting pay? Was Highland land settlement a social issue

---

62. Grigor, 'The Seven Men of Knoydart'

63. Undated 1949 Memorial re Knoydart Estate by Alexander McPhee and others, HF

64. Income listing receipts Mull Wellwisher, 20 December 1948; Eigg Ceilidh, HF, 22 January 1949 etc

rather than purely economic one? And so on. These are themes still pursued today for and against community land buyouts.[65]

James MacLachlan from Clann Albainn wrote to Ewen Robertson at Mallaig. He hoped that many more of his members would visit Inverie and he recommended full support of the Knoydart Seven to Clann Albainn's National Council. Noticeably, their letterhead was now shorn of aristocratic sponsors probably due to their stance on the land 'grab' issue. MacLachlan also represented new settlers on abandoned crofts at Scoraig in Wester Ross. He confirmed his support for the raiders after a reconnaissance to Knoydart. Furthermore, he promised to lobby John McLeod, the Ross-shire MP, another National Liberal, and 'make it hot for him' if McLeod agreed with the Highland panel view that backed John Cameron.[66]

In July, Father Macpherson reported to John Shaw that the men were still in good heart, but that they knew their case in law was difficult, even if morally justified. Shaw noted the priest's conversations with former MP Dr Robert McIntyre, chairman of the SNP, and Reverend TM Murchison of Clann Albainn as being 'rather extreme in their views' but that the memorial he had sent to Woodburn

> has shaken the public confidence in the Cameron Report and the precipitate acceptance of it by the Secretary of State.[67]

Dr McIntyre's pamphlet *State Subsidies for Private Tyrannies – the Lesson of Knoydart* was a thorough-going rejection of Tory and Labour 'centralist reaction in opposition to the development of free communities in Scotland' and noted in passing 'the sheer hypocrisy' of the Communist Party in trying to cash in on the Knoydart affair.[68]

Time passed, and hopes for secure jobs faded. One raider tried to

---

65. *The Scotsman*, HF, 1949 and Rixson, *Knoydart*, 1999

66. Letter – J McLauchlan to E Robertson, 14 April 1949

67. Letter – C Macpherson to J Shaw, HF, 3 July 1949; Letter – J Shaw to C Macpherson, HF, 6 July 1949

68. Dr RD McIntyre, *State Subsidies for Private Tyrannies: The Lesson of Knoydart*, a pamphlet, 1949, I was given a copy by Doc Mac in 1993 along with his support for the Assynt Crofters (see illustrations)

make his peace with the estate, as Ewen A Cameron tells us in the *Oxford Dictionary of National Biography*:

> Brocket was certainly willing to use coercive tactics and did so against one of the raiders late in 1949. Jack Mac-Hardy had been working as a gardener on the estate prior to the raid and in October 1949 sought such employment once again. Brocket demanded, and received, an 'unqualified apology and undertaking never to repeat such acts as those on November 9 1948' before granting MacHardy's request.[69]

And so, families continued to drift away. In 1951, the interdict was handed down without further pleas and each of the men received papers from the Court of Session plus a bill sharing the expenses of the court and the travel costs of the Oban-based Messenger-at-Arms. The defence fund paid up, but the men had to admit defeat. Knoydart continued to stagnate and Brocket sold the whole property the following year.[70] The Church of Scotland gave up on the house allocated by the estate for a minister (to a dwindling congregation) and Father Macpherson was moved on by his church. Writing from St Michael's, Eriskay, South Uist in April 1952 he sent a long overdue cheque for accommodation in Mallaig for a Mr Black in December 1949. In the accompanying letter, the priest commented on his own brief visit to Knoydart, there he found

> that the place seems unchanged. It is still invested with the Brocket miasma – or do I imagine that to be so! I feel sorry for the poor folk. Give me a place open to the fresh air, where people stand independent and unafraid.[71]

---

69. Ewen A Cameron, 'Seven Men of Knoydart (act. 1948)', *Oxford Dictionary of National Biography*, 2007

70. Letter – E Robertson to D Shaw, HF, 21 September 1949; Court of Session writ for expenses to A McPhee and others, HF, 1951

71. Letter – C Macpherson to E Robertson, HF, 4 April 1952

Commemorating the land raid after 40 years

Following 1948, estate jobs were few, visitors and climbers were discouraged as before, shooting deer continued and life on the peninsula decayed under successive short-term owners. My own involvement, years after learning Henderson's stirring 'Ballad of the Seven Men of Knoydart', began as the SNP spokesperson on land reform in opposition to a possible purchase of Knoydart in 1983 by the MoD.[72] But it was the grim determination of one man, Archie MacDougall, which linked the 1948 raid with the hope of future land reform.

Archie's father and grandfather had both been shepherds on the Knoydart Estate. However, his father had left to find work at Monzie near Blair Atholl and this was where Archie was born in 1927. On his mother's death, he was sent to Knoydart to stay with an aunt where he remained till 1952 as an estate gardener, when not in active service as a soldier.[73] In November 1948 Archie was away with the army, but a land claim was staked for him by his neighbour Henry MacAskill. Archie withdrew the claim, fearing army discipline, but attended the Cameron enquiry nevertheless. With the failure of the men's pleas and Brocket's vengeful treatment of them, Archie, like the majority of the others, left Knoydart in 1952. His life as a professional gardener ended in Inverness, where he retired.

For the 40th anniversary of the land raid, Iain MacDonald of BBC Radio Scotland Inverness interviewed Archie who recalled the events and appealed for a permanent memorial to be made to their struggle. I heard the interview and contacted Archie. After that, in February 1989, we set about forming the Land Raid Commemoration Committee. This included myself, then a District Councillor in Ross and Cromarty, and Michael Foxley, Regional Councillor for Ardnamurchan, Mallaig and the Small Isles, whose wife was related to one of the raiders.[74] We were also backed by Archie himself and Councillors Peter Peacock, Sandy Lindsay and Dr Iain Glen, all land campaigners.

---

72. Letters – December 1982 and February 1983, in the author's files
73. Archie MacDougall, *Knoydart: The Last Scottish Land Raid*, Lyndhurst Publications, 1993
74. Press notice, 1991, in the author's files

It took us two years to find a site at Inverie for the proposed cairn. Correspondence with the estate owner, Phillip Rhodes, was stone-walled. Even with help from environmentalist Chris Brasher we got nowhere. Then Foxley thought to ask the local hall committee, who agreed a site just off the tarred road which passed close by.[75] Generous donations, such as one from Father Colin Macpherson, latterly the Bishop of Argyll and the Isles,[76] allowed us to engage Duncan Matheson from Kintail who had built the bicentennial cairn in Mossman, New South Wales, Australia. He designed and built the land raid memorial and topped it out with a broken quern stone, a symbol of a broken community. The Land Raid Commemoration Committee agreed the wording of the metal plaque he built into it.

A considerable crowd gathered at Inverie on 14 September 1991 for the unveiling. We were piped there by Iain 'The Whaler' Macdonald of Glenuig and fiddler Farquhar Macrae while Archie MacDougall un-veiled the cairn. Later in the pub, however, we were met with a muted reaction. Most of the 50 residents of the peninsula were recent arrivals. The publican at The Old Forge told the press that the inscription on the cairn was 'a political statement and not what the Seven Men of Knoydart was about'.[77] Oh, how things would change in just four years.

Incidentally, Knoydart wasn't the last land raid. North Uist men sought to extend their Balmartin crofts after a raid on Balelone farm in November 1952 and negotiations with their laird allowed it to succeed.[78] But Knoydart was still unfinished business by the mid-1990s. By then, the Knoydart commemoration committee wanted to add the names of the raiders and their associates to the cairn. It was agreed that the VE Day anniversary of 1995 was an appropriate date to do so. A second plaque was made and, under the watchful eye of Duncan Matheson, I was to attach it to the cairn. Duncan had been unable to attend the unveiling in 1991 due to a cancelled CalMac sailing from Armadale to

75. Letter – M Foxley to R Gibson, 5 March 1991
76. Letter – C Macpherson to R Gibson with donation
77. *Press & Journal*, 11 September 1991; *Press & Journal*, 16 September 1991
78. MacDougall, *Knoydart*, 1993; James Hunter, *The Claim of Crofting: The Scottish Highlands and Islands, 1930–1990*, Mainstream Publishing, 1991

Mallaig, so we were pleased to congratulate his cairn-building skills in 1995 as Archie MacDougall screwed in the final nail.[79]

At that time the estate was changing hands yet again. Reg Brealey, the new owner, had an obscure jute company called Titaghur, which very soon left estate workers unpaid. So Knoydart was sold once again, this time to Stephen Hinchliffe and Christopher Harrison, who formed Knoydart Peninsula Ltd (KPL). This regime was also short-lived. Residents passed a motion of no confidence in the pair during Hinchliffe's sole visit to Inverie in May 1998. Liquidation of KPL followed in November when Hinchliffe was barred from directorships due to irregular financial dealings.[80]

By March 1999, on the eve of the first Scottish Parliament elections, a partnership called the Knoydart Foundation was set up, similar the one struck up on Eigg. The residents were joined by Sir Cameron Mackintosh, impresario and neighbouring landowner, the Chris Brasher Trust, the John Muir Trust and the Highland Council who bought the remaining 17,000 acres. I, and many others, attended Liberation Day, celebrated on 26 March 1999. At it, the Foundation pledged to ensure the next generation inheriting the estate would see it in better shape than it had been when freed from a string of private lairds.[81]

Knoydart in retrospect

Looking back over the 72 years since the Knoydart land raid, it can seem like decades of frustration were only relieved in 1999. Estate workers – be they gamekeepers, shepherds, gardeners or domestic staff – wanted real security for their families on their own holdings. But long after 1948 acceptance of existing landownership conventions were still ingrained in the minds of law makers. The idea of crofters and estate workers owning their own land was a pipe dream for most of the 20th century. Only the people of Stornoway, who were gifted their parish in 1923 by Lord Leverhulme, or the few hundred small holders in

79. MacDougall, *Knoydart*, 1993
80. *Press & Journal*, 5 November May 1998
81. James Hunter, *From the Low Tide of the Sea to the Highest Mountain Tops*, The Islands Book Trust, 2012

Glendale, whose land was bought by the Congested Districts Board in 1905, were exceptions.[82]

Certainly, the Small Landholders (Scotland) Act of 1911 and the Land Settlement (Scotland) Act of 1919 offered new ways to secure places for families on their native turf. But after World War 1, crofting became seen as a loser's game and emigration rocketed, enabled by the 1922 Empire Settlement Act which saw the government spend huge sums shifting folk to the colonies rather than setting them up with holdings at home.[83]

After the deep Depression of the 1930s and the struggle to beat Hitler, new expectations were fostered among returning servicemen and women in the mid-1940s. Many voted for a Labour Government, and demanded Scottish home rule from that party. But instead they got the NHS and other nationalised utilities. Central control was the norm and the depopulation in north-west Scotland remained a mere afterthought to the establishment. True, Tom Johnston's hydro schemes did offer construction jobs in the Highlands, but officials seemed keener on tourism for the north than small farming.

The Knoydart saga in 1948 threw a shaft of light on to the continuing assertion of the peoples' right to their land made by Highland Scots. Dr Robert McIntyre of the SNP summed up the problem. The Labour Government was quite prepared

> to uphold the rights of personal property of Lord Brocket in the power it gives him over the people in Knoydart... [But] at the same time the government prevent the people of Knoydart from acquiring rights to private property of a very limited kind in crofts and houses. It is this limited property which would give the freedom and stability required to develop a healthy community and which cannot be used to exploit others.[84]

---

82. ibid.
83. ibid.
84. McIntyre, *State Subsidies for Private Tyrannies*, 1949

Such views had been called 'extreme' by John Shaw, the raiders' solicitor. But it can be seen that throughout the 20th century the people of Knoydart had little choice but to leave the peninsula to find work.

From 1965 to 1979, the HIDB, founded by Labour, struggled with the crofting problem, the Gaidhealtachd and the Islands. Its compulsory purchase powers were no greater than a county council's and land settlement was finally binned by Thatcher's Government in 1979.[85]

Yet debate over land reform continued in that Thatcher era as an antidote to her destruction of so many industries and communities. In 1980, Billy Kay edited the BBC Scotland radio series *Odyssey: Voices from Scotland's Recent Past*, which revived the Knoydart story. And thanks to the research of Iain Fraser Grigor, we heard the voices of the dispossessed.[86] The '80s were a time of memorials and commemorations – Glendale, the Braes, Gartymore, Strathnaver and so on. After Archie MacDougall's interview in 1988, why not Knoydart too?

In the '90s folk memory and politics intertwined. The cement had hardly dried on the land raid cairn at Inverie when the news of popular resistance on Eigg and then Assynt opened a new chapter of demands by crofters and communities. The Tory Scottish Secretary Michael Forsyth had prodded HIE into funding the Assynt buyout in 1993. And the prospects of a Labour Government elected in 1997 gave real hope to communities like Eigg and Knoydart – hopes which were realised before the end of the decade.

The Knoydart Foundation set up in 1999 has proved a success. It has increased the resident population by 60 per cent by renewing the estate hydro scheme to power the off-grid peninsula and building houses, a bunkhouse and workshops for new enterprises. Angela Williams, their development manager, told Jim Hunter in 2012 that

> achieving financial sustainability was one of our basic aims. Given all the outgoings we have on wages, maintenance and much else, it's not been easy to get there. But we've managed it – and this matters. After all, community

---

85. Grassie, *Highland Experiment*, 1983
86. Grigor, 'The Seven Men of Knoydart', 1980

ownership can only work long-term if a community owned estate can be made to break even, or, better still, can get into profit.[87]

Angela also told Common Space in May 2016:

> We have succeeded in projects, and understanding where you're coming from is important to understanding why change is happening.[88]

And, concerning the Knoydart land raiders cairn built in 1991, she said:

> It's just a very small monument, [near] the village hall. Yes, that's even further back in the past – but you could argue that what we've achieved has its roots there. Even though the population has changed, that is a daily reminder that what they did wasn't in vain.[89]

The plaque's inscription in Gaelic and English reads:

Justice!

In 1948 near this cairn the Seven Men of Knoydart staked claims to secure a place to live and work.

For over a century Highlanders had been forced to use land raids to gain a foothold where their forebears lived. Their struggle should inspire each new generation of Scots to gain such rights by just laws.

87. Hunter, *From the Low Tide of the Sea*, 2012
88. 'The People's Land: How Community Ownership has Revitalised Knoydart, CommonSpace, 26 May 2016, www.commonspace.scot/articles/8471/people-s-land-how-community-ownership-has-revitalised-knoydart
89. ibid.

History will judge harshly the oppressive laws that have led to the virtual extinction of a unique culture from this beautiful place.

Note: I am indebted to Sandra Henderson, nee Robertson, Fort William for access to many local records of the 1948 land raid. Their details allow us great empathy for that era.

5. Land reform takes off

1999 to 2011

A remarkable degree of agreement is now developing about what needs to change and about the broad approach which should be adopted.
– Rt. Hon. Donald Dewar MP, John McEwen Memorial Lecture, 1998

The reform ideas proffered to the incoming government that had been elected to the new Scottish Parliament in May 1999 contained lengthy to do lists from various activists and political parties. The accumulated wisdom of decades of Activism, in addition to the pent-up expectation stemming from the two-question referendum result of September 1997, was about to collide with the art of the possible.

Referring to the Land Reform Policy Group (LRPG) consultation, *Identifying the Problems*, which was issued in February 1998, Donald Dewar cautioned optimists that

> deciding on an initial programme of Action will of course mean selecting from these options, but even if, after consultation, the list for immediate Action is cut down by half or even more, there will still be a sizeable agenda for the Scottish Parliament to pick up.[90]

And the pace of reform in the first term of the Scottish Parliament reflected Donald Dewar's caution. *Identifying the Solutions* focused on the abolition of the feudal system, rural land reform, crofting

---

90. Dewar, 'Land Reform for the 21st Century', 1998

Community Right to Buy (CRTB) (if necessary without a willing seller) and non-crofting CRTB only with agreement of the seller and a world-leading right to roam law (and consequent pre-emptive rights and responsibilities for land holders and tenement dwellers). Separately, agricultural tenancy law was opened up to allow for new shorter assured tenancies to encourage new entrants and stimulate the sector. Access rights were fully legalised and two National Parks were created, the consensus for change was evident in the support for each measure by all parties – except the Tories. Their MSPs fought for the rights of the lairds and luridly described some reforms as 'Mugabe-style land grabs'. It was a promising start.

It takes several years for new laws – such as the Land Reform (Scotland) Act 2003 – to bed in, not least because literally dozens of pieces of Scottish statutory instruments (SSIs) have to be consulted, debated, enacted and put into practice by civil servants and government agencies. But the pace of land reform was also stalled by the slow decline of the second Labour and Lib Dem coalition. 'Doing less better' lost First Minister Jack McConnell the 2007 election and allowed Alex Salmond to form a minority SNP Government. But from the start, Salmond was subject to Labour jibes that the SNP was not interested in taking land reform to the next stage.

The Land Reform Review Group (LRRG), in 2014, reported examples of Scottish Parliament Acts containing land reform measures from the Labour-Lib Dem regime onwards. In the report, these measures are defined as

> provisions that modify or change the arrangements governing the possession and use of land in the public interest.

Ten of these were passed from 1999 to 2007 and three under the SNP Government of 2007–11.[91] These three were the Crofting Reform Act (2010), which was required to tidy up the overly moderate 2006 measure, the Wildlife and Natural Environment (Scotland) Act and the

---

91. Land Reform Review Group, 2014

Private Rented Housing (Scotland) Act, both enacted before the May 2011 Scottish Parliament election.

But that was far from the full picture. In 2007, the minority SNP Government had relied on Conservative support to pass its budget. And this political irritant, 'buying off' the Tories, occurred as the major land and agricultural holdings reforms of 2003 were bedding in. By 2007, pressure to bring in crofting reform, a policy area that had long stalled, was taking up considerable committee time and resources.

In April 2010, to try and move things along, post-legislative scrutiny of the 2003 Act was commissioned at the behest of the Rural Affairs and Environment (RAE) committee and the Scottish Parliament Corporate Body. The Centre for Mountain Studies based at Perth College UHI, led by Calum Macleod, was selected to carry this out. They proposed improvements to the measures on access provisions, CRTB and crofting CRTB. They also set the study in its political context, concentrating on the three pillars of recreational access, community and crofting community rights to buy.[92]

However, critics still accused the minority SNP Government of having few new proposals for land reform. The most vocal critic, Andy Wightman, marshalled a series of historical land questions and confrontations to challenge the SNP. His proposals for land reform in his influential polemic, *The Poor Had No Lawyers*, had been worked on since the 1990s in close collaboration with Robin Callander and they contained wide-ranging moves such as repeal of the Prescription and Limitation (Scotland) Act 1973 which could cure defective titles to property. He also proposed a form of LVT as an extended exemplar – the very same tax issue that had been body-swerved by the LRPG as requiring 'further study'.[93]

Wightman accused the SNP of having given up on land reform. His critique of the SNP's apparent unwillingness to pursue land reform rests on his interpretation of one parliamentary question from 2009. In the book he adds the reference as a footnote and does not give

---

92. 'Post Legislative Scrutiny of the Land Reform (Scotland) Act 2003', Rural Affairs and Environment committee commissioned report, 2010
93. Land Reform Policy Group, 'Recommendations for Action', 1999

Roseanna Cunningham's answer in full. Reading the Actual question and answer offers a different perspective:

Question S3W-24965: Elaine Murray, Dumfries, Scottish Labour, Date Lodged: 18/06/2009

> To ask the Scottish Executive whether it is concerned that no more than five communities have acquired land since the Community Right to Buy provisions of the Land Reform (Scotland) Act 2003 came into force.

Answered by Roseanna Cunningham (08/07/2009)

> Forty-five community bodies have successfully registered an interest in buying land since the Land Reform (Scotland) Act 2003 was implemented on 14 June 2004. The number of community bodies registering in each calendar year is five in 2004; eight in 2005; nine in 2006; ten in 2007; 14 in 2008; and two in 2009. Within the above figures, one body registered separate interests in 2004, 2006 and 2008. A second body similarly registered separate interests in 2005 and 2007. Two community bodies are currently in the process of registering their interest and their applications are being considered by ministers.

> These 45 community bodies have made some 74 registrations in the Register of Community Interests in Land. Some community bodies have more than one registration (a registration is made in respect of land owned by one landowner).

> As the Community Right to Buy requires a willing seller (it does not involve a compulsory purchase of registered land), there is no certainty that a landowner would want to sell the land during the period when a community body has registered its interest. The purpose of these provisions in the Act is to provide communities with the opportunity

of a pre-emptive right to buy the land in which it has a registered interest should the conditions of the right to buy be triggered. Community right to buy was never intended as the only way that communities achieve ownership of land.

The right to buy has been triggered in respect of 22 parcels of land relating to registrations held by 15 communities. While five registered communities have acquired their desired land using the full provisions of the Act, an additional two have negotiated a successful purchase after having their interest registered. Beyond that, eight further community bodies had the opportunity to acquire registered land when it was offered for sale (ie triggering the right to buy) but failed to purchase. One community body has also successfully purchased, by negotiation, two pieces of land following approval of their application for registration under the Act.

Experience of the practical operation of the Community Right to Buy provisions led to revised guidance being published on 15 June 2009, which provides more hands-on advice on the required processes and procedures for community bodies, landowners, heritable creditors and third parties who may be affected by the provisions. A revised application form with provisions for re-registration, also came into force on that date.

The Land Reform (Scotland) Act 2003 has only been in effect for a relatively short period of time and we are continuing to monitor the Community Right to Buy provisions. If there is evidence that the provisions are not working as Parliament intended, then a review of the Act will be considered.[94]

94. Question S3W-24965, 8 July 2009

The answer reads to me as the government departments were properly applying and adapting the extensive land laws passed in 2003.

This is a useful juncture to remind ourselves of Robin Callander's definition of the three main components of land reform. The first is to reform property law, the legal system of tenure and transfer. The second is to reform administrative law, which includes a wide range of statutes and mechanisms to set up government bodies and environmental laws. The third is to reform the regulations and incentives to promote or control the use of rights over land such as grants and licences. Callander explains these as levels which build on top on one another. The base is the first component, which provides a framework of property law. By this definition, the limited scope of changes to the property law of rural land in the 2003 Land Reform Act immediately limited the advancement of primary legislation. The second layer can be exemplified by the setting up of National Parks by arranging a succession of land funds and enacting access laws. Many of financial incentives, rules for applying the right to buy etc, are examples of the third tier.[95]

Certainly, the areas of property law detailed by Andy Wightman in several publications would require considerable primary legislation preceded by an assessment of European Convention on Human Rights (ECHR) implications and statutory consultation preceding the full parliamentary process.

One can understand Andy's impatience and see his painstaking research – extensive and sustained reviews of necessary policies required to achieve thorough-going land reform. He and others have often listed the programmes the government requires to modernise Scottish land laws. But Wightman's polemic style takes no prisoners. From the claims made in his book, the SNP were back-sliding. And this is a black mark against any government no matter what the political and economic circumstances.

However, Wightman ignores the move by Minister Mike Russell in 2007 to take a few hundred acres on Rum from Scottish Natural Heritage (SNH) to kick-start a community body. Furthermore,

---

95. Callander, *How Scotland is Owned*, 1998

after Wightman's book's publication, Russell's successor Roseanna Cunningham took the bold decision, with ECHR implications, to grant the long-running Pairc buyout the right to buy as a hostile bid. This was the first under the 2003 Act and its saga would struggle through further court cases before the residents finally acquired the land in December 2015. Barry Lomas of Leamington Spa, the reluctant seller, had delayed a change-over of the land in exchange for nearly 13 years of expensive litigation. He negotiated a £500,000 sale price after the hostile bid was withdrawn at his request in 2014. Events and controversies consequent to the 2003 Act, such as Pairc, fuelled the clamour for further land reform action.

The final report of Calum Macleod's team was published in September 2010. It set the parameters for subsequent commitments by the SNP in its Scottish Parliament election manifesto for 2011; to aid community purchases and provide a land fund. The report states:

> We believe it is time for a review of Scotland's land reform legislation. For example, we believe the current period for three months for communities to take advantage of their right of first purchase is too short, and we would wish to see it extended to six months. We will establish a Land Reform Review Group to advise on this and other improvements which we will legislate on over the course of the next five years. We will also establish a new Scottish Land Fund and will set out our proposals in this area by the end of 2011.[96]

The SNP responded in its manifesto by proposing a review of land reform thus far, with a commitment to

> establish a Land Reform Review Group to advise on this and other improvements which we will legislate on over the course of the next five years.

---

96. 'Post legislative scrutiny of the Land Reform (Scotland) Act 2003', 2010

The return of a majority SNP Government in May 2011 brought this about.

The art of the possible and the political priorities of the law makers produced a decade of major change for the better. But it left me with the nagging doubts about the pace of the reclamation of our land needed to answer Donald Dewar's parting shot in his John McEwen Memorial Lecture:

We need to put in place arrangements so that further changes can be worked through and worked up. So that we can ensure that such legislation is not a one-off, but a down-payment.[97]

---

97. Dewar, 'Land Reform for the 21st Century', 1998

6. Deer impact across Scotland

Beyond the common grazing, on the deer ground they call Wild Land, that's our domestic space. It is where we harvest deer, fish, nuts, mushrooms.
– Issy MacPhail, Assynt crofter, Community Land Conference, Stirling 2017

Highlands and Islands MSP Rob Gibson has welcomed the constructive and collaborative approach of the participants in the Responsible Deer Management consultation where the aim is to produce a framework on how to deal with Scotland's burgeoning deer population. Following the passage of the Nature Conservation Act last summer Mr Gibson who has worked closely with Non-Governmental Organizations, responsible estate owners and with colleagues in the Environment and Rural Development Committee in this consultation says that real and sustainable progress is being made...

Any reasonable estate owner who looks at the findings and progress of the deer management proposals contained in the motion lodged for debate in Parliament cannot help but be impressed by its approach. That is why it is galling to read such nightmarish myths and lurid fantasies that are currently being pedalled by those who really should know better.
– Caithness.org, January 2005: 'Gibson hits out at 'irresponsible landowners'

Dear, Deer!
Decades ago, when I began walking the Scottish hills, I was always struck by the Highlanders' claims that taking one for the pot was a basic right. Be it deer, salmon or game bird, you can see the point of

feeding the family. Indeed, the Great Deer Raid in 1887 in the Pairc deer forest on the Isle of Lewis had that aim. It was a direct action against private deer stalking tenancy while nearby crofting villages starved. The charges against the crofters' leaders in South Lochs sparked widespread support across the land from sympathisers such as RB Cunninghame Graham, radical Liberal MP for North West Lanarkshire. He wrote in *The Scottish Highlander*:

> Scotland is a free country – quite – it appears; for the crofter to starve in, or a deer to eat his crops in.

Since many crofters sought work in his Lanarkshire constituency, he knew of their plight directly.

As times changed, the idea of poaching also changed and commercial gangs were known to target whole herds of red deer or poison salmon with Cymag. The chemicals could kill all the fish in a whole river system. But it only poisoned fish, not humans.[98] Wildlife crime has been big business for years. In 1959, a question in the House of Lords to the Scottish Office minister on Cymag came from Viscount Goschen on behalf of Viscount Massareen and Ferrard who was ill that day. The latter Viscount also had the opportunity to introduce the Deer (Scotland) Bill into Parliament in 1966 which set up the Red Deer Commission. As a landowner of some 16,000 acres in the Isle of Mull, and another 20,000 acres in Antrim and Louth, he provides a useful example of the interest their Lordships had, and have, in preserving game for the rich and punishing trespassers and would-be poachers. During the 20th century poachers still played a cat and mouse game with ghillies and lairds. But, unlike in previous times, when you might be transported to the colonies for such offences, the courts had more limited powers. If convicted, you could only be fined, or have your car and gear confiscated.

John Buchan, capitalising on the Victorian craze for blood sports, used the idea of poaching for his light-hearted, adventure novel *John MacNab*. It features bored gentlemen in a shooting lodge one rainy autumn, post WW1, issuing a challenge to three neighbouring estate

---

98. House of Lords Debate, vol. 220 cc 523–24, 17 December 1959

owners where John MacNab might poach a salmon, shoot two deer and avoid detection.[99] This story extolled the popularity of the romantic side of poaching. In the dying years of John Major's Tory Government the Criminal Justice & Public Act 1994 introduced the crime of aggravated trespass.[100] This new law could prosecute those who might wish to disrupt deer stalking and driven grouse shoots. Also targeted were hunt saboteurs who tried to interfere with the then lawful pursuit of fox hunting. The Act arose through increased protests that sought to occupy land which could disrupt other 'peaceful activities' such as the work of nuclear missile installations at Greenham Common or the nuclear submarine facilities at the Faslane Naval Base on the Gare Loch. This new law incensed Scottish novelist Andrew Greig and prompted him to plot *The Return of John MacNab*.[101] It is an exhilarating read that added 'feisty' female characters and a daring plot line, in a way Buchan would never have dreamed. Greig introduced the ultimate poaching incursion on the royal estates in Deeside. I understand that the film rights were acquired but never pursued, more's the pity, because Scottish historical and contemporary themes rarely reach our TV screens. Are they too threatening to the established order?

But, at the end of the 20th century, attitudes to poaching were about to take a subtle turn. Instead of the thrill of outfoxing an absentee laird, the responsibilities of ownership for residents loomed large. With the advent of community land buyouts, many former poachers were turned, not into game keepers, but into owners of their natural resources on what amounts today to over 500,000 acres of community owned lands. Evidence from North Harris, not a stone's throw from Pairc, shows the community buyout arrangements led to the 2009 North Harris Deer Management Plan which was built on a partnership with Ian Scarr Hall.[102] Hall's interest in deer shooting had precipitated his purchase

99. Buchan, *John Macnab*, 1925
100. 'Aggravated Trespass' freebeagles, www.network23.org/freebeagles/ criminal-law/other-laws/misc/aggravated-trespass/
101. Andrew Greig, *The Return of John Macnab*, Headline Books, 1996
102. North Harris Deer Management Plan 2009–12 discussed in Fiona D Mackenzie, *Places of Possibility: Property, Nature and Community Land Ownership*, Wiley-Blackwell, 2012

of Amhuinnsuidhe Castle. However, in 2002, he made a unique deal with the North Harris buyout group where he kept the right to shoot a specified number of stags but the community estate also gained income and some employment from this 'blood sport'. The previously elite sport of stalking was further 'troubled', as Fiona Mackenzie puts it in *Places of Possibility*, by the creation of the Harris Hind Stalking Club in 2004. This gave community members a job in the essential task of hind culling and subsequently sharing the stag shooting with Ian Scarr Hall. Extended hind culling was agreed with SNH to succour resident golden eagles which can eat deer carcasses shot on the high ground. All in all, a neat way to meet several land management goals and fill the freezers of local families with lean, wild deer meat. As we will see this approach did not suit every land buyout group however.

How many deer are there?
The deer population of Scotland has trebled in 30 years. In 2015, when we were debating the Land Reform (Scotland) Bill, I received some evidence from Ninian Stuart, the hereditary keeper of Falkland Palace, and laird of the adjoining estate which he runs on ecological lines. On a Rural Affairs, Climate Change & Environment (RACCE) committee visit to Falkland scoping land reform issues ahead of Stage 1 of the Bill in September 2015, Ninian offered to send me a newspaper cutting discussing his father's resignation as chairman of the Red Deer Commission in 1963. John Crichton-Stuart, 3rd Marquess of Bute, had resigned during his second stint in post. *The Glasgow Herald* of 23 September 1963, explained:

> The last report of the Red Deer Commission complained that lack of co-operation from farmers and landowners could cripple it in its task, which is to reduce the red deer population of the Highlands to manageable proportions.

That was when the red deer population was estimated to be 150,000.[103] Forty years later, when I was elected as an SNP Regional Member for the Highlands & Islands, deer numbers in Scotland were now

---

103. *The Glasgow Herald*, 23 September 1963

estimated to be 450,000. Deer management was now a hot topic. During the passage of the Nature Conservation (Scotland) Bill in the winter of 2003 and spring of 2004 new protections had to be included for Sites of Special Scientific Interest and European designated Natura Sites due to predations by hungry deer.

Arran of the Bens the Glens and the Brave

I first visited Glen Diomhan in August 1965 on a solo hill walk from Pirnmill on the Isle of Arran's west coast. I walked over Beinn Bhreac and followed the Abhainn Mor towards Catacol to catch the bus back to Brodick. I'd heard about a nature reserve created to protect Sorbus arranensis and Sorbus pseudofennica – two crosses of rowan and true whitebeam native only to Arran. The wooden deer fencing erected in 1961 around the steep gully containing the biggest stand of these rare trees didn't strike me at the time as adequate. In 2003, having been elected to Holyrood as MSP for Highlands & Islands, Arran was not in my patch. But, friends such as Malcolm Kerr and Henry Murdo and my cousin, Thea Andrews, made good reasons for regular visits to the island. Inevitably, land ownership and land use questions cropped up between us.

Henry Murdo, a longstanding member of Arran Mountain Rescue had walked and climbed over most of these hills. He had observed Arran whitebeams in precarious ledges and gullies, the few places safe from grazing deer, sheep and goats. To his horror, the fencing around Glen Diomhan was in very bad repair. It had been designated by the Nature Conservancy as a National Nature Reserve (NNR) in 1956 in an agreement with the Duchess of Montrose who owned much of the island at that time. Along with Don MacNeish, Henry photographed and publicised the poor state of fencing, some of which had recently been contracted out by SNH to protect the rare, and increasingly en-dangered, Arran whitebeams in the NNR. It was supposed to preserve flora, fauna, geological and zoological interests.

That's when my partner, Eleanor Scott, and I arrived on the scene. As newly elected MSPs, Henry Murdo was seeking our help to alert SNH to fulfil its duties. On 7 June 2003, we walked the three and a half kilometres up Glen Catacol, the wildcat's gully, to Glen Diomhan, the idle or untilled glen. It is set below Creag na h-Iolaire, the eagle's crag, to the north and Meall nan Damh, hill of the stags, to the west. What we found was broken fencing half repaired with piles of rusting wire and nails lying beside it. Obviously, steps to protect some young saplings had been taken by inserting vole guards which were, alas, no deterrent to the deer. I wrote to SNH and reported the saga in *Reforesting Scotland* magazine of the woeful state of this NNR. The story continued for several years. They included the repair and enlargement of the fenced area and then the removal of NNR status from Glen Diomhan.

Throughout that time the late Mr Stephen Gibbs who owned the Dougarie estate of some 24,908 acres, or most of the north-west of Arran, had done little to divert deer from the area. Since shooting was his main interest you would think that an agreement with SNH could have been struck. Precious little evidence of estate investment has emerged. After the breakup of the Hamilton/Montrose estate in 1956, Mr Gibbs' estate became the second largest on the island. The Forestry Commission with 27,000 acres was the largest and the rump of Arran Estate, under the name of Charles JG Fforde, comes third with 16,300 acres. Fourth comes the NTS owning the Goatfell Massif and Brodick Castle at 5,434 acres, after their transfer in lieu of death duties by the Duchess of Montrose.

Arran Community Land Initiative reported in March 2015 that Henry Murdo was growing specimens of Sorbus arranensis in a plot at his garden in Corrygills. He had showed me these hard to propagate saplings the previous year. I am glad to note the campaign to save and spread these endangered native trees is alive. When RACCE made deer management proposals in 2013, Arran was in our minds.[104]

Glen Feshie

Deer management conflict reached a new pitch in February 2004 when a compulsory cull in Badenoch drew the ire of some shooting estate owners and their game keepers. Emotions erupted after seven trained marksmen hired by the Deer Commission were airlifted by helicopter

104. http://arranland.org/our-campaign-to-help-the-critically-endangered-arran-whitebeam-tree/

to upper Glen Feshie to kill 80 red deer which were steadily munching their way into vulnerable remnants of native pine woods. A lurid video claiming it was a massacre of red deer was filmed by game keepers and showed the carcasses lying, gralloched outside the estate lodge. This display was shown on BBC Scotland without any proper explanation.

The recently installed laird of Glen Feshie, Flemming Skoube, a Danish businessman, who bought the 42,000-acre estate in 2001 for a reported £8.5m, had been cooperating with the Deer Commission. Their official, David Balharry, was trying to apply the powers the agency possessed to reduce the herd from 1,500 to 1,000. However, concern for the scattered remnants of Scots Pines in upper Glen Feshie, under siege from hungry deer, prompted the compulsory cull under emergency powers. This led to the demonstration by game keepers from across Scotland. Many attended, presumably with their employers' permission. They voiced fears for potential loss of jobs in scattered communities if blood sports were to be curtailed by government interference. They railed against unnecessary deer culling which they claimed was traumatising local ghillies and their families.[105] Some month later, I joined two other MSPs from the Environment & Rural Development committee to visit Glen Feshie. In August 2004 we witnessed the progress the Deer Management Plans (DMPs) were making. The committee convener, Labour MSP Sarah Boyack, and I were impressed. The late Alex Johnstone, a Tory MSP, was less so. For my part, the vast shooting estates of the Highlands were a major challenge to biodiversity which had been protected in recent Acts of Parliament. This would be a recurring theme in the Land Reform Scotland Bill in 2015.

Poor relations between shooting interests and the majority of MSPs continued to be aired over the next decade by the SGA. They had in their sights various environmental NGOs and the Deer Commission, now subsumed into SNH, through the Wildlife and Natural Environment Act of 2011.

---

105. 'Protest at Deer 'Massacre' On Estate Demonstrators Fear Cull Will Threaten Gamekeepers' Jobs', *The Herald*, 30 March 2004, www.heraldscotland. com/news/12511749.Protest_at_deer__apos_massacre_apos__on_estate_Demonstrators_fear_cull_will_threaten_gamekeepers_apos__jobs/

In 1986, Creag Meagaidh in nearby Brae Lochaber became a NNR and for over 20 years it has had its ecology deliberately rebalanced to exclude sheep and reduce deer (red, sika and fallow deer) to manageable numbers.[106] Directed by Dick Balharry, who had been highly praised for his pioneering work at the original NNR at Beinn Eighe in Wester Ross, the policy of this NNR was to balance deer numbers with woodland regeneration in the 10,000 acres reserve. The land had originally been bought by the Nature Conservancy Council and became a publicly funded success story. Much of that success was achieved without major new fencing being erected. By chance, it was Dick's son David who led the compulsory action to reduce drastically deer numbers in Glen Feshie in 2003.

Glen Feshie was bought by Danish billionaire clothing magnate Anders Holch Povlsen in 2006 and would become an outstanding example of private sector planning to rebalance deer and trees. The transformation, under Povlsen's local land manager, Thomas Mc-Donnell, continued and accelerated the work begun under Skoube.[107]

Raasay deer management

In each of RACCE's periodic work programme announcements aspects of land management featured in many forms. Early in 2013, a question to Environment Minister Paul Wheelhouse exposed the removal of the fishing and shooting rights from the Raasay Crofters' Association (RCA) to a South Ayrshire stalking firm. The subsequent loss of income and control angered the Raasay community. This led, on 28 February 2013, to the First Minister announcing that, following an intervention from the Minister for Environment and Climate Change, the contract with South Ayrshire Stalking had been withdrawn by mutual consent and the RCA's lease had been extended for a year. This would allow Ministers to work with the wider Raasay community to find a long-term

---

106. 'The Story of Creag Meagaidh National Nature Reserve', Scottish Natural Heritage, www.snh.org.uk/pdfs/publications/nnr/The_Story_of_Creag_Mea-gaidh_National_Nature_Reserve.pdf
107. www.glenfeshie.scot/Glenfeshie_Nature.html and https://treesforlife.org.uk/blogs/article/glenfeshie-reborn/

solution to the issue. The details were expanded on by a motion lodged a week before by Jean Urquhart, Independent MSP for Highlands and Islands:

> The Parliament notes with concern the transfer of fishing and shooting rights on the island of Raasay from the Raasay Crofters' Association to a South Ayrshire stalking firm; further notes that the association, which represents 11 crofters and has paid an annual fee of £650, was set up in 1994 to manage these rights on behalf of the local community; understands that the association held the lease from 1995 until November 2012 and that during that period it made the enterprise a success through its investment in training and facilities; queries if this success, which, it understands, resulted in a profitable butcher's trade operating on the island, is one of the primary reasons that the lease was put out to tender for the first time in November 2012; understands that the Scottish Government informed the association that ministers were not obliged to accept the highest offer, and expresses concern at what it sees as this loss of local control and community involvement.

This drew cross-party support of 29 MSPs. An amendment in the name of Angus MacDonald, SNP MSP for Falkirk East, was lodged on 27 February 2013:

> As an amendment to motion S4M-05704 in the name of Jean Urquhart (Raasay Crofters' Association), leave out from first 'notes' to end and insert '[The Parliament] recognises what it sees as the success that the Raasay Crofters Association has had since acquiring the transfer of the local fishing and shooting rights on the island; appreciates that local control of the Raasay sporting rights has, in its view, been the cornerstone of the association's success in recent years; understands that the initial sporting rights on Raasay were leased to a private landowner,

then subsequently assigned to the Highlands and Islands Development Board in November 1981 for the remaining 31 years of a 50-year lease and reassigned to the Raasay Crofters Association in 1995, with the lease ultimately expiring in November 2012, as specified in the lease; further understands that the decision taken to award the sporting rights to the highest bidder was not a decision taken by ministers, but was taken on their behalf by the Scottish Government Rural Payments Inspectorate Division; believes that the decision has been met with widespread disapproval; welcomes what it sees as the prompt action taken by the Minister for Environment and Climate Change to review procedures and ensure that, in future, community and conservation interests are always fully taken into consideration; understands that the minister has taken action to instruct Scottish Government officials that any decision that would result in a local community failing to secure a renewal of a sporting lease, where they had been the sitting tenant, should be referred to ministers, and supports the Scottish Government's decision to consider options and to do all that it can to restore the Raasay community's access to sporting rights on the island.

The amendment gained the support of 22 SNP MSPs.

The Raasay shooting lease was another reminder that promoting local control required government departments and agencies to align their policies and land management rules.

Ardvar loss of biodiversity leads to tougher deer management

In February 2013, my attention was drawn to a simmering constituency issue in Assynt. SNH has refused a licence to cull excess deer on the John Muir Trust's (JMT) Quinag estate. The charitably owned property of over 9,000 acres sits amid the local deer range that is the responsibility of the West Sutherland Deer Management Group (DMG). This deer sub-group contains owners of various sorts. Ardvar,

Inchnadamph and Loch Assynt Lodge are engaged in private sport. The Assynt Foundation is a charitable trust, as is the JMT. Finally, the Assynt Crofters Trust estate in north Assynt was the first modern crofter-owned buyout, won in 1993.

The JMT's head of land and science, Mike Daniels, had been seeking a solution to the long-running degradation of the native woodlands by deer grazing on and around Quinag. Quinag is a conspicuous multi-topped hill that rises to Sail Gharbh at 808m/2653ft. The JMT argued that Ardvar and Loch a'Mhuillinn woodlands to the north of Quinag, as a Special Area of Conservation (SAC), were most threatened. These woods contain the northernmost remnants of sessile oak in Scotland as well as birch, aspen, rowan and alder. The JMT's proposed cull was opposed by all but the Assynt Foundation. The shooting estates all claimed it would prejudice the number of deer available for sport.

During summer parliamentary recesses I used to visit nature reserves. On 7 August 2013, I arranged to visit the Ardvar woodland with the local Highland Council ranger, a representative from the Scottish Wildlife Trust (SWT) and local JMT personnel. We saw that the woods were seriously diminished. Small saplings marked for study in the steep sided, predominantly birch clad slopes, were grazed to the ground. On open slopes higher up, we could see young trees bitten off and browsed to the height of the heather. Regeneration was impossible without further intervention.

As the issue dragged on, disturbing allegations emerged of bitter altercations between employees of shooting estates and the JMT workers. I concluded that a report was needed for the RACCE committee to consider in the autumn of 2013. I released the bones of my report to the press, who are always on the lookout for blood sport stories in August. As the local MSP, the weekly *Northern Times* was interested as was David Ross, the seasoned Highland correspondent of *The Herald*. The *Northern Times*, known locally as the Raggie, duly obliged with a page one splash, 'MSP reignites deer cull row.' The paper took exception to my passing comment that deer shooting was elitist, saying, 'Sutherland politician accused of living in the past'. However, my call for a 'cool-headed review' was agreed to by Andy Hibbert, the proprietor of Assynt Lodge, who concluded that it was certainly time for all groups to sit round the table and try to understand and reach a balance between everyone's individual objectives.[108]

The Herald, on 23 August, headlined 'Deer cull groups to face MSP challenge', with the subtitle, 'Landowners may see limiting of powers in deciding fate of herds.' Next day's headlines included 'Gamekeepers warn of red tape' and subtitles such as, 'MSPs to debate taking control of the deer management system.' The familiar line-up of the estates and SGA on one side with the JMT, the Royal Society for the Protection of Birds (RSPB) and SWT on the other proved that the prolonged stand-off begged for exploration in parliament.

On 27 August, most RACCE members attended our away day visit to the Glenlivet estate in the Cairngorm National Park where comprehensive deer management strategies were being formulated. The following morning, we discussed our suggestions for committee business that autumn. My colleagues agreed to recommend that the full committee should confirm evidence taking on contentious deer management issues when parliament reconvened in early September. However, the SGA warned, in *The Scottish Farmer*, that 'a statutory system of deer control would be a practical and political disaster.' Under the headline, 'Deer divide opens wide', Gordon Davidson reported that 'hostilities commenced when habitually maverick Highlands MP [sic] Rob Gibson returned from Assynt' with evidence of 'open hostility' by local stalking interests who were not culling enough deer to protect forestry.[109] On the same day the Raggie led with: 'MSP claims backing for deer management stance' as the RACCE committee was set to discuss the future of deer management. This was duly confirmed on 11th September by RACCE in its work programme and dates in November were earmarked for two sets of hearings.[110]

Despite my call for a 'cool-headed review', an open letter, 'to whom it may concern', from the shooting proprietors of Assynt, was published on 1st October which raised the matter of temporary fencing. This

---

108. *Northern Times*, 23 August 2013
109. *The Scottish Farmer*, 31 August 2013
110. *Northern Times*, 6 September 2013

issue had previously stalled moves to protect the overgrazed Ardvar woods. They highlighted their view that,

> JMT as a matter of policy are opposed to temporary fencing. JMT prefer to cull deer indiscriminately to assist regeneration. This policy of culling deer without regard to age or numbers brings JMT into conflict with the undersigned neighbours and also the wider Community.[111]

A scatter gun allegation such as this was far from conciliatory. A spokesperson for the neighbouring estates to Quinag went on:

> The management of deer numbers in Scotland is through Deer Management Groups. These are voluntary arrangements and are a tried and tested method of controlling deer numbers and are supported by the Scottish Government.

The open letter also claimed that the JMT declined to attend the local DMG meetings or share information about deer culls.[112]

It was mooted that the impasse at the DMG was due to open hostility from these estates to the JMT. This was claimed by JMT CEO Stuart Brooks, in his response to the open letter. He also said the open letter was 'threatening'.[113] This made it even more important for MSPs to review deer management issues: the association of DMGs (ADMGs) felt that the voluntary approach was working well and that Assynt was an exception.

Written evidence received ahead of the first two subject panels at RACCE on 13 November suggested that 321 out of 1203 designated

---

111. Rural Affairs, Climate Change & Environment Committee official report, 11 September 2013

112. Open letter to John Muir Trust from Ardvar, Inchnadamph, Loch Assynt Lodge and Assynt Crofters Trust estates, 1 October 2013

113. Letter – Stuart Brooks signed in addition by Middle Inver Estate, 4 October 2013

conservation areas in Scotland were classed as being damaged by deer. In SACs, 28 of 44 protected woods were damaged by deer and other herbivores, such as sheep and goats. It was also reported that the National Forest Estate conducted 28–30% of deer culling per annum on only 9% of the deer range.[114] Detailed ideas for more regulated deer management were suggested by the Scottish Environment Link. They represent up to 30 organisations. In contrast, the ADMGs felt that more time was needed for DMPs to take effect.

At that time, I received an interesting email from Lisbet Rausing, a member of the Swedish Tetrapac dynasty, who owns the 50,000-acre Corrour estate in the Central Highlands. She began, 'You are right that much of the Highlands are ravaged by too many deer'. Speaking out for a Swedish approach to a wider range of natural predators, such as eagles, bear, lynx and wolves, to control deer numbers, Ms Rausing praised her 'fantastic team of Scottish stalkers and foresters who are totally onside ecologically'. She added that they were

> pursuing other necessary goals of local employment and industry, treasuring their own traditions of stalking, welcoming visitors and so on. But it is not so easy – we have neighbours with 55 deer [sic] per square kilometre in SSSIs [Sites of Special Scientific Interest].

In conclusion Ms Rausing commented:

> landowners are a varied lot, and there are many of us – the Scandinavians and Germans not least – who would love to support Scotland's efforts to re-wild the Highlands, while respecting the people who live there.[115]

I sought out the SNH map of the Ben Alder Deer Count of July 2013 which showed the density per square kilometre. It looked ominous in

---

114. Tom Edwards and Wendy Kenyon, 'SPICe Briefing: Wild Deer in Scotland', SPICe, 2013, www.parliament.scot/ResearchBriefingsAndFactsheets/S4/SB_13-74.pdf

115. Email – L Rausing to R Gibson, 6 November 2013

various areas. When asked by the press about my thoughts following the Assynt open letter and other evidence, such as the Corrour information, I responded ahead of the RACCE hearings, stressing that these were personal views and that RACCE would make up its collective mind in due course. This did not stop the SGA and Jamie McGrigor MSP, the Tory environment spokesperson, from accusing me of 'trying to sway [the] deer cull debate'.[116] My comments had been printed between the two hearings, and Jamie contended that 'it was quite possible that such an opinion expressed in a newspaper could influence the proceedings.' I responded:

> We heard evidence on the basis that it was without fear or favour. To underline that, there are nine people on the committee and the other eight, in particular, had a great opportunity to ask a wide variety of questions and raise a wide range of concerns.

The committee hearings created a new record for us. So many people attended that tickets were required for access. The packed gallery, along with a full house of MSPs, heard how only 16 out of 40 DMGs had proper DMPs, how the groups only met twice a year which made planning progress extremely slow and how the two-year-old voluntary Code of Practice was just bedding in.

Since the days of the Red Deer Commission, shooting estates had been urged and cajoled to organise sustainable plans, but progress was evidently proceeding at a snail's pace. We were assured that DMGs were changing. We were also assured by SNH that voluntary and compulsory culls had been used in other places and that, under the most recent law, agreements were used, but that the application of compulsory action under Section 8 provisions had yet to be applied. Accusation about my own or other MSPs' partiality nevertheless drew commendably favourable comment from Playfair Walker on the ADMG website. He summed up the hearings:

---

116. *Northern Times*, 15 November 2013

Overall it was a fair debate. The majority of the panel remained in favour of the current system but that it could be improved, particularly if SNH was better resourced. The Committee gave little away although, despite the strength of evidence presented over the two sessions, they do I suspect remain highly sceptical that 'voluntary' can deliver, let alone that 'voluntary' is best. It is difficult to gauge where this goes next, but certainly the effectiveness of DMGs, the current system, and the uptake of the Code will be in the spotlight for some time to come.[117]

As a riposte to the complaints of shooting interests, the RACCE committee unanimously concluded that progress had been too slow in the creation of effective, environmentally responsible DMPs. A letter to Paul Wheelhouse stated that the patchy and inconsistent picture of DMG plans across Scotland, highlighted by RACCE, clearly showed that new management plans had to be in place by the end of 2016. Also, DMGs should be required to be more transparent and include persons with expertise in deer and habitat management in their membership. Due to reduced sheep stocks and greater afforestation, deer numbers had increased. Deer are a woodland animals and need woodland habitats to thrive. We strongly argued that it was critical for the Scottish Government to consider appropriate measures to enforce deer management. Since the Code of Practice had been in place for only two years it was premature to judge its effectiveness. Therefore, it was too soon to introduce statutory regulation, though that should not be ruled out. The committee agreed to monitor the situation's progress and return to the issue within the following two years. Finally, since the Scottish Government's 2008 strategy for managing deer 'Scotland's Wild Deer: A National Approach', was due for review in

---

117. Playfair Walker, 'Report on the Deer Management Debate at the Rural Affair Climate Change and Environment Committee – 20 November 2013', Association of Deer Management Groups, 21 November 2013, www.deer-management.co.uk/report-on-the-deer-management-debate-at-the-rural-affairs-climate-change-and-environment-committee---20-november-2013/

2014, RACCE asked to be kept informed about the scope, timing and process of this critically necessary review.[118]

On the same day as the RACCE deer management letter was published, Wheelhouse reviewed the Native Woodland Survey of Scotland. It was the product of eight years of work by Forestry Commission Scotland (FCS) and it showed that 46% of native woodlands were in a 'satisfactory' condition for biodiversity. Scotland has around 17% forest cover and around 4% of its land supports native woods. Unsurprisingly the survey found that the biggest threat to these native woods was overgrazing by deer. The losses in 40 years were significant even though 20,000 acres of native trees had been planted in the past 30 years to try and counter these losses. Shooting estates and gamekeepers continued to grumble that the balance of deer and trees was being reached, while environmentalists saw that any reversal of decline in habitat health would require a rethink of the voluntary approach to deer management.[119]

The RACCE members were pleased that we had opened the way through parliamentary initiative to a new era. Parliament would now focus SNH and DMGs on a step change to achieve the goal of transparent, enforceable deer plans aimed at both sporting and sustainability outcomes. The minister's commitment to a late 2016 deadline lead to £100,000 of funding for speedier progress and to ensure there could be no hiding place for the laggards. Best practice was to be shared and some of the slow coaches could then catch up. What it did not do was solve the vexing issue of Assynt deer damage.[120]

It needs to be understood that any move by an agency or government department takes a considerable amount of time. In the case of Ardvar, SNH was drawing up a management plan for the JMT. This had then to be opened out to wider consultation and, if agreed, pressed into action. Meanwhile at national level, the LRRG was entering the second phase of

118. Letter – RACCE to P Wheelhouse, 5 February 2014
119. Letter – P Wheelhouse to R Gibson, 5 March 2014, www.parliament. scot/S4_RuralAffairsClimateChangeandEnvironmentCommittee/General%20 Documents/2014.03.05_-_Ministers_response_on_Deer_Management.pdf
120. *The Herald*, 4 February 2014

its work and was also reviewing deer management. RACCE, as promised, kept a watchful eye. We sought a review of deer management progress at an informal briefing by Susan Davies, acting CEO of SNH, when she met the committee on 22 April 2015. Of the several issues discussed we were aware that progress on Ardvar SAC was hardly moving. In a follow-up letter dated 18 May, Davis gave us an insight into the approach adopted by her agency.

The SNH aim was to apply a voluntary agreement that would include at least temporary fencing and an agreed cull. Ardvar Estate, the Assynt Crofters Trust (ACT) and the JMT were the main parties concerned. An SNH contractor had reported in March that his proposed solution was agreed by SNH and FCS. Their final report was then sent to the three main interested parties. Some areas of native woodland were found to be regenerating. Others needed to be enclosed to secure an 'unfavourable recovering' category across the whole site. The picture did get more complicated despite public funding for fencing being available through the Scottish Rural Development Programme. ACT also agreed to the plan. The JMT, however, remained opposed to fencing on a designated site.

A meeting to break the deadlock was scheduled for June 2015 between FCS and the JMT. Susan Davis argued that if this failed, enforcement action under the older Deer Commission scheme, i.e. a Land Management Order (LMO), would be needed because a compulsory Section 8 order would not pay for fencing. Before an LMO could be served, SNH would have to offer the JMT a Management Agreement. It was about to offered to all the other parties by the end of May. This would then trigger a six-month consultation period and if not agreed the SNH board had indicated it would pursue the Section 8 route. So, the saga was to roll on into 2016.[121] In the event, the dissolution of Parliament in March 2016, put any actions off during the purdah period. An SNH board meeting had been scheduled for a few days after the Scottish election. But it emerged that the board did not have the confidence to use its undoubted powers at that time.

Two years earlier, the LRRG had reported to the Scottish Government

---

121. Letter – S Davies to RACCE, 18 May 2015

in Section 32 of its report – 'Wild Deer'. This report built substantially on the RACCE inquiry and the ministerial response. It saw red and roe deer as an important national asset that must be sustainably managed. Further, it recommended that

> improvements should be made to the current statutory framework governing the hunting of deer in Scotland to ensure appropriate culls are carried out to adequately safeguard public interests.[122]

The Ardvar case showed MSPs that they were more than justified in taking a detailed interest in the Assynt Sub-Group deer management issue. While JMT seemed to block progress and SNH seemed to be hamstrung by the rule book on funds for fences, a way forward was found when the draft deer management plan for the area was researched and published by the contractor Vincent Clements. ACT and other shooting partners in the Sub-Group found that Forest Enterprise Scotland (FES) could fund fences and that was said to be underway in the 2017 plan.

Had the Ardvar problems not appeared so acute, and had I not been the local MSP, the engagement of the Scottish Parliament and Paul Wheelhouse would not have set the deadline for producing local DMPs across all DMG areas. And we might not have found a way to protect vulnerable trees. Fencing of several small blocks on Ardvar was the practical solution that was eventually found, despite the apparent impasse that SNH presented to MSPs in 2016.[123]

---

122. Land Reform Review Group, 'The Land of Scotland and the Common Good: Report', 23 May 2014, www.gov.scot/publications/land-reform-review-group-final-report-land-scotland-common-good/
123. Ray Mackay and Victor Clements, 'SNH must heed the lessons of Assynt', *Am Bratach*, April 2018

7. Tenant farmers, factors and landlords

It's the land. It is our wisdom. It's the land. It shines us through.
It's the land. It feeds our children. It's the land. You cannot
own the land. The land owns you.
  – Chief Seattle 1855, adapted by Dougie Maclean, Solid
  Ground

Control of agricultural land has, for centuries, been heavily weighted in favour of landowners and against the rights of tenant farmers. From the Agricultural Holdings (Scotland) Act of 1883 to the present day, the policy of owners is clear. These lairds sought to retain as much control over their land as possible. That is a constant theme through various crises and acts of Parliament. It has had a major impact on the nation's food producers and, in my view, was as live an issue in 2016 as in the centuries before.

In 2011, most of my colleagues on the Rural Affairs, Climate Change and Environment committee (RACCE) wanted to see radical changes to stabilise farming in Scotland. But without a widespread right to buy – and a powerful dose of human rights law – we wouldn't see the overbearing behaviour from the landed proprietors and their agents curtailed any time soon. It has a long history and tradition stretching back centuries which has proved difficult to uproot.

In the 1880s, the depression of agricultural prices bit deeply on farming at home. The import of cheap grain, mutton and beef from the British Empire, Argentina and the USA was the main cause. Tenants were forced to accept unrealistic rent rises to retain their holdings or lose their considerable investment and move on. Gladstone's Liberal government set a bare minimum of compensation in the 1883 Act in a modest attempt to help crofters survive. Further, lengthy campaigns followed the legislation in the hopes of improving the tenant farmers' and farm servants' lot. Through all the economic ups and downs, world wars and depressions, the need for vigilance against landlord power was still evident.

I see the potential for something similar happening amidst the UK Brexit boorach. Free markets outwith European Union safeguards could wreck high quality British farming and crofting. Unacceptable standards of feedstuffs and intensively reared and chemically treated meat could truly threaten the repopulation Scotland. The only counter to industrialised farming is family farming, backed by fair prices that reflect production costs and a safety net of a tailored support scheme as practiced by the EU for its least favoured areas. Crofting and a heartening rise of organic farms and farm shops require special support on the grounds of biodiversity and healthy food production. Our overweight, under exercising citizenry need more options to shop locally.

However, figures supplied in 2013 by the Scottish Government to the LRRG show that farms were being amalgamated, sometimes managed 'in hand', and that tenant farming was in sharp decline. Data for 1913 show 5,648 owner run farms and 71,740 tenanted holdings. By 1980 the respective numbers were 17,139 owned and 14,274 tenanted.[124] Between 1990 and 2013, farm ownership rose from 27,949 to 36,670 while tenancies fell from 21,740 to 14,937. In terms of acreage over the same period, the totals owned and rented changed from a ratio of approximately 3:2 to 4:1. Reasons for this include the demand for increased output which led to amalgamations. Considerable, compared to rental income, public subsidies encouraged landowners to take some tenancies in hand. Landowners also became increasingly reluctant to create new tenancies if the security of tenants' rights, gained in 1949 and confirmed in 1991, was likely to be further enhanced.

Less secure tenancy vehicles such as limited partnerships also became fashionable in the 1980s. This galvanised the Scottish Tenant Farmers Action Group.[125] Organised in 2001, it lobbied hard during the debates around Agriculture Holdings (Scotland) Bill as it passed through Holyrood in tandem with the Land Reform (Scotland Act)

---

124. LRRG Part 7 Chapter 28 p194 et sequi
125. Scottish Tenant Farmers Action Group, see Case for the right to Buy

2003. The counterblast was to demand more land for tenant farming and encourage new entrants. Out of the Bill's passage the Action Group claimed some gains from the Scottish Executive's initial proposals. These included a range of technical measures to help maintain tenants' incomes and compensation. But their big ask of the right to buy (RTB) in a research paper, *The Case for a Right to Buy*, did not come to fruition despite considerable parliamentary debate and support.

As the principal opposition party, the SNP MSPs made a strong case in Bill's committee to support the RTB for secure tenant farmers. The Stage 1 Report noted the committee voted by six to three that, in Fergus Ewing's words, it was

> sympathetic to an absolute right to buy for secure tenants under the 1991 Act but reserves judgement on this issue pending amendments to be brought forward by the Scottish Executive at Stage 2.[126]

An amendment (No. 134) in Stage 2 was put forward by Ewing but the Coalition Government decided it was too contentious – ECHR could be breached as a result of the amendment. The result of the committee vote was seven (4 Labour, 2 Conservative and 1 Lib Dem) against and four (3 SNP and 1 Lib Dem) for with no abstentions.[127] Because the committee vote was decisive the SNP members declined to bring it back at Stage 3. Instead they focused on parrying the efforts of landlords who were trying to turf out limited partnership tenants. Limited partnership tenants would become entitled to secure tenancies in the Bill after the Scottish Executive proposed its own 11th hour amendments, later known as Sections 72 and 73. This left a legacy of 'what ifs' especially for general partners of limited partnership tenancies.

After the bill was passed in 2003, the Scottish Tenant Farmers Action Group then became a permanent lobbying body as the Scottish Tenant Farmers Association (STFA). It joined the newly formed industry-led round table, the Tenant Farming Forum (TFF), alongside

---

126. Fergus Ewing, Rural Development Committee, 3 December 2002
127. Scottish Parliament OR Agricultural Holdings Committee, Stage 2 amendment 134

representatives of Scottish Land and Estates (SLaE), the National Farmers Union of Scotland (NFUS) and the Royal Institute of Chartered Surveyors (RICS). The TFF commenced to work over the next six years seeking some agreed tenant farming improvements.

Richard Lochhead and I, as shadow spokesperson and his deputy, attended a briefing in Parliament with the TFF early in 2007. We heard first-hand of the struggle to find any common ground: it had been acting like a wartime naval convoy. The pace was that of the slowest ship, namely SLaE. Eventually, during the 2007 to 2011 minority Scottish Government, the TFF proposed some minor and non-contested changes in tenancy law and succession.

In the early days of the majority SNP Government (2011–2016) these were enacted in the Agricultural Holdings (Amendment) (Scotland) Act 2012 which was scrutinised by RACCE. The majority of the committee sought a wider range of possible successors to tenancies but agreed to get those already proposed onto the statute book. The government's frustration with the slow progress in the TFF led it to form the Agricultural Holdings Legislation Review Group (AHLRG) in November 2013. This new body would be led by Richard Lochhead, the Cabinet Secretary, himself, instead of being an industry-only creature.

Succession law reform – long sought, still to be achieved

One of the bastions of Scotland's concentrated pattern of land ownership was, and is, the hereditary principle of primogeniture. This practice ensured landed property including farms would pass to the eldest male successor on the death of the owner, unless previous provision had been made by the family. It maintained the size and extent of many holdings in very few hands.

In 1951, as the removal of feudal dues were being discussed, the Mackintosh Commission recommended an end to the legal distinctions between the sexes in succession law. The Succession (Scotland) Act was passed by Westminster in 1964 but signally failed to redress the heritable (land) and moveable (houses and other possessions) division of property. The Scottish Law Commission repeatedly reported in 1986 and 1990 to the government recommending changes. But the longstanding opposition of the Scottish Landowners Federation (SLF) and NFUS had stymied change under successive governments before devolution. So, with the advent of the Scottish Parliament, it was hoped that reform would be proposed. Yet the Scottish Executive failed to do so.

In June 2006 I launched a consultation paper as a possible Member's Bill on Succession Law Reform. I cited favourable examples in several European countries and in North America. As a result, several law firms contacted me with a range of caveats to my Bill, while land reform campaigners saw the abolition of the distinction between heritable and moveable property as a key aim to modernise which would hopefully prise open land ownership in what was supposed to be post-feudal Scotland. But as the final months of the session closed in, and time started to run out to launch a Bill proposal, I had hopes that it might be launched in the following parliamentary term after the next round of proposals by the Scottish Law Commission, which was set to report to government in 2009. Ministers of the minority SNP Government 2007–2011 were reliant on Tory votes to pass the budget. Yet a wider array of parties could support succession law reform if it was prioritised. So, I was less than impressed with the ministerial answer to my parliamentary question.

> Rob Gibson (Highlands and Islands) (SNP): To ask the Scottish Government what plans it has to legislate in relation to the Scottish Law Commission's 'Report on Succession', published in April 2009.

> The Minister for Community Safety (Fergus Ewing): The 'Report on Succession' recommends significant reforms to the law. I provided an initial response in July. Subsequently, in answer to a parliamentary question from Ian McKee, I confirmed that I had also met the commission's chairman. The Scottish Government is now having a dialogue with and consulting stakeholders to inform the way forward. Plans for legislation will be finalised in the light of that work, taking account of all relevant perspectives.

> Gibson: Succession was last legislated on in the 1960s,

and indeed the Scottish Law Commission's 1990 review was not acted on in the Parliament's first eight years. I am delighted with the indicated timetable, which I presume means that an answer will emerge only after 2011. However, it is important, that as far as equality in family law is concerned, the interpretation of heritable property succession rights is legislated on as early as possible.

Ewing: Rob Gibson is entirely correct to say that the current law rests on the Succession (Scotland) Act 1964, which, although it has served Scotland well, now needs considerable updating. We hope to take that forward through consultation, and in that regard I am delighted that the Justice Committee has responded positively to my suggestion of meeting the commission informally to discuss the report. Given the complexity of the issues, not least the recommendation to abolish the distinction between heritable and movable property –something, indeed, that Rob Gibson raised in his member's bill in 2006 – the widest consultation should be carried out to ensure that we maintain a consensual approach. With that in mind, it is more likely than not that legislation will emerge only after the end of this parliamentary session.[128]

And yet years passed. Till this time, late in Session 4 of the Scottish Parliament, it was agreed that the Subordinate Legislation Committee should be transformed into the Delegated Powers and Legislative Reform Committee. That way primary legislation, such as Succession Law Reform, could fall within its remit. The Scottish Government consultation on succession law was launched in the Spring of 2015.[129] Given

---

128.   Oral question on 21 January 2010, www.scottish.parliament.uk/business/officialReports/meetingsParliament/or-10/sor012102.htm#Col22993
129.   https://consult.scotland.gov.uk/civil-law-reform-unit/consulta-tion-on-the-law-of-succession/user_uploads/consultation-paper---final-as-at-26-june-2015.pdf-3

the complexity of the proposals which could have multiple effects on successors, the hope for early abolition of heritable property rights has not yet emerged. The aim was to move to a Bill after the 2016 elections. However, at the time of writing that is still not yet on the horizon.[130]

Tenant farming – erosion and disquiet or excellent relationships?

From the outset of the RACCE committee work programme in 2011 we reviewed the plight of the tenant farmer. Members received informal briefings from the STFA and others. Officially the TFF, the industry-led body, had been meandering through a maze of seemingly intractable sessions for six years. At the root of this delay, it appeared to MSPs that there was an unbridgeable gap between the tenants' aspirations and the views held by landowners and their agents. By 2011, the SNP Government decided that the problems for such a key group of innovative farmers had to be a land reform priority.

The Agricultural Holdings (Amendment) (Scotland) Bill, introduced to Parliament on 31st October 2011, appointed RACCE as the lead committee. Such a modest proposal referred to a slight extension of possible successors as tenants, the conduct of rent reviews and ruled out VAT costs on variation of tenancies. This was the sum total of seven years' work by the TFF. Primary legislation was required to pass some proposals already agreed by consensus in the TFF that could not be included in the Public Service Reform (Scotland) Act 2010. These had been scrutinised by RAE, the predecessor committee to RACCE, and pinpointed the fragility of consensus in the TFF by the paucity of subjects agreed to. Any talk of extending the range of succession beyond grandchildren to nephews and nieces exposed this fragility. It drew a familiar view from landowners. One TFF member from RICS, Richard Blake stated:

> The bill clarifies that succession by grandchildren is now permitted and we do not have any particular objection

---

130. https://www.abdn.ac.uk/law/blog/landlocked-the-continuing-separate-treatment-of-moveable-and-immoveable-property-by-the-law-of-succession-in-scotland/

to that. If, as a matter of principle, we are looking at extending the definition of 'near relative' beyond direct descendants, it could be argued that that takes away from landlords more rights that they have under existing legislation.[131]

However, evidence presented by the TFF to RACCE sought to portray optimism in the face of awkward evidence to the contrary. They were concerned that a transition period between the death of a tenant and a successor prompted questions about the retrospective nature of the clause. After questioning the Cabinet Secretary, Richard Lochhead MSP, Conservative and Liberal Democrat members of the committee were, nevertheless, satisfied with the Government response. Of the 16 submissions to the RACCE committee's call for evidence three were anonymous.

The issue of land agents was raised:

> The recent tactics of some agents have left tenants in shock and can only be described as bullying behaviour which has had a very negative effect on landlord/tenant relations... The actions of a few land agents who operate nationwide (and are gradually replacing resident factors), combined with the actions of some legal advisors over the last decade, have damaged landlord and tenant relations to such an extent that it is difficult to see good relationships ever being restored.[132]

The NFUS told the committee that the way in which land agents act on behalf of some landlords in discussions with tenants could give rise to tension and conflict within negotiations. It went on to recommend that a code of practice should be established and enforced to better govern the role of land agents. (For a worrying example of the work of land agents see below in connection with the Isle of Bute.) In response RICS

131. RACCE oral evidence col 521, Richard Blake 18 January 2012
132. Written evidence anonymously private papers to RACCE S4/12/1/1(P)

confirmed that its members had 'rigorous guidance' on how agents should behave and conduct themselves but added that this did not apply to all land agents, as not all agents were members of RICS. RICS confirmed that it had produced a guidance note on a code of conduct for its members and that this would be revisited within the TFF. During his evidence to the committee, Lochhead stated that he did not feel the development of a code of practice in this area was the responsibility of Government, but was supportive of the industry itself developing a code:

> A code of practice to address some of the issues with land agents would be a good thing, as long as there is a way in which the professional organisations of which the agents are members can enforce it internally.

In its First Stage Report on the Bill the committee supported the development of that code of practice which would ensure a greater consistency of practice and behaviour amongst those providing land agent services. However, it was essential that any such code be applicable to all land agents operating in Scotland, whether acting on behalf of landlords or tenants, and irrespective of their membership of RICS, and that the code had some 'teeth' to ensure it could be appropriately enforced. And, on land agents' conduct, the committee recommended that the Scottish Government closely monitor the development of a code within the industry, via the TFF, to ensure that any code is fit for purpose.[133] This was to prove a major irritant in subsequent years as the land reform consultation unfolded and instances of strained tenant and landlord relations came to the surface.

Another anonymous submission to RACCE expressed fears about speaking out during tenant and landlord disputes:

> It is difficult to find tenants willing to represent tenants' interests, not just because of continual daily hands-on farming commitments which prevents most tenants taking time off from their farming duties, but also because

---

133. RACCE report paras 105-109, 2012

of the fear that any tenant who dares to stick his or her head above the parapet will draw unwelcome interest from land agents, factors, and landlords. It is clear that tenants who represent other tenants' interests by sitting on the STFA board or the NFUS's Tenants Working Group are often the ones who are singled out and pursued to the land court by landlords who clearly want to put tenants off the idea of taking part in any debate regarding the tenanted sector. For a similar reason [sic] it is hard to persuade tenants in difficult and unpleasant situations to allow their problems to become public, as they rightly see that doing so will only make their situation worse. If government is to encourage a debate over the tenanted sector, consideration should be given to these difficulties which will prevent many tenants from making a valuable contribution to this debate.[134]

To break the ice, the new AHLRG would report back early in 2014. Scottish Government research, conducted by IPSOS MORI in 2014, also took the temperature of tenant/landlord relations. This led to the oft-quoted figure of 82% of tenant farmers being happy with their landlords.[135] This figure was repeated time and again by Tory MSPs and landed interests to counter and limit the importance of evidence of tenant/landlord flashpoints which we heard of in various submissions to the consultations and the eventual bill proposal in 2015. The seven years' snail's pace in the TFF suggested that major problems were affecting many more than the 18% who were less than happy with their tenancy arrangements. Even modest proposals by the ministerial-led AHLRG had to be wrung out ahead of the full land reform bill. These revealed the underlying demands of a significant minority of tenants who were living with smouldering concerns that prompted some, even if it was costly, to try and purchase their farms if they could.

Meanwhile, MSPs were assessing ministerial proposals to resolve

---

134. Written evidence anonymously private papers to RACCE 2012 S4?12/1/1 (P)

135. http://www.gov.scot/Publications/2014/11/8975/4

the historic consequences of the Scottish limited partnership tenancy crisis. This was a hangover from clauses offering security of tenure to a range of limited partnerships in the 2003 Act. The Salvesen v Riddell judgement would spawn a high-profile campaign on behalf of affected tenants that petitioned Holyrood for redress. As a committee, RACCE members had our fill of tenant farming issues from the outset.[136]

Bute – a tale of two surveys

A prime example of tenant farmer and landlord conflict was gleaned by RACCE members even before the modest Agricultural Amendment (Scotland) Bill was given unanimous approval in Parliament on 7 June 2012. On 28 and 29 May of that same year, a committee fact-finding visit to the Isle of Bute saw three MSPs, including myself, and their committee clerks walk unawares into a heated controversy.

The planned itinerary of day one of our trip began with presentations and visits hosted by the Mount Stuart Estate Trust staff and a senior CKD Galbraith factor, Christopher Addison Scott. Later that evening tenant farmers from Bute, Islay and Arran accompanied by Angus McCall, STFA chairman, met with us at our hotel in Rothesay. On the morning of the 29, Mr McCall and John Dickson, the NFUS Bute chair, conducted a tour examining the tenant farmers' points of view.

The surprise revealed to us on our arrival at Mount Stuart was an NFUS survey of its Bute members who composed 98% of the island's farmers. Thirty-four of Bute's 52 farmers had responded including 85% of this island's dairy farmers, a key sector which was under strain. The results were highly critical of the estate management showing that 80% of the respondents had poor to bad views of their relationship with their landlord. The survey had been prepared for us. Margaret McDougall, Dennis Robertson and I expected to interrogate its findings on our visit. Instead we found that the estate had been given copies before our arrival at Mount Stuart where the factors who greeted us immediately counter attacked. The tenants were incensed; they did not know the results as the NFUS HQ at Ingleston had passed the findings to the landlord's agents.[137]

---

136. Appendix and Briefing from NFUS 24 and 25 May 2012 to MSPs
137. Appendix and Briefing from NFUS 24th and 25th May 2012 to MSPs

A fortnight later *The Scottish Farmer* presented the controversy as 'A tale of two surveys! Landlords – all is well; Tenants – crisis of confidence'. Its leading article headed 'The need to know!' noted that land reform matters continued to dominate the news and letter pages. While some saw constant publicity of the issues as injecting 'too much emotion into the debate', others saw publicity as the 'only vehicle available to get their point across'. It went on to claim that many tenants felt let down by the system' so 'publicity is their most potent weapon'.[138] Referring to the Bute spat, *The Scottish Farmer* claimed:

> The lack of publicity given to a recent tenants' survey on Bute by NFU Scotland has angered some of the island's tenant farmers and union members. What has angered them even more, however, is the apparent leaking of the results to their landlord's representatives before a crucial meeting [with MSPs] and even before tenants themselves know the contents. If true, this is unacceptable![139]

We reported back to our colleagues on our return to the Scottish Parliament and the committee agreed to keep a close eye on any developments. Some days afterwards, an extremely frosty exchange occurred at the Royal Highland Show when I met Luke Borwick – an Ayrshire landowner and, at that time, chairman of SLaE – along with James Galbraith – the principal of CKD Galbraith who provided the Bute Estate factors. My parting remarks to them were that the public interest would be much more prominent in forthcoming debates in Holyrood. No, I was not seeking land nationalisation as Mr Borwick angrily accused, but much more diverse ownership of Scottish land. The letter pages of *The Scottish Farmer* reverberated with further heated comments and then, on 14 July, *Scotland on Sunday* ran a story 'MSP hits out over Bute's "absentee landlord" Johnny Crichton-Stuart.' Journalist Marc Horne retold the tenants' story and my response to it. On a wider tack, he quoted the plight of Aidan Canavan, a secondary school teacher who

---

138. Scottish Farmer 16 June 2012
139. ibid.

had contacted me when the MSPs visited the island. He described, to me, how his partner had received a 'golden hello' to work as a doctor in a practice on the island but that they couldn't purchase a house site. Having moved from Glasgow, they did not wish to dwell in Rothesay. Mr Canavan told Marc Horne that 'their dream of buying a home in the countryside had been thwarted'. He went on:

> There are a number of derelict houses on the island which have been left to crumble over a number of years. We would be happy to buy one and invest in it and the island, but we can't because we are being impeded every step of the way by the estate.

The feudal nature of Bute was made plain to us by the estate's opposition to installing wind turbines which could reduce the considerable electricity bills incurred by dairy farmers. Derelict houses which we had spotted on our rounds, some empty for a decade, were as clear an indication as possible that Mount Stuart would only tolerate tenant farmers' housing in their demesne, not other rural residents.[140]

Following the *Scotland on Sunday* article, James Galbraith challenged me by letter to corroborate points he had discussed by an email reply he claimed to have received from Marc Horne prior to the substantive article appearing. These points, he claimed, did not match my remarks printed in the paper itself. He then made an accusation that I had told Mr Horne that 'individuals representing CKD Galbraith had acted, on occasion, "with a degree of menace".' On that matter Mr Horne quoted one tenant farmer who spoke on condition of anonymity:

> I've been warned that my future on the island could be affected if I spoke out. But it is no exaggeration to say that people on the island are living in fear.

As CKD Galbraith provided the factoring service to Bute estate, James

---

140. Scotland on Sunday, 14 July 2102

Galbraith was keen to link my alleged remarks to be a direct accusation against his firm. He concluded his initial letter:

> CKD Galbraith is a professional business which provides a livelihood to over 200 partners and employees and our reputation is critical to our continued ability to do so. We cannot tolerate any parties making unsubstantiated slurs against us... As you spoke to Marc Horne in your capacity as RACCE chairman [sic] I am circulating copies of this letter to all committee members.[141]

I responded on 13 August on return from my annual leave:

> You say your firm takes seriously the remarks made in *Scotland on Sunday* of 14 July concerning Bute Estate. I take very seriously the views of the Bute tenants which you dismissed as 'a measure of dissatisfaction with the Trust'. The facts show deep concern and dissatisfaction as you well know. As the estate factors your conduct of business requires further enquiry.[142]

Another round of correspondence ensued in which Mr Galbraith continued to probe my responses to Marc Horne. Another point he made was this:

> When you visited Bute Estate you did so as a member of and Chairman [sic] of RACCE committee. I understood that it was normal for members of parliamentary committees to set aside their political agenda in order to gather facts so that the committee can jointly assess them and thereafter report to parliament. It seems to me, given your interview with Marc Horne, you are acting in a

---

141. CKDG LLP by James Galbraith letter to RG 18 July 2012 (circulated to other RACCE members)
142. RG letter to JG 31 August 2012

manner which is evidently partial and neither fair minded not balanced against normal practices of parliamentary committees.[143]

I replied briefly saying that there had been three MSPs and clerks taking copious notes of the tenant farmers' views. We all concurred. I repeated the evidence we heard of a depth of feeling about the tactics of his staff. I replied:

> It paints a sombre picture of the way your staff conduct the factoring business on behalf of Bute Estate.

As to Mr Galbraith's aspersion about partiality of MSPs, I suggested that

> various investigations such as the TFF and the Land Reform Review Group will be most interested in the evidence we collected.[144]

Subsequently, I understand that Mr Galbraith wrote to the First Minister, Alex Salmond, seeking redress. Nothing further was heard of his allegations. However, calls for a statutory code of conduct for land agents became an important thread in RACCE evidence sessions through further committee hearings and the Land Reform Bill Stage 1 hearings in the autumn of 2015.

Measuring farming confidence – was it dented or upbeat?

Measuring the confidence of farmers and the condition of Scottish farming was undertaken for 19 consecutive years by the Bank of Scotland, part of the Lloyds Banking Group. The bank's redoubtable chief economist, Professor Donald MacRae conducted these surveys by sampling over 2,000 of the bank's farming customers. For several years, each January, his findings were presented to MSPs at breakfast briefings in Holyrood.

---

143. JG letter to RG 22 August 2012
144. RG letter to JG 5 September 2012

The December to January survey of 2013/14 saw 2,205 farmers mailed. 359 (16%) responded. It was conducted on a random basis and was anonymous. Prosperity and attitudes were probed. In the 2014 report three questions were included concerning the right to buy for tenant farmers. Unsurprisingly, a majority were opposed to a right to buy for all tenants. The figures showed a slight rise from the previous year. Of those who answered, strongly against rose from 46% to 51% while strongly for rose from 10 to 11%. When separated into mainly owner occupiers and mainly tenants 56% of the former and 32% of the latter were strongly against, with 7% and 23% strongly in favour. An automatic right to buy for 1991 Act tenants was contained in a new question for 2014. 43% strongly against and 12% strongly for. Again, comparing mainly owner occupiers and mainly tenants 49% and 22% respectively were strongly opposed while 6% and 31% were strongly for. Donald MacRae significantly highlighted that 42% of tenants supported the right to buy.[145]

So, what can be made of these attitudes?

The business of farming is complex. The number of individuals who are both owners and tenants forms one element. That way a business can be developed, and extra ground found to produce more crops, whilst retaining the owner-occupied unit as collateral for bank loans. Owners want options to bid for shorter term leases to suit their business plans. Therefore, less leased land available would stymie such plans.

The price of land also plays its part. The LRRG, in its final report in 2014, looked at the capital value of agricultural land with good arable land at nearly four times the price in 2013 compared to 2003.[146] It noted that 'the value of all types of agricultural land increased significantly over the period.' The LRRG went on to compare the price of land to other commodities in the same period. From an index of 100 in 2003, gold rose to near 400; English and Scottish farmland to 300; FTSE 100 index to 150; and UK house prices 140. Land has outperformed most other commodities for at least 25 years! No matter how confident or

---

145. Lloyds Bank Farm Survey 2013/14
146. LRRG Chapters 38 and 39 p175

profitable farmers consider their businesses, the price of land has risen sharply because many uses can be made of such investments, over and above short-term economic gains. Therefore, questions arise about the public benefits of tax reliefs on agricultural and forestry land:

> The Group recommends that each of the exemptions and reliefs should be reviewed and reformed as necessary, to ensure that there is a clear and transparent public interest justification for public expenditure through revenue foregone.[147]

For farmers and crofters building sustainable businesses, the changes in Common Agriculture Policy payments from single farm to area-based payments loomed large at that time. With hindsight, there's also the threat to European market access; Brexit will remove Scotland and the rest of the UK from the EU Single Market. To the LRRG, sustainability went hand in hand with increasing the numbers of landowners in rural Scotland, in the public interest.[148]

Many tenants are interested in buying their farms but the rise in land prices could never match the economic value of these acres. This makes farm purchases hugely problematic for mortgage seekers. A major corrective between land purchase prices and realistic returns might tempt some tenants to buy. The Land Reform Review Group state that there had been 1,463 registrations of interest to buy by tenants early in 2014, of which 906 were still active. That amounts to a full quarter of secure 1991 tenancies. No information is available on the reasons behind the 557 registrations which have come off the register. My points above are germane to this. The LRRG report states that:

> Some registrations would have been removed because they had lapsed, while others may have been rescinded for inaccuracies. In some cases, the right may had been exercised or the tenancy may have ended for other reasons.

147. LRRG Part 6 Section 25 para 43, p177
148. LRRG Part 6 Section 25 para 48 p178

> The Review Group's understanding is that, while no pur-
> chases have apparently taken place by a tenant exercising
> their right under the legislation, the existence of the right
> has facilitated that outcome in some cases.[149]

The edginess of relations between tenants and landlords is real. And since the AHSA03, the tension has far from died away. Raw nerves were exposed by the slow progress of the TFF. The Salvesen v Riddell case upset the hopes of several hundred limited partnership tenancies when the Supreme Court ruled in 2012 that parts of the 2003 Act were *ultra vires*, as we shall see.

Protection for tenant farming in Land Reform Bill 2015?

When 11,065 responses to the Scottish Government consultation on the draft Land Reform Bill were analysed, 64% of individuals who replied were in favour on including improvements to the potential for tenant farming in Scotland in the Bill. In contrast, 65% of organisations were opposed.[150]

In 2011, Richard Lochhead decided agricultural holdings were part of land reform and would be handled in one bill. Thus, agricultural holdings formed nearly half of the bill launched in 2015. Many landlords thought they should be kept separate and made it plain that more time was needed to set out the best approach – if necessary, in the following session of parliament. Such a delay was an unacceptable and a stalling tactic that bedevilled real farm tenancy reform for far too long.

Landlord power plays pressed on during the consultation and scrutiny of the Land Reform Bill. RACCE had also to face the consequences of the flawed, but well-meaning clauses from 2003 as MSPs weighed against some real tenancy reform.

---

149. SPICe and LRRG
150. Responses to Land Reform Bill consultation.

8. Most of Scotland is under water

Not even our rivers run free.
- Misquote from Mickey MacConnell's 1965 song, *Only Our Rivers Run Free*

The Scotland that lies under water has a special place in the whole land reform story. Until recently, it has been largely ignored that six times more of Scotland's territory is under the sea than above it. And when you add in our river and loch systems, and their contribution to the health of our ecosystem, their importance to the land reform story becomes clear. During my three terms at Holyrood we addressed several ways to reform the control and management of our rivers, lochs and seas. We set up a coherent direction, albeit only the early steps, towards the goal of a democratic and fair use of our natural resources under sovereign control. As they are such key resources, transparent management of their biodiversity will immeasurably aid Scotland's sustainable future.

A Europe-wide agenda to create marine protected areas (MPAs) had serious implications at a local level in Scotland. The Scottish Parliament was conscious of the reported fall in numbers of wild salmon and sea trout, so new proposals for wild fisheries were brought forward for consultation. Because aquaculture has been greatly increasing in importance to consumers over recent decades, its footprint now affects our marine ecology to a greater extent than ever before. Farmed fish now make up the biggest percentage of food exports from Scotland. In contrast, river angling interests have been exercised over dwindling catches. When I was an MSP, some saw a direct link between these two activities where others saw more complex factors. Nonetheless, a Bill to tighten regulation of the aquaculture industry was passed in 2013 and all of these natural resource components were addressed in the National Marine Plan for Scotland of 2015 proposed by the Scottish Government. As the relevant Holyrood committee, myself and the rest of the RACCE spent considerable time and effort to understand and streamline this plan to make it effective.

In one of the early years of my mandate, as a regional member for Highlands and Islands, the issue of protecting marine features, such as in the Firth of Lorne, were subject to SSIs. These government orders were, in this case, to regulate fishing – especially scallop dredging which needed to be excluded from pressured areas. I had a strong impression that cavalier, unscrupulous fishing had to be curbed to protect the spawning grounds that regenerated many fish stocks, be they langoustine, haddock or cod. In my huge region, particularly in the Minch, the lack of fin fish (as opposed to shellfish) was a strong sign of overfishing. So I welcomed an opportunity to bring this debate to parliament after a visit to Arran. Although this was not in my constituency, the land and water was already familiar to me from my visits over many years.

In 2005, my old friend Henry Murdo – bagpipe maker, hill walker and environmental watchdog – introduced Eleanor and I to key members of the Community of Arran Seabed Trust (COAST). One member, Don MacNeish, as well as being a fellow hill walker, was a keen diver. Along with Howard Wood, another member of COAST, they had sought to protect a portion of Lamlash Bay from scallop dredging for over a decade, but without success. Their focus was saving rare maerl beds. Maerl is a form of cold water coral which is found on the seabed of Lamlash Bay. We all met at the home of Tom Vellaboyle in Whiting Bay and agreed a plan. Our advice was to lodge a reasoned petition at Holyrood where the Public Petitions Committee (PPP) would give it a fair hearing. We suggested that if they were asked to give evidence, they should alert us so that we might suggest to PPP members they should think to involve the RAE.[151] And that's what happened.

The committee was due an away day to plan the programme for session 2006–07 during the August recess, so Eleanor and I persuaded

---

151. Public Petition No.

the rest of the committee to hold it on Arran. As part of the trip we would review the maerl beds and to take some time to assess the plight of small land holders at Sliddery on Arran's south coast. The latter issue was still ongoing at the time of the 2015 Land Reform Bill.

On Arran, we duly donned waterproof gear and embarked on a fast rib owned by Arran Adventures from Brodick to Lamlash Bay. The exhilarating, wave-splashed ride round Clauchlands Point took us into the calm of the bay where Wood met us in another rib over the maerl beds. His dive to the seafloor brought us small samples of the coral so that we could discuss how solutions to end their destruction by dredgers could be ordered. The committee agreed to write to the Environment Minister and suggest a 'no take' zone for the Lamlash maerl beds. This met with the approval of the Scottish Executive and it fell to Richard Lochhead, the incoming Cabinet Secretary, to move the regulation in 2007.

Ten years on, in 2018, despite sporadic arguments with Clyde-based scallop dredgers, the success of the No Take Zone was celebrated. Breeding stocks of langoustine, haddock and cod all benefitted from maerl regeneration, and also the Scottish Parliament's willingness to tackle degraded marine habitats. Indeed, the tail end of the 2011–16 session saw the adoption of 30 MPAs, including the South of Arran MPA, much to the delight of COAST and many others. These barred scallop dredgers from a much wider area.[152]

In 2012, in another public petition, RACCE took evidence on the removal of Marine Stewardship Council accreditation for creel fishing for nephrops, ie langoustine, in Loch Torridon. This exposed not just the conflicts between creelers and trawlers but the excessive laying of creels in the protected area. A petition lodged at Holyrood by Richard Munday of Shieldaig exposed this dilemma.[153] The committee held a roundtable evidence session in June 2012 and considered the petition again in September 2012 after correspondence with the Scottish Gov-

---

152. See below, January 2016
153. Public Petition No. PE01386, 'Establishment of further static gear only inshore fisheries', www.parliament.scot/GettingInvolved/Petitions/petition-PDF/PE01386.pdf

ernment.[154] The petitioner agreed that the Scottish Government was demonstrating an attempt to address many of the issues raised by his petition, though not necessarily as a direct response. The gear conflict and fragility of fish stocks would be a constant refrain in our deliberations and led to scrutiny of the Aquaculture and Fisheries (Scotland) Bill in second half of 2012. The Bill aimed, according to the Policy Memorandum, to

> ensure that farmed and wild fisheries – and their interactions with each other – continue to be managed effectively, maximising their combined contribution to supporting sustainable economic growth with due regard to the wider marine environment.

We made two visits in November 2012 to other sites of marine interest. The first to the River Dee and a salmon netting station near Montrose. The second outing to Lochaber enabled members to see, first-hand, the issues and tensions between fish farms and freshwater fisheries that were at the heart of the Bill. These visits helped to inform our Stage 1 scrutiny.

On our first visit – arranged through the good offices of the River Dee Trust and the local salmon fisheries board – we were able to see, with our own eyes, where the female salmon scrape a shallow depression, a redd, on the riverbed to lay their eggs. Thereafter the male salmon fertilise the eggs and cover the redds with gravel. Yet what struck me most was that the fishery was also seeking funds from the Scottish Government to plant trees close to the banks of the River Gairn. That place was what can only be described as a devastated landscape. Formerly clothed in Scots Pine and Birch the land had been cleared for sports shooting on any land 500 metres above sea level. The riverbanks of the fishery were located beside large areas of land bared and recently charred with the dead white stocks of burnt heather roots. RACCE was asked to support their initiative to replant this riverside area. The angling trust hoped to cultivate dappled shade which would cool the

---

154. 19 September 2012

river and encourage salmon spawning and to diversify the local flora and fauna. And, by ensuring a greater salmon population, they would also be able to provide catch and release sport for wealthy anglers. For this privilege, anglers would pay handsomely to riparian owners, the private landlords of the riverbanks downstream.

The next day, we drove over the Cairn O' Mount from Deeside down to the sea near Montrose to visit Usan Salmon Fisheries, a mixed stock wild salmon fishery. With fixed nets man-handled and harvested on cobles, this historic occupation had become the fulcrum of a clash of cultures at the heart of a dispute with the Esk District Salmon Fishery Board. In times past, long before the Scottish Parliament was founded, coastal salmon netting had coexisted peacefully with river angling. Often they were interchangeable, in terms of ownership of riverbanks or licenced fixed nets in the sea. But ancient netting rights for salmon and sea trout around our coasts had dwindled from several hundred in the middle of the 19th century to a handful of active fishing stations by 2012. However anglers, and their rich clients, began to question the drop in catchable salmon and confrontations between the two sectors flared. Legal restraints were sought against netsmen, such as Usan. Other sectoral clashes also developed with the spread of farmed salmon pens sitting in the firths and bays of the west coast; the very routes through which salmon undertook their perilous return journey to and from Greenland. The Scottish Government saw the need to streamline aquaculture regulations and to modernise salmon fishery boards to make their meetings transparent and, for the sake of biodiversity, to extend their remit to include all species in their river catchment.

RACCE members visiting Lochaber a week later saw smolt spawning in contained tanks at Glenfinnan. Some fish were for release to restock the River Lochy, others for farming, grown to full size in adjacent pens on nearby Loch Shiel. Clothed in regulation protective gear we went on the loch to see these large pens for ourselves. Biosecurity was becoming paramount. An SSI in 2009 had already regulated responses to a contagious salmon disease, Gyrodactylus salaris, commonly known as salmon fluke, which was wiping out fish on river systems in Norway. Strict rules for anglers moving between countries were brought in. The problem of sea lice, however, continues to challenge the industry to this day. While sea lice parasitise wild salmon, farmed salmon are far more vulnerable and the use of chemicals to control the problem remains controversial. After seeing the scale of the fish processing factory at Inverlochy, we had a sense of the size of the aquaculture industry. As part of this visit, we looked into nearby Loch Leven. Marine Harvest were using lice-eating fish called wrasse and lump fish to clean their pens of sea lice. Could these be caught or bred in numbers to meet the demand of salmon pens spread along the west coast from Scourie in the north to Kintyre and Arran in the south?

The committee's Aquaculture Bill Stage 1 report recommended far tougher rules for river catchment reporting systems for sea lice while also detailing ways to curb and prevent escapes for salmon pens. Publishing sea lice numbers was essential for public confidence when dealing with a very defensive salmon farming industry led by the Scottish Salmon Producers Organisation. We demanded a considerable increase in the number of river catchments from which data was to be collated. There was also public concern about the number of seals being shot as an element of 'predator control' on the fish farms. We considered this should be a last resort. It was stated in our report that humane methods such as seal scaring should be applied first.

The proposals outlined in the Bill were a necessary step to improving the accountability and transparency of District Salmon Fishery Boards. It was a necessity that board members should declare any financial interest that they might have had in board decisions. The introduction of a carcass tagging scheme with individually numbered tags would also be required to establish the credibility of overall statistics. This applied to salmon netting and also to close times and days at sea. Processes for conflict resolution had to be made clear by the government, RACCE argued. We had been disappointed to hear about the breakdown in the relationship between netsmen and the Esk District Salmon Fishery Board. Although the committee appreciated the difficulties netsmen could encounter at trying to adhere to weekly close times in challenging weather conditions, rules to aid conservation of salmon were essential even if a degree of flexibility was needed. These issues raised big questions about inland waters and offshore management. They also exposed vested interests and flagged up the pressing need for biodiversity in an age of extreme weather due to climate change. Such concerns would have to be grasped if economic uses of species were to be sustained.

The question of who controls our waters, and who benefits from good resource management, spurred us to think further about this aspect of land reform. Related matters were set to tax our patience and understanding for the rest of the parliamentary session, in fact, to the very last committee meeting in March 2016.[155]

At RACCE, on 23 September 2015, I convened a controversial session on the plans for MPAs. An emergency MPA order was passed to set up the Wester Ross MPA covering the area from Gairloch up to Stoer in Assynt because of a series of scallop dredging incidents. Prior to the committee sitting, Clyde fishermen let off a smoke cannister while demonstrating against MPAs outside the Scottish Parliament; unacceptable behaviour to my mind. Our government's urgent action, reining in unchecked scallop dredging and the despoliation of spawning grounds was a turning point for the management of inshore waters. A counter demonstration by COAST remained peaceful. At last the parliament was moving towards full-scale marine protection. To underline the intensity of the confrontation over these issues, and for the only time in my tenure, police constables were stationed in the committee session for fear of trouble.[156]

In committee, Duncan MacInnes, the secretary of the Western Isles Fishermen's Association, spoke his mind:

> On the shared marine environment, we have what we consider to be a balanced fleet that has been sustainable. We have a creel fleet. We are the largest association with static gear members in the whole of Scotland. We have been at the leading edge of conservation. For the past ten years, we have been asking Marine Scotland to introduce a pot limitation scheme, and we are seeing light at the end of the tunnel. We do not want to see more creels go into

155. RACCE OR, 23 September 2016
156. 'Passionate Debate on Marine Protected Areas, says Lochhead', BBC News, 27 January 2016, www.bbc.co.uk/news/uk-scotland-highlands-islands-35412565

the sea. I was a fisherman myself. I started fishing with 240 pots and finished 15 years later with 750 pots. If I was still at sea today, I would need 2,000 pots to catch the same amount that I used to get.

We need a sensible balance on the way forward if we are to have a shared, successful and sustainable marine environment that benefits all industries. Marine renewables are coming into that environment, and there is increased fish farming with larger fish farms that want their own section of the seabed. It is right and proper that we should discuss protecting marine features within the overall framework of future marine planning.

As I said, no fisherman wants to destroy the marine environment. Fishermen have shared that marine environment for the past 50 or 60 years. The marine features are there, and it is not as if the fishermen have destroyed the marine environment; they have been fishing it commercially and sharing it for a generation. Fragile communities such as those on the west coast, from the Clyde all the way up to Kinlochbervie, are now faced with a dilemma about how to take forward the management of the marine environment.

No one is against MPAs; it is their management that needs to be sorted out.

I asked Mr MacInnes to comment on the necessity of bringing in an emergency order for the Wester Ross MPA. I wondered how that squared with his assertion that trawlers were interested in maintaining the marine environment seeing as one of his boats had been accused of flouting fishing restrictions in the Summer Isles. MacInnes replied that the skipper had made a full statement to the fishery office in Ullapool and that there was a total misunderstanding about the different zones in that area. He went on:

There was a zoning approach that meant that scallop dredging should be kept deeper than 20m, yet there was one zone that had a total prohibition in it. There were seven different zones. Marine Scotland did not have the courtesy to send details of those voluntary measures to the scallop vessels that had scallop entitlements. In my opinion, it should have done that.

The skipper of the vessel was unaware that he had a fishery cruiser beside him that Saturday morning. The fishery protection vessel did not tell him that he was operating in a voluntary closed area. In the area where he was fishing, he did not go shallower than a depth of 30m, so he was well within the agreed 20m zoning. He has requested that Marine Scotland show photographic evidence that he caused any damage in that area, and that evidence has not been given to him.

There was a total misunderstanding and that has been conveyed to Marine Scotland. If nobody in life ever misunderstood anything, this room would be empty. We are dealing with a misunderstanding or an interpretation of the information available.

This confusing catalogue of assertions was but one of several such infractions of the ban in the Summer Isles waters. Boats from Northern Ireland and elsewhere had been implicated in the same place thus mounting up evidence for urgent regulation. In committee, another panel member immediately begged to differ. Alasdair Hughson, who was representing the Scottish Scallop Divers Association, was also a local scallop diver. What he said was damning:

I am afraid that I must take issue with the evidence from Duncan MacInnes. I was made aware of the incursion into the voluntary zone by the Siarach III within 15 or 20 minutes of it happening because I had phone calls from local residents, who were out taking photographs of the vessel. Within an hour, I had been sent the photographs by email and it was decided between me and some local residents that, if it was to be proven that the infraction had taken place, we had to get evidence from the sea bed, because we were aware that the vessel might well have been just towing its dredges below the boat – they might not have been on the sea bed.

It was arranged that a local vessel would take me out to the area and that I would dive on it. I dived in the area on the Tuesday and found the dredge marks on the sea bed. The shallowest point of the dredge marks was 19m. I have video evidence of that, which has been submitted to Marine Scotland.[157]

What more public corroboration of infraction could be had? The behaviour of mobile gear fishermen – a scallop or prawn dredger in this case – had resulted in this MPA being brought forward earlier than it might have been. The committee was left in no doubt about the urgency to meet European targets for marine protection and, following the SSI lodged in January 2016, held a high-pressure session. RACCE finally recommended that Parliament introduce 30 MPAs around Scotland's coasts. The recommendation was carried by a vote of seven to two (SNP and Labour versus Tory and Lib Dem).

A particularly sensitive issue was flagged up on our committee work programme: the ownership of quotas to fish for white fish species such as haddock and cod and for the truly mega scale pelagic fishery for mackerel conducted by fewer than 25 large trawlers. Strong suspicions had arisen over the years, following each annual Common Fisheries Policy agreement, that only a few companies owned much of the available quota. These few were dubbed 'slipper skippers'. They sold their rights to actual fishing boat owners for a set number of catches. Due to pressing business from all our other responsibilities, RACCE members

157. RACCE OR, 23 September 2015

were unable to find time for a committee enquiry. Suffice to say that, in 2018, it was revealed that around five families owned the bulk of available quota in Scotland. So much for the idea that Scottish fishing communities are bastions of our coastal economy.

The interaction of salmon that live in rivers, lochs and high seas became a fitting culmination of the RACCE session regarding aquatic policy. It produced a lengthy debate triggered by a petition to the European Commission lodged by Salmon & Trout Conservation (S&TC) suggesting that the Scottish Government was not protecting wild salmon from offshore mixed stock fisheries. The Salmon and Trout Association which had been founded in 1903 claims to 'have been a voice for the UK's watery places and the wild fish that live there'. Its website explains:

> Previously Salmon and Trout Association, we received charitable status in 2008 which allowed us to specialise as a campaign based, science-led, lobbying organisation under our new identity, Salmon & Trout Conservation.

> Wild salmon and trout are natural indicators of a happy and healthy water environment. Their wellbeing is a fundamental interest for everyone with a love of rivers, lakes and their wildlife. With this belief at our heart, we were established as the Salmon and Trout Association in 1903.

> We fight to keep UK waters wild. We do this without the use of taxpayer's money, so we are not compromised in challenging governments. All our work is a product of your passion and support, which enables us to be your voice and to stand up openly for wild fish and water with no strings attached.[158]

Needless to say, ST&C has a Scottish arm and it claims success in halting mixed stock salmon netting as well as hastening the most

---

158. Salmon & Trout Conservation, www.salmon-trout.org

recent Scottish Parliament enquiries into salmon farming practices in Session 5 (2016–21). In 2016, the Scottish Government had to respond to the possible consequences of any financial penalties that could be demanded for negligence in safeguarding wild salmon, if proven by the European Commission regulators of the European Environment Agency. The Scottish Government's response to the ST&C challenge was to be the final subject of RACCE deliberations in our last meeting in March 2016.

At that time Marine Scotland had devised a scheme which composed three classes of fishery districts. The bulk of Scotland's west coast rivers were deemed Grade 3, the most threatened, Grade 2 would allow limited catch and release and Grade 1 gave the greatest cause for hope. Grades 1 and 2 were scattered along our east and north mainland river catchments. It emerged, as we questioned the Cabinet Secretary, Richard Lochead, that these could be reclassified if evidence of improvement was to hand. The big caveat was a three-year moratorium on coastal netting of salmon and sea trout by firms such as Usan near Montrose and that of the Mackays of Armadale in north Sutherland. Committee members quizzed Lochhead at length and found him hampered from full answers to our questions. His deputy Dr Aileen McLeod was unable to attend due to illness and, for several months, any previous informal dialogue with her we had held had probed the Marine Scotland plan.

Our proposed plan was to assess and classify the conservation status assigned to each river district. This would inform further management measures and actions that might be considered at a local and national level. The options listed were conservation, restoration, enhancement and management of wild Atlantic salmon stocks considering the best scientific evidence available. The conservation plans would detail existing and future local initiatives to address the current assessment of the fishery district and identify (and where possible quantify) other factors that might have a material impact, such as marine renewable energy, predation, aquaculture and other barriers.[159]

Several MSPs, including Jackie Baillie, with specific interests in

---

159. RACCE/S4/16/8/1

angling clubs in central Scotland, asked questions. Joan McAlpine supported the recreational fishery of Haaf netting on the Solway.

I had been lobbied strongly by coastal netters in my constituency. Most of our rivers were in Grade 1 conditions but all would be subject to a three-year moratorium, a ban that some thought would be permanent. Mr Skinner at Balintore could not accept that netting could occur inside the Cromarty Firth, two miles away from his business. James Mackay on the north coast had worked with the River Naver Board collaboratively for many years. His livelihood was threatened. Ian Paterson from a family steeped in coastal netting for a century had produced verifiable statistics from Scottish Government data showing that from 2009 to 2014 rod and line angling had caught 159,731 fish while mixed stock coastal netting accounted for 118,366 fish.

I was seriously exercised by this issue. Not only because constituents' livelihoods were at stake but there was a deeper disquiet. Sport fishing was posing in the guise of conservation and had forced the Scottish Government to 'meet EU and international obligations' in response to growing concerns about Scotland's salmon stocks.[160]

Certainly, mixed stock coastal netting was not immune from responsibility for interference with salmon returning by tortuous routes to the rivers of their birth. However, seal predation, climate change warming our seas, indiscriminate fishing efforts around Greenland and the disputed mortality figures for catch and release by anglers all had a part to play in the overall picture of wild salmon population health.

The SSIs we debated that day were vital to meet Scotland's international obligations. However, it meant the end of sales of wild salmon, which had Label Rouge accreditation in France as anglers who catch salmon and sea trout cannot sell them by law. A whole new set of regulations were set to govern the harvest of our rivers and coasts whether for sport or commerce. The difference as of March 2016 was that the Scottish Parliament had to agree less than palatable terms to satisfy EU environmental imperatives. Had the committee rejected the SSIs then the parliament would have held a vote. It is inconceivable that MSPs would have willingly opened the door to large fines levied against

---

160. Letter – Dr A McLeod to RACCE, 19 January 2016

Scotland. In the end, searching questions arose about the ability and capacity of Marine Scotland to monitor, assess and police our waters.

My own concerns about sport angling posing as the guardian of salmon and sea trout had to be weighed against the accusation from Europe of infractions. Party politics close to an election brought the committee to split five against annulment of the order and four in favour. Basically, it amounted to SNP versus Tory, Lib Dem and Labour members.[161]

As a codicil to this chapter, the Scotland Act 2016 passed in Westminster devolved management of the assets of Scottish Crown Estate. While the Smith Commission recommended complete devolution of the Crown Estate, the future relationship of the Scottish Crown Estate with local authorities and Holyrood would have a beneficial effect on licencing and planning powers over fish farms. These had been uneasily set some years earlier but offered coastal communities more scope in future to gain from licences near their areas. A future Crown Estate Scotland Act would lay out the way ahead in the fifth session of the Scottish Parliament. As I previously stated in debate, devolution of the Crown Estate moved more slowly than glaciers. Only we now know glaciers are melting much more quickly than we previously thought!

---

161. RACCE OR, March 2016

9. Human rights to our land

Is it legitimate to disturb property rights? Is it legitimate not to?
– Dr Kirsteen Shields, *New Statesman*, 14 December 2015

The ECHR was built into the founding statute of the Scottish Parliament. It places Scottish laws in the broader mainstream of European jurisprudence. That concept is consequent on the transmission from the UK's membership of the Council of Europe, which is much wider than the transcription of EU law into Scottish practice. The consequences of applying EU law into Scottish property law has been problematic. In this respect Article 1 on respecting rights and Article 8 on privacy have been the worst offenders. This issue loomed large in deliberations on the Land Reform Scotland Bill 2015 which followed debates on human rights when MSPs scrutinised the Community Empowerment (Scotland) Act 2015.

We can see that the Brexit debate has the potential to interfere with these agreed concepts of human rights. You only have to witness the attempts to curb immigration into the UK to find a fundamental challenge to the human rights that we have carefully built upon in Scotland. The work of the Scottish Parliament before 2016 applied ECHR and went further to explore the United Nations' concept of universal human rights.

It had been understood for many years that Article 1 of ECHR balanced the principles of rights to enjoy private property while meeting the public interest. This is justiciable in civil law and could be costly to infringe. In the second John McEwen Memorial Lecture, in 1995, James Hunter presented his case to use ECHR. He believed that his list of land reform proposals could 'be shown to be compatible with that injunction'.[162] In the Scottish Parliament, during debates on rural land reform and agricultural holdings in 2003, these issues were also raised. But it was in the context of a late clause in the Agricultural Holdings (Scotland) Act passed in 2003 that ECHR compliance was tested and, ten years later, the landlord's interests were upheld. This would become a major headache for the Scottish Government and RACCE committee in 2013.

The background to this debacle was summed up concisely by a Scottish Tenant Farming Association (STFA) written submission to the Agricultural Holdings Remedial Order proposed by the Scottish Government following the loss in the Supreme Court of the Salvesen v Riddell case in 2013:

> Limited Partnership (LP) tenancies evolved during the 1970s as a means to circumvent the security provisions of 1991 traditional tenancies. By the 1990s they were, by and large, the only vehicles for letting land. LP tenancies were usually let for a specified period of time and if not extended they usually continued by tacit relocation (on a yearly basis). In most cases LP tenancies were regarded as long-term prospects.
>
> In early 2003 the Minister of the day, Ross Finnie, was presented with evidence that some landlords were dissolving their LP tenancies due to fears about right to buy legislation. In February the Executive decided to take preventative action and introduced measures to grant added protection to LP tenants. In an avoidance measure many landlords served notices to terminate LP tenancies the day before the lodging of the new legislative measure to the Rural Affairs Committee. At the time it was estimated that 200 notices were served on 3 February.

---

162. James Hunter, 'Towards a Land Reform Agenda for a Scottish Parliament', John McEwan Memorial Lecture, 1995

What eventually emerged were Sections 72 and 73, which became incorporated into the 2003 Act. These provisions gave added protection to tenants in Limited Partnership tenancies and enabled those who were given notice during the 'relevant' period to claim full security of tenure providing it could be shown the intention behind the notice to quit was to deprive the tenants of any rights accruing to them to them from the new Act.[163]

In 2014, SPICe summarised the court action and its effect:

The Supreme Court recognised that the legislation has had effect from 2003 and that a number of parties that were not involved in the Salvesen v Riddell court case may have been affected. To be in the affected group a party would need to have served or received a dissolution notice for a Limited Partnership between 16 September 2002 and 30 June 2003. The Scottish Government identified a number of groups affected by the defective sections of the 2003 Act, including that a tenant may now have a full 1991 tenancy; or that the landlord may have sold either to the tenant exercising a pre-emptive right to buy, or to a new landlord. The Scottish Government consultation sets out the different groups that could be identified as being affected by the defect in its consultation on the remedial order.[164]

RACCE took evidence ahead of the passage of the Remedial Order hearing that the number of tenancies affected had been reduced to seven cases. Of all the parties identified a very few indeed were expected to suffer. Of course, tenants as well as landlords would be very likely to

---

163. See timeline
164. Tom Edwards and Wendy Kenyon, 'SPICe Briefing: Tenant Farming', SPICe, 25 July 2014, www.parliament.scot/ResearchBriefingsAndFactsheets/S4/SB_14-52.pdf

seek compensation for the actions of the Parliament in 2003 – in which all but the Tories had supported the Scottish Executive position.[165] The Lord Advocate's appeal to the Court of Session on the ECHR point was rejected by the court due the 'inflamed language' of Alan Wilson MSP, the deputy minister. This was prompted by the heightened atmosphere of tension among LP tenants by the serving of notices by their land-lords to end the partnership. At Stage 2 of the Agricultural Holdings (Scotland) Bill the Scottish Executive had introduced the amendment to enhance the security of these tenants for the period after the intro-duction of the Bill in September 2002 until February 2003.

Limited Partnership tenancies – The fallout!

Timeline

April 2003	Agriculture Holdings (Scotland) Act, as enacted, contained the controversial Sections 72 and 73 which offered a route to security of tenure for Limited Partnership Tenants (LPTs) if notices of termination were served between 16 September 2002 and 30 June 2003.
2008	Alastair Salvesen served notice to Andrew Riddell and took his case to the Land Court after the Peaston LPTs was due to end in 2008.
29 Jul 2010	Land Court Order upheld the legitimacy of the Agriculture Holdings (Scotland)

---

165. 'Judgement: Alastair Salvesen Against John Riddell and Andrew Riddell and the Lord Advocate', Scottish Courts and Tribunals, 6 January 2015 www.scotcourts.gov.uk/search-judgments/judgment?id=3c7dbfa6-8980-69d2-b500-ff0000d74aa7

	Act 2003 in the case of Salvesen v Riddell.
15 Mar 2012	In the case of Salvesen v Riddell, the Court of Session decision challenged the Land Court ruling on grounds that Section 72 of Agriculture Holdings (Scotland) Act 2003 was outwith the powers of the Scottish Parliament. Salvesen appealed to the Court of Session.
5 Oct 2012	Andrew Riddell committed suicide after his last harvest and days ahead of his eviction.
24 Apr 2013	The Scottish Government joins the case and appeals to the Supreme Court in London on behalf of potentially 20 allied cases which confirmed the Court of Session decision that Section 72 breached ECHR Article 1.
22 Nov 2013	The Scottish Government lodged Draft Agriculture Holdings (Scotland) Act 2003 Remedial Order 2014 and consulted on it from 27 November 2013 to 7 February 2014.
Apr 2014	RACCE took evidence on the case and its report was responded to by the Scottish Government and passed by Parliament.

5 Dec 2014	Tenants affected by Agriculture Holdings (Scotland) Act 2003 had to lodge final compensation claims by this date.
Mar 2015	Seven affected tenants lodged a motion in the Court of Session for compensation.
12 Aug 2015	A Scottish Government mediator was appointed to the case. The *Our Land* campaign was launched to highlight many land injustices, including the plight of LPTs.
25 Sep 2015	A legal stalemate without a time bar prompted RACCE to seek Scottish Government action at the earliest possible date.
10 Nov 2015	Demonstrators backed by *Our Land* outside the Scottish Parliament hand over 20,000 signatures on a petition on behalf of LPT Andrew Stoddart, Coulston Mains. Sarah Boyack MSP and I accepted the petition on behalf of RACCE committee.
22 Nov 2015	Iain Gray MSP asked Cabinet Secretary Richard Lochhead to soften Mr Stoddart's eviction. Mr Lochhead answered that he was seeking land for the tenant to farm.

26 Nov 2015	An agreement was reached for compensation for tenant's improvement to the holding was paid by landlords, Coulston Trust. Mr Stoddart was given leave to remain till January 2016 before quitting.
17 Nov 2016	A further demonstration outside Parliament organised by *Our Land* and the campaign group 38 degrees supported the Paterson brothers facing imminent eviction as LPT from Glenree Farm, on Arran Estates.

Human rights tested, and universal rights invoked

In 2003, Ross Finnie MSP, the then Cabinet Secretary for the Environment, was bombarded by news that hundreds of LPTs had received notices to quit. Finnie believed his limited proposal for security was ECHR compliant, as did the parliament's lawyers who allowed the proposed amendments to go forward. Ten years later this move had unravelled spectacularly.

Alastair Salvesen, one of the richest businessmen in Scotland, was determined to retrieve vacant possession of Peaston Farm near Ormiston in East Lothian from his tenant Andrew Riddell whose family had farmed there to a very high standard since 1902. Mr Salvesen had purchased the estate in 1998 and had other ideas for the LP tenancy that Mr Riddell and his brother enjoyed. The Scottish Government inherited the implications of the decision of its predecessors. Ross Finnie's attempt to protect this group of LPTs had Labour, Lib Dem and SNP support but was struck down in the landlord's favour in the Court of Session in 2012. This raises the key question about the means whereby a substantial majority of MSPs can offer protection to tenants from eviction by voting in the national parliament to do this, believing it to be in the public interest. The interpretation of Article 1 Protocol 1 and Article 8 of ECHR by Lord Gill to uphold the landlord's rights lays severe tests for any future laws that might be proposed (eg to seek to give secure tenancies held under the 1991 Act as a right to buy their farms). It had been widely debated in 2003 having been common in other EU states in previous times.

The basedrones blog on 2 April 2014 commented on the Salvesen v Riddell remedial proposals constructed by the Scottish Government to correct an ECHR breach that had been handed down by the UK Supreme Court. After a summary of the legalese in Richard Lochhead's statement of intent, it went on:

> Good luck to the civil servants drafting the plain English guidance. If I was to have a go myself, I would probably opt for, 'general partners who thought they were getting an upgrade because a landowner tried to end a farming Limited Partnership between 16 September 2002 and 30 June 2003 are now treated roughly the same as any tenants with a landowner that acted after 30 June 2003.'

> One final point. In the comments to a post on this topic last year, I supposed this might affect a hundred or so cases. The Scottish Government today suggests the figure is as low as 25. While that may be a low number, and this may seem like an awfully complicated way to deal with things, if human rights mean anything the numbers and the complexity matter not a jot. A society that cares about human rights ought to do all it can to ensure those rights are respected in all circumstances.[166]

This last remark by the blogger, Malcolm Combe, then a law lecturer in Aberdeen University, lies at the heart of the conundrum legislators must face. Firstly, how does the Scottish Parliament's responsibility to

---

166. Malcom M Combe, 'Salvesen v Riddell – Remedial Order, base-drones, 2 April 2014, www.basedrones.wordpress.com/2014/04/02/salvesen-v-riddell-remedial-order/

apply ECHR principles in Scottish laws protect its citizens? Secondly, what impact on such situations can the UN Convention on Economic, Social and Cultural Rights (UNCESCR) make to our laws which the parliament is also obliged to apply? This latter convention had been adopted into UK law in 1976. Being UK international obligations, the Scotland Act 1998 included its observance and implementation. But, unlike ECHR, the UNCESCR is not directly justiciable.

Mindful of the difficulties ECHR and other constraints, in August 2012 the Scottish Government gave the LRRG a radical remit which could collide with ECHR. In a key section of its final report entitled *The Land of Scotland and the Common Good*, the Review Group linked these ideas to that of the public good. They argued that their remit encouraged a detailed development of ideas for a comprehensive land reform programme because:

> The term 'common good' describes a comprehensive and complex concept which brings into its embrace questions of social justice, human rights, democracy, citizenship, stewardship and economic development. These are all terms which have expansive, ambitious horizons. Yet each of them can be interpreted in a narrow way which limits its value. The Review Group considers that bringing them together under the common good helps to point towards outcomes that are healthy, rounded and robust.[167]

The LRRG explained that social justice was centred on fairness and equality values that were embedded in their remit. They went on:

> Human rights have traditionally been a prominent part of the land reform discourse, with the UN Covenant on Economic, Social and Cultural Rights and the European Convention on Human Rights (Protocol 1, Article 1) providing a framework which seeks to balance the right of the population to an adequate standard of living, with the

---

167. LRRG, 'The Land of Scotland and the Common Good', 2014

right of the individual to the peaceful enjoyment of his or her possessions. A respect for democracy (and democratic accountability) is also a key component of the common good, as is the concept of citizenship – active citizens pursuing not just their own ambitions, but also goals that are for the good of society as a whole.[168]

During the period of the LRRG deliberations from August 2012 till May 2014, which was followed by the Scottish Government consultation and publication of the Land Reform (Scotland) Bill 2015, the ECHR breach played out sensationally in the courts, tragically at Peaston Farm, and vocally outside the Scottish Parliament. It was addressed thoughtfully in the RACCE committee which processed and quizzed ministers on the remedial order and encouraged the incorporation of international examples of human rights into the Community Empowerment (Scotland) Bill and Land Reform (Scotland) Bill 2015.

In my role as convener of RACCE I continued the well-established practice of encouraging wide-ranging participation from all parties, even though the committee's work programme was often fashioned round the time needed to process government Bills. Members agreed to business that led us into greater understanding of key aspects of the Bill's contents through preparatory work and visits. The pressures of time always left us wanting to get out more to meet the people we were trying to serve. But, in the case of human rights issues, the urgent business came at us through events, dear boy, events. The Supreme Court ruling on Salvesen v Riddell in April 2012 and the death of Andrew Riddell, by his own hand, in October 2012 followed his final harvest. Each was greeted with shock and sadness in parliament and across the farming industry. Calls for an equitable solution were mixed with anger at the loss of a progressive farmer and a well-liked man. The case underlined the strains created by complex landlord and tenant laws and their long history of conflict and entrenchment of the landlord interests by the extensive and costly use, often at great length, of the civil courts.

---

168. ibid.

Cabinet Secretary Richard Lochhead MSP, soon to become the longest serving minister in one portfolio, longer even than his predecessor Ross Finnie, had extensive experience of agricultural matters. He generated new urgency by personally chairing the Agricultural Holdings Legislative Review Group to speed up solutions that might ensure tenant farmers were better protected and to encourage landlords to let more land. Yet the need for a remedial order to meet the UK Supreme Court's judgement would dog Richard's last years of the 2011–16 parliament.

David Balharry, from the Agriculture Directorate, was the civil servant tasked with producing a form of words to identify those affected, propose changes to the Agriculture Holdings (Scotland) Act 2003 and set out ways for LPTs and their landlords to reach compensation agreements without any Scottish Government liability to particular sums of money. The groups likely to be affected were surveyed and the numbers reduced to seven tenants who were directly caught by the ruling. In the event, there was little room for manoeuvre for RACCE or the Scottish Government. An order was agreed, laid before Parliament, and conveyed to the Supreme Court for its approval.

Concerted action to assert human rights

The Scottish Human Rights Commission (SHRC) had been established by the Scottish Parliament in 2006. It has UN accreditation and was led from 2007 till 2016 by Professor Alan Miller. Alan Robertson observed in 2016 that Miller's appointment

> came at a time when any discussion around human rights seemed to be entangled with criminal justice.

The decision to release convicted Lockerbie bomber Abdelbaset al-Megrahi on compassionate grounds in 2009 – one that the commission supported very publicly – was perhaps the most emphatic example of that. Miller went on:

> As chair of the European Network [of National Human Rights Institutions] and vice-chair of the global network,

I am constantly in circulation and Scotland's stock rose enormously around the world as a result of that decision.[169]

Happily, a whole new area of human rights activity opened with huge international bearing when community empowerment and land reform were on the table. We had the great pleasure to question Alan Miller and discuss many aspects of human rights with him. From this there emerged a cluster of concerns to embed human rights in land reform issues. These became talking points following the LRRG Final Report. Lobbying by human rights activists prompted Mike Russell MSP to introduce an amendment to the Community Empowerment (Scotland) Bill when RACCE was asked by the Scottish Government's business manager to shepherd Part 4 of the Bill through parliament. Decisions under Parts 2, 3 or 3A of the 2003 Act would require ministers to have regard to the International Covenant on Economic, Social and Cultural Rights argued Mr Russell. He explained:

> If we fail to recognise those wider rights and are mindful only of, for example, the European Convention on Human Rights, we are promoting – always promoting – the concept of individual rights and never promoting the concept of community rights. It is important, at least at the base of decision making by ministers, that they should be mindful of those wider obligations.
>
> In the area of land reform, it is also important that they are mindful of those wider obligations, because, as we can see in the developing debate over land reform, the issue will, at times, become a debate between the rights and

---

169. Alan Robertson, 'Outgoing Scottish Human Rights Commission chair Alan Miller on "toxic" Westminster debate, the referendum and Supreme Court "stooshie"', *Holyrood Magazine*, 19 February 2016, www.holyrood.com/inside-politics/view,outgoing-scottish-human-rights-commission-chair-alan-miller-on-toxic-westminster-debate-the-referendum-and-supreme-court-stooshie_6517.htm

expectations of an individual and the rights and expectations of a community. Ministers have to be able at least to consider the wider obligations that the parliament and the government owe to a community.

The Minister, Dr Aileen McLeod MSP, agreed that this was a useful addition to guide ministers. Only Alex Fergusson, the Tory MSP, abstained at the vote to reserve his position for Stage 3 debates on the Bill.[170]

Arguments aplenty were taking place about the right to buy, whether by communities, tenant farmers or crofters. Regarding the latter, when the UK Crofting Reform (Scotland) Act 1976 gave crofters the right to buy at 15 times their annual rental, no application of ECHR was mentioned. No attempts were made to stop the measure which had cross-party support. No appeals were made to the UNCESCR although it was ratified that year in UK law. Perhaps this shows a mindset among law makers at the time and landowners, then and now, that while crofting was a burden to them, tenant farming was, on the other hand, a major source of income.

On 25 March 2015, RACCE was reviewing the Agricultural Holdings Legislative Review Group final report published that January. We quizzed a panel of witnesses who gave evidence on the report that ran to 49 detailed recommendations. Whether these could be legislated for in the current parliamentary session was a moot point. The fragility of a rural business consensus was exposed when the SLaE (Scottish Land & Estates) representative mentioned ECHR. Many committee members raised eyebrows on the topic of succession and conversion of leases on which SLaE considered the review groups recommendations to be 'not appropriately balanced and represent a substantial erosion of the landlord's rights'. This allegation was led by Stuart Young, factor of Dunecht Estates, and chair of SLaE Agricultural Holdings Strategy Group. Most RACCE members saw this as another threat to the hard-won agreement. Mr Young's explained:

---

170. RACCE OR, 11 March 2015

We have taken opinion from senior counsel, and counsel's firm view is that the proposals represent a breach of the European Convention on Human Rights and will ultimately leave the government with the prospect of a hefty bill of circa £600 million for paying compensation to landlords.

That is pretty blunt and fundamental in terms of the position of Scottish Land & Estates and how we see things. Clearly, we do not want to go into any new legislation that would create a period of conflict and court action that was a repeat of the Salvesen v Riddell case. We should see whether there is a better way of going forward.

Mike Russell immediately challenged the SLaE threat of 'the big stick' which brandished ECHR as a matter of opinion suggesting there might be other opinions. He went on:

A different perspective could be taken, which is that the freedom to assign has gradually been eroded since the 1948 legislation, but the pendulum is beginning to swing back to a more reasonable set of arrangements by which assignations should take place in the best interests of the tenant and the landlord, provided that that will lead to the continuing safe and secure operation of the farming business.

Mike Russell concluded that Mr Young's remarks were 'not a helpful contribution to the debate'. Stuart Young replied that it would be irresponsible of SLaE to have identified the difficulty 'but not brought it to the attention of the Government and the committee'.[171] Scroll back 13 years to the 12 weeks when the Land Reform Scotland Act 2003 was being consulted on. The *Press & Journal* reported that the same Stuart Young, 'a leading north-east estate factor', had said 'the pre-emptive

---

171. RACCE OR, 25 March 2015

right to buy was likely to kill the letting market dead'.[172] The trajectory of SLaE strategy is plain to see. Along with the Royal Chartered Institute of Surveyors (RICS) they sought to threaten the Scottish Parliament ahead of its law making. Mr Young claimed in the same piece that this pre-emptive right to buy (RTB) 'threatens to destroy the agreement reached by the Scottish Landowners Federation and NFU Scotland on new agricultural tenancies.'

In 2002, Hamish MacDonnell reported in *The Scotsman* that RICS was estimating that 'nearly £500m will be wiped off the value of farm land'. He noted that the SNP, which was campaigning for the Bill to be tougher, were pointing out that 50 tenant farmers had already been served with eviction notices by landlords trying to dodge the provisions of the Bill. This was seen by MacDonnell as

> an escalation in the war of words over the Bill that was supposed to be uncontentious, but which had now become the latest battleground over land ownership.

The tactics of landowners and their agents have become all too familiar. First you overplay the rhetoric to assert your self-proclaimed property rights and then apply the big stick to beat any hard-won concession that might be agreed with their 'partners' in rural businesses. Certainly, the Agriculture Holdings (Scotland) Act 2003 had not been the last word on tenants' rights. The late amendments to the Bill to try to protect LPTs exploded by the end of the decade.

The SNP took over the reins as a minority government in May 2007 and the *Press & Journal* reported on 20 October that, according to land agents Savills,

> Farmland prices continue on an upward path – values are now 50% above peaks in the 1990s.

The paper calculated that the reasons for 50% of farm sales were either death, retirement or other domestic reasons. It expected farmer buyers

---

172. *Press & Journal*, 17 April 2002

to be the majority of purchasers while so-called lifestyle farmers could account for the balance of farm and land purchases. As RACCE members well knew, investment in land and farms continued to produce the best return, as the LRRG were to reference in 2014.

Fast forward to an important footnote to the '£600m compensation claim' raised by Stuart Young in April 2015 at the RACCE hearing. This was contained in the SLaE supplementary written submission at Stage 1 of the Land Reform Scotland Bill later that year which laid out the legal advice that argued the ECHR implications of widening succession to farm tenancies. In that advice it referenced possible compensation for landlords but offered no mention as to the potential sum involved. When David Johnstone, the recently elected chair of SLaE, represented the landowners' body at the Stage 1 hearing on 16 September 2015, he did not mention compensation or amounts of compensation in his evidence.[173]

International human rights to the fore

NGOs and the SHRC were formulating a much wider approach to human rights over land reform along with sympathetic MSPs. Their focus would go beyond individual property rights and towards community rights, which had become a durable part of international law. They sought for land reform in Scotland to use that wider armoury of argument to boost its radical intent.

Under the auspices of the United Nations Organisation various declarations have been adopted by the international community, such as UNCESCR. Another key text was the UN Food & Agriculture Organisation's Voluntary Guidelines on Responsible Governance of Tenure of Land, Forests and Fisheries (VGRGTLFF). Each was adopted in response to bad practice and increased pressure on land across the globe. The eradication of hunger and poverty by promoting sustainable development was required by the recognition of the centrality of secure tenure rights. This first crystallised in a Developing World focus. But Scotland's concentrated land ownership pattern and inequalities of opportunity to access our most basic natural resources

---

173. RACCE OR, 16 September 2015

made these measures highly relevant in one of the oldest nations in Europe. Enhancing human rights would be brought to bear in the cause of transparency of ownership in the Land Reform Bill.

10. Land reform in Parliament at last
Too far or not far enough?

The landlords have given to the people no satisfaction but have told us to have patience. We told them that our forefathers had died in patience until now, but we can wait no longer – our forefathers got nothing by their patience but a constant worsening.

– John Macpherson of Glendale, evidence to the Napier Commission, 1882.

With a Land Reform Bill promised by 2015, the lairds' network once again amassed a substantial war chest to mount a sustained campaign of opposition. They had deployed such a strategy each time land reform appeared on the political agenda. During the early stages of the LRRG's work group its members engaged in meeting many estates and landowners, among others. This was cast up by some land reformers as a sign of bias in the lairds' favour.

SLaE produced 238 pages of a 'Response to the Scottish Government's Land Reform Review' which was published in January 2013, ahead of the evidence taking sessions.[174] This blockbuster document, compiled by a range of members and consultants, set out to show the strength of their case for extensive land ownership in rural Scotland. Of the 60 recommendations they made, several would require considerably more taxpayers' spend, to the benefit of existing owners. One pointed example was a demand for

> a critical economic evaluation of community buyouts to be carried out, looking at their successes, failures and

---

174. Scottish Land and Estates, 'Response to the Scottish Government's Land Reform Review', 2013, www2.gov.scot/resource/0043/00432805.pdf

their cost effectiveness in achieving their business plan objectives.[175]

Surely SLaE with its friendly welcome of community ownership was indeed skin deep?

Despite stating it would be willing to work along with Community Land Scotland, the umbrella body for community landowners, SLaE, landlords and land agents returned time and again to downplay community land ownership. Right-wing newspapers and journals had been targeting communities such as Eigg, and more recently Gigha, often distorting facts about their economic viability. I raised the Gigha issue in my speech on Nicola Sturgeon's first Programme for Government in November 2014 (see below).

Scotland's private estate owners have never been slow to denounce land reform measures brought forward by the Scottish Parliament. The 2003 Land Reform Act was branded a 'Mugabe-style land grab', which Tory MSPs duly voted against. By 2013, ten years' experience of the further need for strengthened land reforms had set in train a two-part process of inquiry by the Scottish Government's LRRG.

Its interim report seemed underwhelming to longstanding land reform campaigners, but the beefed-up approach to Phase Two drew a stark headline in *The Scotsman*, 'Lairds warn Holyrood over new land buyout powers'.[176] What had triggered such divergent views on the state of Scottish land ownership and use?

Disquiet arose during the LRRG's early months. It has been suggested that clerical and organisational back up was slow off the mark. Reform-minded campaigners noted a preponderance of meetings with estate owners. Alarm bells rang out when Jim Hunter left the team (for personal reasons) before the interim report was compiled by Alison Elliot and Sarah Skerratt and published on 10 May 2013. This led Andy Wightman to speculate that the two remaining group members were interpreting their remit as community empowerment not full-scale land reform.

---

175. ibid.
176. *The Scotsman*, 1 August 2013

Further concerns mounted when news broke that Sarah Skerratt had decided to return to her work at the Scottish Rural University College – mapping the problems of rural Scotland issue by issue at biennial intervals.[177] It all seemed pessimistic for the task set for the LRRG by Alex Salmond in July 2012, namely:

a)   Enable more people in rural and urban Scotland to have a stake in the ownership, governance, management and use of land, which will lead to a greater diversity of land ownership, and ownership types, in Scotland;

a)   Assist with the acquisition and management of land (and also land assets) by communities, to make stronger, more resilient, and independent communities which have an even greater stake in their development;

b)   Generate, support, promote and deliver new relationships between land, people, economy and environment in Scotland.[178]

Andy Wightman's blog *Land Matters* assessed the lack of progress under a lurid headline 'It's Over – Unconditional Surrender'. Within hours of the interim report's publication, Wightman noted that Alison Elliot, the LRRG chair, was giving a keynote speech at the SLaE AGM at Perth Race Course. He went on:

No doubt she will receive a warm welcome and a rousing cheer from the landed class and its legal and financial advisers as the latest attempt at kick-starting land reform withers and dies on the vine of complacency and ignorance.[179]

---

177.   Sarah Skerrett, 'Rural Report 2012' and 'Rural Report 2014', Scottish Rural University College
178.   Land Reform Review Group, 2012
179.   Andy Wightman, 'Land Matters', speech at Scottish Land and Estates AGM, 21 May 2013

Andy Wightman's comments are seldom likely to be mistaken for a ray of sunshine. He tore into the LRRG's work having questioned at the outset how its interpretation of the remit would guide its actions.

Those of us at Holyrood were concerned about the bad press and criticism of the LRRG's interim report. We noted, however, that the report was only the group's initial thinking. We also noted that the work of Phase Two and Three was laid out over the coming months. As well as details of the visits and of the evidence received (and published sometime later) other than the interim report, we welcomed the focus on the means to take forward the full remit to a conclusion by April 2014. The subjects listed provided strong indicators of a fully-fledged response to the expectations raised by Alex Salmond's original proposition.

A competing claim came from the Scottish Conference of the Labour Party held in Inverness in April 2013. The party's leader, Johann Lamont MSP, called for radical action on land reform. She said:

> land reform had stalled under the SNP, if it is in the public interest, communities will have the right to purchase land, even when the landowner is not a willing seller.[180]

Lamont's speech suggested that the LRRG lacked ambition. This may well have been the first sign by the main opposition party of a co-ordinated move in a bidding war with the Scottish Government's land reform programme.

Concerns about a lack of progress from the SNP's choice to initiate an independent advisory group had been fed by Jim Hunter's resignation and Wightman's speculations. Misgivings about the group's focus were confirmed five days before the publication of the LRRG interim report and a month before the Labour opposition decided to secure a short debate at Holyrood on 5 June to raise their own concerns. Hunter was speaking at the unveiling of a new Land League monument at

---

180. Malcolm M Combe, 'Labour Towards Land Reform, base-drones, 22 April 2013, www.basedrones.wordpress.com/2013/04/22/labour-towards-land-reform/

Bhaltos in Lewis. His stinging attack was relayed widely:

> We're now six years into an SNP Government which has
> so far done absolutely nothing legislatively about the
> fact that Scotland continues to be stuck with the most
> concentrated, most inequitable, most unreformed and
> most undemocratic land ownership system in the entire
> developed world.[181]

Hunter proposed that the Cabinet Secretary, Richard Lochhead, should take over the chair of the review group, as Labour ministers had done in 1997. He listed a range of actions required for a radical approach to ensure the review group explored LVT and got serious about a RTB for tenant farmers, as the Labour Party had indicated the previous month. He demanded that the SNP Government should commit to legislate in 2014–15.[182]

Hunter's demands ignored Labour's own selection of land reform topics for development from among the total recommendations of their LRPG's findings in 1998. What would be included in forthcoming legislation, that became the 2003 Acts on land reform and agricultural holdings, had far fewer subject heads than previously consulted on. For example, LVT explored in 1998 was dropped from the draft Bill being deemed to require 'further study'. Hunter failed to remember the Scottish Executive orders to whip Labour and Lib Dem Rural Development committee members (John Farquhar Munro rebelled) to vote against the absolute right to buy (ARTB) when the SNP had attempted to bring it forward as an amendment at Stage 2.

It became clear in 2013 that out-manoeuvring the SNP via a Westminster land reform enquiry by the Scottish Affairs committee (SAc) was part of the Labour tactic. On the morning of 5 May, ahead of

181. Torcuil Crichton, Whitehall 1212, 4 May 2013, www.whitehall1212.blogspot.co.uk

182. Andy Wightman, 'The Most Concentrated, Inequitable, and Undemocratic Land Ownership System in the Entire Developed World', Land Matters, 4 June 2013, www.andywightman.com/archives/2757

Labour's planned land reform debate in Holyrood, the *Daily Record*'s London political editor, Torcuil Crichton, announced in his blog, Whitehall 1212, 'MPs to launch "who owns Scotland" investigation'. He went on:

> Ahead of the debate on land reform in Holyrood today Scots MPs at Westminster have signalled they are to launch an investigation into the shady offshore companies that own vast tracts of land in Scotland.
>
> The Commons Scottish Affairs committee is due to start an inquiry into land ownership and tax avoidance after campaigners slammed the SNP Government's lacklustre commitment to the land reform agenda.
>
> Ian Davidson MP, the Labour chairman of the Scottish committee, said he hoped the inquiry would 'establish who owns and controls the great landed estates in Scotland, in order to minimise tax avoidance'.[183]

In the event this enquiry soon looked like it would be complimentary to Holyrood's land reform review process. But it was political gamesmanship which, later that summer, afforded Jim Hunter a chance to compile a wide-ranging set of land reform proposals as a starter paper for the SAC. He authored the paper on behalf Peter Peacock, Michael Foxley and Andy Wightman thus playing on the multi-party concerns to broaden the debate beyond powers available to the devolved Scottish Government. It is a thread I will pick up after recounting the outcome of the 5 June debate in Holyrood.

Claire Baker MSP led the charge for Labour in this debate by pointing out the inadequacy of the LRRG interim report saying:

> the interim report has been met largely with disappointment and criticism from land reformists because of the group's lack of expertise in many key areas, the decision

---

183. Torcuil Crichton, Whitehall 1212, 5 May 2013, www.whitehall1212. blogspot.co.uk

that it took to narrow the remit and the dearth of radical proposals or options for further development.

She pressed on:

> I fail to understand how this review of land reform can take place without considering land tenure... An opportunity is being missed for the LRRG to highlight to the government the need to address best land use and tenure in Scotland in the next decade and beyond... There is now a strong and justifiable mood of cynicism amongst tenant farmers that they have been side-lined and an opportunity is being missed to provide vision and direction for this neglected rural community of Scotland.[184]

Paul Wheelhouse MSP, Minister for Environment and Climate Change, responded for the government by proposing a simple amendment to point out that the LRRG was indeed an independent advisory group and then underlined how he intended to enhance its work:

> A key theme will be land reform in urban Scotland. As that is closely associated with the developing community empowerment and renewal Bill, we will ensure that that Bill takes on the review group's ideas in furthering the Scottish Government's desire to empower urban and rural communities and in resolving problems identified with current legislation.

He followed this with a discussion about the proposed land agency which "is another key consideration and I am intrigued by the possibilities that it might deliver." Mr Wheelhouse assured MSPs that:

> The group will look at community engagement with landowners and community energy projects and at how we ensure that the right support and advice are in place

---

184. Claire Baker, Scottish Parliament, 5 May 2013

for community landowners. It will recommend how the Community Right to Buy legislation, which currently makes life unnecessarily difficult for communities in a number of respects, can be simplified and amended to be more accessible, and further work will be commissioned on common good land, taxation, public interest issues and issues with regard to the Crown Estate.

He went on to announce further resources needed to complete the work. He had previously agreed with Alison Elliot to expand the group from its original three members to five. Ian Cooke, a director with Development Trusts Association Scotland, was appointed as vice-chair to ensure that there was expertise on the community sector, and John Watt as the second vice-chair following his role as a recent director of HIE with a wealth of experience on state aid and public sector support for communities. This was a welcome step up for Watt who was already an adviser to the LRRG. Furthermore, the Minister stated that two additional appointments would be announced in due course to complete the expanded group. Additionally, Richard Heggie and Malcolm Combe had been appointed as new advisers so that the group would be fully resourced to carry out Phase Two of its review. Thus, he concluded,

the additional expertise available will allow it to come up with clear, informed and workable proposals in its final report.[185]

In reply to Labour's debate, I questioned if Johann Lamont's conference speech were more than 'fiery words', arguing:

As has been said, land reform is a process, like constitutional reform, and the background to the current inquiry must be understood so that other members can have the chance to comment.

---

185. Paul Wheelhouse, Scottish Parliament, 5 May 2013

Clarity on the issues was not helped by Johann Lamont telling the Scottish Labour spring conference in Inverness in April that a compulsory right to buy should become available to urban and rural communities if they so wished. Those were fiery words, but there was not one single detail to allow that to be taken seriously.[186]

The outcome maintained the overwhelming consensus for radical land reform. A Tory amendment, proposed by Alex Fergusson MSP, sought to water down the LRRG's work. It concluded, the parliament

> agrees that, while community ownership is to be encouraged, a willing buyer and willing seller are paramount, and welcomes the group's decision not to examine land tenancy issues, which are currently being scrutinised by the Tenant Farming Forum.

This was defeated by 98 votes to 12 and the motion amended with inclusion of the government phrase about the LRRG being independent and advisory was accepted by Labour and passed by the same margin. The amended motion then read:

> That the Parliament notes the publication of the Land Reform Review Group's interim report; recognises that the Land Reform Review Group was appointed by the Scottish Government as an advisory group independent of Scottish ministers to offer a 'radical review of land reform'; believes that ownership of land is an economic and social issue; recognises that the Scottish Government has the power to deliver further land reform now; supports greater diversification of land ownership in Scotland, and calls on the Scottish Government to demonstrate a commitment to radical and bold land reform.[187]

---

186. Rob Gibson, Scottish Parliament, 5 May 2013
187. Amended Motion on Land Reform, Scottish Parliament, 5 May 2013

Following his announcement in the land reform debate on 5 June, Paul Wheelhouse appointed Pip Tabor, project manager for the Southern Uplands Partnership, to join the other three LRRG members. She brought to the table practical expertise from the south of Scotland.

Land review – Phase Two goes wider and lairds dig deeper

The second appointment in June 2013 was Robin Callander as an independent special adviser to the LRRG. This signalled radical intent by the Scottish Government to strengthen and deepen the LRRG in its Phase 2 work. Callander's credentials were widely acknowledged as highly appropriate. His work at Birse Community, previous publications and collaborations, and indeed advisory posts to local authorities in the Highlands and Islands on the Crown Estate and the Scottish Affairs committee in Westminster marked him as a driver for radical and comprehensive change. He underlined this when appearing at my committee with the LRRG chair Alison Elliot on 26 June 2013. We could see his depth of knowledge and drive in a series of answers that guided MSPs to have confidence that a big step up in output by the review group could be expected.[188]

It was during that summer of 2013 that I took up the deer culling issues to protect threatened woods in Assynt in my constituency, as described in a previous chapter. The RACCE involvement in the wider deer management issue played into important moves by the government to put Deer Management Groups under notice. Get your plans up and running or expect tougher action!

In anticipation of beefed-up LRRG's conclusions, the landed classes again mobilised. They correctly anticipated the mood for enhanced reforms which a substantial Holyrood majority was expected to back. The Earl of Seafield commented on this new energy for change. In the forward to *Seafield & Strathspey Estates News Review* in the summer of 2013 he wrote:

> Johann Lamont took the land reform concept to a new level in her speech to the Labour conference this spring.

188. Robin Callander, Scottish Parliament, 26 June 2013

She said that 'land reform had stalled under the SNP', and
then declared that 'if it is in the public interest, communities will have the right to purchase land, even when the
landowner is not a willing seller.' That seems a dramatic
extension of compulsory purchase – but full marks to her
for laying her cards on the table.[189]

As one of the leading lights of SLaE, Seafield was serving notice that a
major counter offensive was being planned against the likes of shooting
rates and further farm tenancy reform.

Ahead of the grouse shooting season, Tom Peterkin, writing in *The
Scotsman*, obliged the SLaE publicity machine by reporting that 'breaking up their sporting estates could have a "disastrous" effect on rural
communities'. And that

the Duke of Roxburghe and other representatives of the
nobility had taken the rare step of putting their heads
above the parapet to express reservations about moves to
help individuals and communities buy land that had been
in their hands for generations.... a host of Scottish aristocratic families have made their views known in a series of
documents published this week. [190]

Peterkin then selected quotes from the Duke of Roxburghe (65,600
acres), the Earl of Seafield (101,000 acres), Atholl Estates (145,000
acres), James Carnegy-Arbuthnot, Balnamoon Estate near Brechin
(3,250 acres), 15th Earl of Hume, Douglas and Angus Estates (40,000
acres), Lord Lyell, Kinordy Estate (10,500 acres). His selection of
quotes encompasses a wish to promote tenant farming, land management benefiting wildlife and assertions that some moves such as an
ARTB for tenant farmers had 'no place in any democratic system'.

---

189. The Earl of Seafield, 'Foreword', *Seafield & Strathspey Estates News Review*,
Issue 12, 2013, www.seafield-estate.co.uk/newsletters/Seafield%20News%2012.
pdf
190. *The Scotsman*, 1 August 2013

The tie up in *The Scotsman* with SLaE strategy was completed by an 'analysis' of the proprietors' submission to the LRRG by Sarah-Jane Laing, director of policy and parliamentary affairs at SLaE. Laing had often appeared as a witness at the RACCE committee throughout recent years. Reflecting the 'disappointment' of the 2,500 members of SLaE across Scotland, Laing concluded:

> We believe responsible use of land – whether in public, private or community ownership – should be the determining factor in the policy landscape. Land in the ownership of private organisations is overwhelmingly employed productively. It benefits local communities through tourism, job creation, agriculture, housing and more. Private and community ownership should not be viewed as opposite ends of a spectrum – both ensure the viability of our rural areas.[191]

The gauntlet was well and truly thrown down at the LRRG, it had to be wary that its invigorating second phase of investigation could be severely mauled.

House of Commons Scottish Affairs committee probe land reform

In the House of Commons between 2010 and 2015 its SAc completed 11 inquiries on the theme of The Referendum on Separation for Scotland. It reviewed the role of the Crown Estate twice and felt its probe naturally led on to the wider issue of land reform in Scotland which required 'to be looked at'. It led to conclusions reported in the March 2014 listing revealing, in the main, the UK barriers to change.

The composition of SAc in that session was five Labour, two Lib Dem, two Tories and one SNP. Led by Glasgow MP Ian Davidson, it was no friend of the SNP Government in Edinburgh. Amidst some controversy, the SNP member Eilidh Whiteford MP for Banff and Buchan, one of six SNP members in that parliament, resigned. She refused to continue attendance at the committee after alleging personally threatening

---

191. *The Scotsman*, 1 August 2013

behaviour by the chair. With an incumbent Tory and Lib Dem coalition Government in power there was precious little likelihood of the SAC findings being applied. Indeed, it appeared to be more of a meddling bystander, or commentator, than a serious influencer in the actual land reform process. The timing of its enquiry ahead of the independence referendum on 18 September 2014 led to the publication of its Eight Report of Session 2013–14, entitled an interim report, in March of that year.

When Jim Hunter, the distinguished land reformer, left the Scottish Government's LRRG, commentators saw the LRRG as stuck in a narrow rut. However. Professor Hunter had been given another chance to approach the issue, and on a more expansive canvas, by Ian Davidson for the SAc. Hunter took up the commission with relish. As a long-time land reform campaigner, he held a thorough definition of land reform, some of which would have to be delivered from London. This starter paper coincided with Hunter's exit from the LRRG. Hunter wrote:

> The paper's purpose is to inform the SAc as to the current state of the land reform debate in Scotland, to connect the debate with wider concerns about growing inequality and wealth and, in particular, to underline the extent to which SAc – in the context of UK and international efforts to combat what a recent EC [Edinburgh City] Council resolution calls 'tax fraud, tax evasion and aggressive tax planning' – is well-placed to explore ways in which fiscal and related arrangements contribute to and underpin inequality in Scottish land ownership.[192]

Hunter steered the forthcoming committee process towards the big issues of tax and company law which were, and still are, reserved to Westminster. This was confirmed by the SAC's Interim Report that

---

192. James Hunter et al, '432:50 – Towards a Comprehensive Land Reform Agenda for Scotland: A Briefing Paper for the House of Commons Scottish Affairs Committee', 2013, www.parliament.uk/documents/commons-committees/scottish-affairs/432-Land-Reform-Paper.pdf

contained 22 conclusions and recommendations, 18 of which were clearly UK powers. The report argued for further investigation or early intervention by a UK Government although committee members knew this would be dismissed by the Treasury.[193]

Evidence of growing inequities of wealth and opportunity were a pivotal reason to pursue radical land reform solutions, the report concluded. So, Ian Davidson's committee came back to the subject to probe a further four issues after the result of the independence referendum of September 2014. The four issues were:

- whether the ownership of estates through charitable companies set up by private owners is in the public interest and how governance of such organisations should best be organised;

- how the fiscal framework of agricultural land might be reformed to meet the concerns of tenant farmers;

- how the new Common Agricultural Policy framework can best support farmers;

- and the extent to which land is owned in offshore jurisdictions as part of individual corporate tax planning.[194]

People centred land governance

In Scotland, the LRRG Final Report entitled 'The Land of Scotland and the Common Good' arrived at an impressively wide set of recommendations compared to predictions by the doubters in April 2013. The 262-page tome contained a lucid argument, supportive data, concerns

193. Scottish Affairs Committee, 'Land Reform in Scotland: Interim Report', 18 March 2014, www.publications.parliament.uk/pa/cm201314/cmselect/cmscotaf/877/87702.htm

194. Scottish Affairs Committee, 'Land Reform in Scotland: Final Report', 24 March 2015, www. publications.parliament.uk/pa/cm201415/cmselect/cmscotaf/274/27402.htm

about constrained time for research, but a challenging set of 62 recommendations. It was presented to Scottish Ministers in May 2014 inducing considerable public interest in its proposals, not least from campaigners for radical change.[195]

For MSPs with an interest, a careful reading of this blockbuster signalled major proposals for legislation which we would expect the Scottish Government to reflect and consult on. The independence referendum delayed progress till the winter of 2014 into 2015. Apart from the complexities for officials to absorb and recommend potential for law making, the referendum campaign reached its pitch, or denouement, if you will, by mid-September 2014.

Scotland's future – Your guide to an independent Scotland

The definitive case of the Scottish Government for a Yes vote in the independence referendum had been published in November 2013. Running to 649 pages of detailed policies, Part 3 Chapter 8 ('Environment, Rural Scotland, Energy and Resources') explained the thinking on land and communities at the time. Empowering communities and local government, committing to a target of 1,000,000 acres in community control by 2020 and the reviews of land reform and tenant farming were said to be part of

> building a fairer society for which independence is required, for example, taxation powers are needed to encourage land to be made available for new tenant farmers and address wider land reform.[196]

In the Q&A section of the manifesto, a commitment was made to bring the Crown Estate into Scottish control and to decentralise both management and revenues for local benefit.[197]

These complex matters would be developed in the next two years,

---

195. LRRG, 'The Land of Scotland and the Common Good', 2014
196. Scottish Government, 'Scotland's Future', 2013, www.gov.scot/publications/scotlands-future/pages/15/
197. ibid.

despite the No vote on 18 September 2014. In that respect, various far-sighted commentators were proven correct.

Objections to change by private landowners

Voices hostile to change among SLaE and other landowners pepper the chapters of this book. Wherever deer management, shooting rates and tenant farming conditions arose, so did threats aimed at the Scottish Government citing huge costs to the public purse and of likely recourse to ECHR. These threats hinted at redress being sought through the civil courts if certain policy options were adopted. The volume of comment cranked up during the lead up to the independence referendum which was played out in the two years leading to the decisive vote.

Two stories penned within weeks of that first Scottish independence referendum voiced the concerns of the propertied classes. Successive land reform measures and the fears among the great landowners were exposed as a speedier pace of land reform and community empowerment were expected if Scots voted Yes.

First, let's hear from Sophia Money-Coutts. She wrote for *Tatler* in August 2014, going 'beyond the wall' to see why 'Scottish aristocrats are fiercely opposed to independence'.[198] Secondly, in August 2014, Merryn Somerset Webb asked readers of the *Financial Times* Weekend was this 'The twilight of private ownership?'[199]

The buggers are out to get us!

Sophia Money-Coutts embarked on a breathless romp from big house to big house across Caledonia stern and wild. She found many plummy voices ready to raise fears of a Yes vote, but would Scotland's old lairds 'really abandon their ancestral mountains and ancient customs' she pondered and would the new landowners, not only land rich but cash rich, be concerned for the future of their huge holdings?[200]

---

198. Sophia Money-Coutts, 'The Future of Scotland?' *Tatler*, 8 August 2014, www.tatler.com/article/the-future-of-scotland

199. Merryn Somerset Webb, 'The Twilight of Private Ownership in Scotland?', *Financial Times*, 1 August 2014, www.ft.com/content/c7c0e662-133a-11e4-8244-00144feabdc0

200. Money-Coutts, 'The Future of Scotland', 8 December 2014

While poking gentle fun at kilts, reeling and haunted castles, Money-Coutts, a scion of the private banking family, detected class differences between aristocratic lairds and the nouveau riche. She heard of the former group's fears about likely land reform moves. The Duchess of Argyll told her how Inveraray Castle 'eats money… what if Salmond imposes a mansion tax? We're done for.'[201] Money-Coutts concluded,

> Given the fairly feudal distribution of land in Scotland,
> you can perhaps see why big landowners are nervous.[202]

She pinpointed what she deemed to be 'Old Scotland' whose hereditary lairds seem 'definitely panicked, as if they can already hear the tumbrils approaching'. As for 'New Scotland', the 'arivistes' often foreign, not always so, such as Anne Gloag and Paul Dacre are 'insulated by their immense wealth' and not able to be blamed for the Highland Clearances of the 18th and 19th centuries like 'Old Scotland'.

By December 2014, having seen off the immediate threat of independence, Money-Coutts reported a new burst of lairdly apoplexy when Nicola Sturgeon, the First Minister, announced radical land reform proposals following her predecessor Alex Salmond resigning after the Yes voters were defeated.

The direction of land reform travel had been correctly forecast by Merrin Somerset Webb before the fateful referendum vote in 'The twilight of private ownership?' Essentially, Webb was looking at the prospects for large landowners in the wake of the final report of the LRRG in the summer of 2014. Writing in the *Financial Times* ahead of the grouse shooting season, she also detected a slowdown in the land and property market in the three months leading to the referendum. She commented:

> The talk around independence doesn't pander much to
> the wealthy. There's much talk of a new Scotland having
> better values than the rest of the UK.[203]

---

201. Money-Coutts, 'The Future of Scotland', 8 December 2014
202. ibid.
203. Webb, 'The Twilight of Private Ownership in Scotland?', 1 August 2014

Real fears of progressive taxes, of land redistribution would likely fall on those with the broadest shoulders. But, she noted,

> The Scottish Government already has the powers to do most of the things you might be nervous about. Land and Transaction Tax, the Community Empowerment Bill (enacted in 2015) and concerns about absolute right to buy for farm tenants in the wake of powers already available to crofters.[204]

The property market, Webb went on, was influenced by the LRRG Final Report with concepts such as 'wellbeing', 'sustainability', 'greater diversity of land ownership' and 'social justice' indicating serious threats to landed proprietors. In sum, this legislative focus

> represents a change in broad policy from a focus on expanding the number of people who have access to land to one on expanding the numbers of people or communities who own land.[205]

On alleged woes for investors, Webb quoted legal firm Gillespie MacAndrew saying it was likely that reform would

> impose a far greater degree of public involvement in and control over land ownership, together with substantially increased visibility of the use made of that land.[206]

She concluded:

> Whichever side you choose to take, this all matters for the Scottish economy, for confidence in the sanctity of property rights and for social cohesion. But it has nothing

---

204. ibid.
205. ibid.
206. Webb, 'The Twilight of Private Ownership in Scotland?', 1 August 2014

whatsoever to do with the independence vote. It's going
to happen anyway.[207]

The questions Webb posed, reflected the fear among proprietors of
diversity of ownership. It perceived a wide-open market for bolt holes
and shooting estates coming to a grinding halt. Old landed power was
being systematically challenged and the privileges of the lairds, which
stretched back centuries, was challenged not only for economic and
social reasons but also for environmental reasons by our devolved
Scottish Government.

The steps along that democratic road would certainly be contested
in the courts. Considerable legal business had passed to the Supreme
Court, invented by Tony Blair, which had been handing down rulings
that narrowly interpret ECHR, so far too often in landlord interests.
If ECHR had been in force in 1976 then crofters ARTB probably would
have been challenged in the courts. But their scraps of land could have
been seen as a burden to estate factors and the Scottish Office, while
land agents could see valuable assets for future speculative sales to
holiday home prospectors.

Devolution in 1999 opened the debate on what land reform could
do. By 2014 it also became clear to investors here and abroad that the
'sacred rights of property' were going to be eroded, whether the lairds
liked it or not.

Fallout from No vote leads to more radical land proposals

Immediately after the No vote in September 2014 came the resignation
of Alex Salmond as First Minister. His commitment to land reform had
been longstanding. From the mid-1990s when he initiated the SNP's
own Land Commission to the setting up of the LRRG with a stretching
target of doubling community ownership to one million acres by 2020,
he had been a staunch proponent of a fairer and more diverse Scotland.
The arrival of Nicola Sturgeon as First Minister would bring a new
Programme for Government in November 2014 which included land
reform commitments.

---

207. ibid.

In parallel, the SAc concurred with the Scottish Government for once when the new First Minister put her stamp on the land reform journey with the following statement:

On the 26 November 2014, the First Minister, as part of the Programme for Government, set out the Scottish Government's vision that Scotland's land must be an asset that benefits the many, not the few. This vision promotes a strong relationship between the people of Scotland and the land of Scotland, where ownership and use of land delivers greater public benefits through a democratically accountable and transparent system of land rights that promotes fairness and social justice, environmental sustainability and economic prosperity.[208]

I spoke in the debate on the Programme for Government. My speech was as follows:

Rob Gibson (Caithness, Sutherland and Ross) (SNP): To underline the fact that we have a radical government, radical land reform is rightly at the centre of the social justice debate.

The Land of Scotland and the Common Good: Report of the Land Reform Review Group sets the tone for the wide range of land reform policies that are contained in the SNP programme. We can transform our nation's fortunes through optimum use of our most basic natural resource. Land reform will deliver participation, prosperity and fairness but, above all, we must diversify ownership to create social and environmental sustainability.

Inequalities in Scotland are summed up by the most concentrated pattern of land ownership in Europe. Land reform is based on the public interest and has overwhelming support in the Parliament. First, we need to know who owns Scotland. Next, we need to build

---

208. Scottish Government news, December 2014

local capacity to own the land and use it sustainably. Crucially, the proposed land reform commission could facilitate the best transfer of public or private land to a new set of non-traditional owners.

A good example of the new hope in land ownership received unjustifiably mixed coverage this week. The community buyout of the Isle of Gigha in 2002 has transformed the island, which has a growing population and a variety of new commercial activities to complement farming and tourism. Nevertheless, the BBC hinted this week at financial trouble for the Gigha Heritage Trust, which took over the island for about £4 million in 2002, saying that it was almost £3 million in the red.

The trust replied that it 'has invested in the housing and other developments on the island some of which has been borrowed, some granted from supporting organisations and some raised from the island's own businesses and efforts... In addition to improving our housing stock, £1m was paid back to lenders within a year of the original purchase of the island; over £800,000 has been raised through Trust's renewables companies; and the value of the island has increased to over £7m.'

It has also recently carried out a strategic review with the support of Highlands and Islands Enterprise.

A typically hostile press has focused on a grumpy farmer, alleged divisions among islanders and implied incompetence among community leaders, not on their successes. The islanders are due to take part in a vote of confidence in the chairwoman of the trust this week.

That stands in stark contrast to the conduct of the private estates that sprawl across our landscape. We never know how much in the red they are, and the media rarely asks. Also, the families who live on large estates such as those owned by the 432 individuals and trusts that control half of rural Scotland are never asked their opinions about the future of the land.

Lairds avoid taxes through skilful accountants. James Hunter and company suggested to the Scottish Affairs Committee at Westminster that huge landholders offset losses on land through tax accounting via non-landed enterprises.

All those powers are still reserved and not on offer by the Smith Commission.

Liz Smith: Does Mr Gibson acknowledge that, nonetheless, many of those private landowners are doing a highly successful job when it comes to Scotland's economy?

Rob Gibson: As Andy Wightman said in *The National* newspaper today: 'these ideas... will be opposed every bit of the way by powerful vested interests.'

There is a powerful vested interest. In some cases, the lairds have had 1,000 years to build their domains, so it will take community bodies such as those in Gigha, Eigg, South Uist and Knoydart a few more than ten years to sort out the mess that the lairds often left behind.

The North Harris Trust has successfully built new homes, and it runs the deer shooting and creates renewable energy income, as Fiona Mackenzie has charted in her recent book, *Places of Possibility*. That sums up the intent of the government's land reform package.

The review of local government finance can take land value tax seriously and look at many other possibilities. Like many members, I want tenant farming reform to be included in the proposed Land Reform Bill, and I want real powers to be given to the Land Commission to chart the how as well as the what of sustainable land ownership.

We could measure the success of land reform against the number of members that Scottish Land & Estates has. At present, it has 2,000 members. In ten years' time, perhaps it should have a membership of 20,000, which should comprise a vibrant mix of communities, smaller landholders and reduced-scale sporting estates. Why not? As the land leaguers used to say, the land is before us. I commend the ambition and common sense in the Scottish Government's plans.[209]

Smith Commission offers Crown Estate devolution

The aftermath of the referendum reverberated and a three-party

---

209. Rob Gibson, Scottish Parliament, November 2014

Unionist vow was made on the eve of the vote. The London Government responded by appointing Lord Robert Smith to propose more powers for the Scottish Parliament. Among these, to pass control of the Crown Estate Commission Scottish assets to Holyrood. All this was to be completed by St Andrew's Day 2014. It, in turn, led to a new Holyrood committee being formed to review Smith and the Scotland Bill that followed it.

I had been a member of the previous Referendum Bill committee which saw its major proposal agreed to enfranchise 16-year-old Scots to vote for the first time. This contributed to the huge engagement of voters across Scotland in the exciting referendum summer in 2014. The committee morphed into the Devolution (Further Powers) committee which was to recommend whether the Smith proposals were met by the London Government's Scotland Bill and whether we could recommend that the Scottish Parliament should pass a Legislative Consent Motion to allow the Scotland Bill 2016 to be enacted in Westminster.[210]

London committee concurs with Holyrood

During this period before and after the independence referendum, the SAc scrutinised Scottish land reform matters. This involved many new witnesses, including Alison Elliot and others concerned with the final report of the LRRG. The Scottish Government consultation on the Future of Land Reform in Scotland launched in December 2014. The final report of the Review of Agricultural Holdings Legislation published in January 2015 was also a focus. These were preparatory to the publication of the draft Land Reform Bill in June 2015.

The SAc finished its land reform scrutiny in March 2015, ahead of the dissolution of Westminster's elected chamber for the forthcoming general election. This led to 15 conclusions and recommendations aimed mainly at the incoming government. They all required UK action, the repository of reserved powers. In its conclusion the SAc noted its pleasure

that the Scottish Government is taking forward work

---

210. Smith Commission and consequent Scotland Bill, March 2016

on land reform in line with the findings of our interim report.[211]

The committee urged the UK and Scottish Governments to work together on areas of mutual interest, such as land tax reliefs to ensure a tax system that supports the Scottish Government's stated aim of increased community ownership of land.[212]

Intergovernmental relations (IGR) became a major ask of the Smith Commission in November 2014 so as to adjust the Scottish Fiscal Framework. Alas the history of Joint Ministerial Council meetings was one of conflict and impasse, and emphasised the real barriers to Scotland's wish to exert tax and other powers over landowners, whether resident or not. IGR was to become a special study area for Holyrood's Devolution (Further Powers) committee in its final report in March 2016 ahead of the vote on the Legislative Consent Motion to trigger the Scotland Act 2016.

SAc had observed the main barriers to change without any likely means to effect that change. In the event, all the Labour and Lib Dem MPs of its membership were defeated in the 2015 electoral 'tsunami'. A majority Tory UK Government came in and had no intentions of implementing the land reform agenda, either in Scotland or England.

Landowners prepare for Land Reform Bill

In anticipation of the critical proposals in the final LRRG report *The Land of Scotland and the Common Good*, published in May, SLaE went into overdrive. A month before publication they made further substantial claims asserting the contribution of landed property to the countryside's benefit. With the collaboration of Rural Solutions and Scotland's Rural College Research, their report was published. Entitled 'Economic Contribution of Estates in Scotland – An Economic Assessment for Scottish Land & Estates', it boasted authorship by five reputable academics.[213]

---

211. SAc, 'Final Report', 24 March 2015
212. ibid.
213. R Hindle et al, 'Economic Contribution of Estates in Scotland: An Economic Assessment for Scotland Land & Estates', Scottish Land & Estates, April 2014, www.scottishlandandestates.co.uk/sites/default/files/library/Economic%20Contribution%20of%20Estates%20in%20Scotland.pdf

The SLaE report addressed 'key challenges for land use, land owners and land management'.[214] The body's members, the report claimed, represented approximately 65% of all of Scotland's private estates, from which an in-depth survey in the early months of 2014 gleaned 277 useable responses. These had been thoroughly and professionally analysed.[215] Responses had been sought from estates and landowners who collectively managed over 1.25 hectares of land, owned 7,645 houses and provided 1,563 tenancies (23% of all tenancies in Scotland). Then a diverse subset of 35 respondents answered 'semi-structured' interviews to augment the findings.

The Scottish Field assured in January 2015 that private land in Scotland owned by SLaE members contributed £471m in revenue per annum. This figure was more complex than just a bald claim. It was derived from calculations from the SLaE database, not the above sample. This showed 1,351 members holding 2.27m hectares. It was estimated that annually SLaE membership directly generate £272m revenue, which contributes £471m or £207 per hectare to Scotland's output after indirect and induced impacts are included. An additional estimate of the impact of SLaE members is said to contribute £91m (£40/hectare) to Scottish household incomes, maintain 5,919FTE jobs (91FTE per 385 hectares) and contribute £186m (£82/hectare) to Scotland's GVA.[216]

As with many of these calculations SLaE members and supporters could regurgitate these figures to anyone who questioned the value of estates, large and small. For insight, from a political point of view, there was the open section in their final survey question. This shows respondents' views about key barriers and challenges to future opportunity. Of those nearly half cited land reform and political uncertainty, while a quarter raised concerns about bureaucracy and excessive regulation. Planning, taxation, uncertainty over Common Agriculture Policy, grants and subsidies, access to finance, managing public assets and managing heritage assets trailed off into single figure concerns.[217]

---

214. ibid.
215. ibid.
216. Hindle et al, 'Economic Contribution of Estates in Scotland', April 2014
217. ibid.

SLaE used the deep purses of its members to set down markers for their determination to contest, in a robust fashion, a land reform process they did not want and to assert that best land use practice, rather than disturbing the rights of private property, should be the government's focus.[218]

Wild land or devastated terrain?

Many policy areas affect the delivery of radical land reform. When Scottish Planning Policy gave a place to core wild land areas – of which there are 42 mapped out and described by SNH in 2014 – it was aimed at halting any development of onshore wind turbines in or near, as it was beginning to be interpreted by some, these extensive but artificially drawn zones. They total 1,537,247 hectares or 3,843,117 acres of Scotland.[219]

As a comparator, the Royal Commission on the Highlands and Islands, better known as the Deer Commission, reported in 1896 that 1,782,785 acres should be returned from deer forest to extend existing grazings, new holdings and in some cases modest sized farms.[220] Many of these areas are adjacent or overlap the wild land (non) designation. I drew attention to this with a comparison of my map of Clearances trail areas and many of the core wild land areas. The controversy prompted a debate in community land circles where the concept of repopulating previously inhabited areas was taking shape. I was invited to address Community Land Scotland's annual gathering in Inverness on 22 May 2015. I took the theme of books that had guided my thinking on land issues and homed in on the Clearances Country controversy.

---

218. Linda Nicholson, The Research Shop, 'A Consultation on the Future of Land Reform', Scottish Government Social Research, 2015, consult.gov.scot/land-reform-and-tenancy-unit/land-reform-scotland/supporting_documents/land%20reform%20analysis.pdf
219. Scottish Natural Heritage Core Wild Land designations, 2014, www.nature.scot/wild-land-2014-maps
220. Royal Commission on Highlands & Islands, 1896

Speech: Community Land Scotland, 22 May 2015
Health, Beauty, Permanence?

Forty-three years ago, on a rainy, midge ridden evening in September 1972, the Skye crofting community of Strollamus demonstrated against an overbearing new landlord. That demo was followed by court cases, planning issues and the widespread publicity occurring as a result were widely reported in the fledgling West Highland Free Press and many other places.

Across the country, political ferment was high at the time in the middle of Ted Heath's Tory Government which had plans for centralising local government, crofting right to buy debates, building of a new torpedo testing range in the Sound of Raasay and the early news of oil rig construction at nearby Loch Kishorn in the dawning days of North Sea oil. Along with members of the FSN, Skye Crofting Scheme based in Glendale, my friends joined forces with locals to highlight what was wrong and suggest ways to make a difference. I wrote up the story in my 1974 pamphlet, *The Promised Land?*, in which concluded with a clarion call for community control:

> Although the Crofters Commission has locally elected area assessors, there needs to be real on-the-spot control in the townships and communities where crofters live and work. Till the people control the land they live on there can be no hope of achieving a satisfactory and more just way of life for the Gael.

> Much eloquent and sound work to back up the cause of COMMUNITY CONTROL has been produced by interested departments in our universities. But intellectual alternatives need sound common sense determination on the ground would be a useful starting point to assess and guide our actions today.

This salvation for crofters is in co-operative action.

I was struck, on reflection, that some of the ideas I drew on then, beyond the obvious history of the Land League, would be a useful starting point to assess and guide our actions today.

Books I refer to include *Small is Beautiful* by Eric Schumacher, *Government by Community* by Ioan Bowen Rees, *The Politics of Environment* by Malcolm Slesser and *Land Reform and Economic Development* by Peter Dorner in the Penguin Modern Economics Texts. These were my biggest influences along with understanding why it took till 1970 to erect the Glendale Land League Monument. Greater clarity came along in 1976 when James Hunter's ground-breaking work was published on *The Making of the Crofting Community*. Also, I attended and applauded the first performance of John McGrath's ceilidh play *The Cheviot, the Stag and the Black, Black Oil* which is quoted with relish in my book.

In the long years of land reform discussions since then, the first lines in Schumacher on the proper use of land stand out:

> Among material resources, the greatest, unquestionably, is the land. Study how a society uses its land, and you can come to pretty reliable conclusions as to what its future will be.

There I've said it again! Around the world Dorner pointed to one key to land reform:

> It is quite clear that under a system of private property in land, a small farm agriculture can absorb more labour than a large-farm agriculture.

He went on:

> Agricultural production processes, as mentioned, have characteristics which invalidate many comparisons with developments in industry.

So why are agriculture and industry so different? Schumacher wrote:

on a wider view, however, the land is seen as a priceless asset which it is man's task and happiness 'to dress and keep'. We can say that man's management of the land must be primarily orientated towards three goals – health, beauty and permanence. The fourth goal – the only one accepted by the experts – productivity, will then be attained almost as a by-product.

He explains that

the crude materialist view [much discussed in the EEC Mansholt plan for bigger farms and more flight of redundant people to the cities] sees agriculture as essentially directed towards food production.

Other doubters of the primacy of productivity spoke out. One was the chemical engineer and climber Malcolm Slesser who identified the forces that damage communities saying:

science is largely accurate observation coupled with common sense. The man in the street is, because of this, scientist enough to sense that something is going badly wrong.

It is dawning slowly that the use of scientific knowledge and technological skill for the conquest of poverty and disease does not of necessity mean enslavement to expansionist economics...

He then argued that we must tackle

the more complex issue resulting from the conclusion that economic growth is a doomed philosophy and a practical disaster.

I was hooked. Then Slesser described the starting point:

> with those small nations not yet committed too far along the Gadarene slope. Let them be allowed to make themselves practical examples of realignment to balanced development, in co-operation, and by humbly scientific use of their physical and mental resources.

What did he mean by a range of resources?

> We must allow for these unacademic terms 'community spirit', 'national morale' at all times, not just in the practical emergencies of war.

Alas the story of Strollamus has sputtered on over decades so that when the JMT was making a partnership with the Luib township of the estate ten years ago it was reported that the crofters did not know who they were sending their rents to. The recipients are probably the beneficial owners of private trusts that are still protected in law from public scrutiny. If the UK Tory Government refuses to agree that beneficial owners of private trusts should be revealed it will be another snub to the EU and the fourth Money Laundering Directive that must be agreed this year and it will severely curtail our efforts to find out who owns Scotland.

* * *

Ioan Bowen Rees had a long career of public service in Wales where he championed the governance structures in Swiss cantons such as Grisson as the ideal for decision taking. Jim Perrin picked this up in an obituary for Ioan in June 1999 praising

> his natural inclination was to view people as indissociable from place, and to insist on the centrality of their voice in determining policies that might affect it.

I have been banging that drum to this day. That's why I see community land as a major example of how to do the governance of localities fairly and progressively. That's not to say that every community should adopt a standard approach, but we now have examples from the pre-devolution era of Stornoway, Assynt, Knoydart and Eigg plus the post 2003 buyouts in Lewis (most recently in Pairc), Skye, the Uists and Harris as well as a scattering of Lowland Scots cases to build on.

Over time both 'community spirit' and 'national morale' have played a big part in the demands for land reform. In the decades before the creation of the Scottish Parliament it was emblematic of our powerless condition. Today, by increments, we are getting to grips with radical change.

During the protest years, morale boosting events mounted up like the contested cairn building in 1991 to honour the unsuccessful Knoydart land raid of 1948. Many symptoms of support for land reform in Scotland came also with acclaim for the victory for free Eigg. I recall during the Assynt crofters' struggle in 1992 that people were watching the TV for news in pubs and family homes across Scotland. A friend of mine was a barman in Carrutherstown near Dumfries and reported punters asking, 'Have these crofters got that land yet?'

In 1995 the monument to the Duke of Sutherland on Ben Bhraggie received worldwide coverage due to an outline planning application to topple the duke. Then the mining millionaire Dennis Macleod who hailed from Marrel, Helmsdale suggested that it was better to put up a statue to the cleared people than to seek to tear down the Mannie. Sutherland District planning committee inevitably threw out the outline application by Peter Findlay and Sandy Lindsay. But Dennis proposed a Clearances museum and trail at Helmsdale. After complications with land acquisition he scaled down the plan and the Emigrants Statue was unveiled in 2007 by former First Minister, Alex Salmond MSP. However, Dennis endowed the fledgling history department of the UHI in Dornoch with the rest of the funds to employ its first professor, our own Jim Hunter!

Morale boosting as such stunts were, the development of land reform ideas of the 1997 Labour Government opened the door to the community land purchase model which drew the ire of Andy Wight-man. He saw this 'fashionable idea of community' as 'muddled think-ing' about true land reform. His critique said these ideas are suitable in some circumstances and asserted that CRTB 'is a proposal born out of an acceptance of the current division of land and the unregulated market.'

However, in 2013, Alex Salmond, the then First Minister, announced at the Community Land Scotland conference in Sabhal Mòr Ostaig that it [the Scottish Government] wants to extend the 500,000 acres already in community control to one million acres by 2020.

* * *

I will now explore some of the reasons why this suits the condition of Scotland today and why the impact must consider global concerns about climate change and biodiversity as prime measures of sustaina-bility that impacted after the 2003 phase of land reform.

The ground-breaking Scottish Climate Change Act of 2009 set tough targets. These include decarbonising transport, moving away from fossil fuel uses, sequestering carbon in deep peat, reducing the emissions by agriculture and planting many more native woods and forests. Each year they are tougher to achieve. But Scotland is on a good trajectory. We are held up as an example to other parts of the UK, especially in renewable energy production and energy efficiency. But be warned, if we are not successful the landscapes, fauna and flora we cherish are likely to disappear in 50 short years.

Biodiversity targets set at EU level have been missed, but again Scot-land is blessed with many species which are rare elsewhere. Arising from a concern for the natural heritage which is said to be under 'deep threat', some NGOs have taken it upon themselves to campaign for draconian restrictions on development and call for wild land to be designated in planning law and government policy.

In the meantime, some charities like RSPB, JMT and SWT have become substantial landowners and claim millions of pounds from the public purse for their agri-environment and biodiversity work. Other groups demand more national parks and a marine park fed by the success of Loch Lomond and the Trossachs and Cairngorm National Park models. But the philosophy has been imposed on communities just like the range of conservation designations adopted since the 1950s.

In a significant pamphlet, *Beyond National Parks: Conserving the Landscape of a Democratic Wales,* Ioan Bowen Rees wrote in 1995 about conservation by command and his wish to see conservation by consent saying:

> Worst of all is the way in which communities, districts and counties are deprived of clear responsibility for the places in which they take greatest pride.

Recently we are indebted to Fiona D Mackenzie in *Places of Possibility: Property, Nature and Community Land Ownership* for exploring the concept of social nature – not separated but integral to all life. She quotes Bruce Braun:

> It is about disturbing the norm of nature as external to the social and opening up meanings of the term 'nature' and 'the social' to allow new ways of thinking critically and creatively about how to move forward.

Her study of North Harris Trust has shown how a fragile community can develop remarkable means to bring nature and community into a new relationship which applies Schumacher's mantra of promoting 'health, beauty and permanence'.

However, we should never underestimate the obstacles to achieving step changes in development in so many varied communities across Scotland. One of these barriers, noted by Fiona Mackenzie, is about the relationships between public and private property and the commoditisation of nature. In conservation practices, which she notes are 'subject to environmental designations whose provenance lies elsewhere', we see an enemy of social nature.

Nothing compares to 'no trespassing' more than the call to map core wild land areas. SNH duly delivered a desk top exercise which was given token recognition of this in Scotland's Third National Planning Framework which states:

> Onshore wind will continue to make a significant contribution to diversification of energy supplies. We do not wish to see wind farm development in our National Parks and National Scenic Areas. Scottish Planning Policy sets out the required approach to spatial frameworks which will guide new wind energy development to appropriate locations, considering important features including wild land.

Some other wild land guidance from SNH to Scottish Government in June 2014 included this advice:

> Scotland's wild land is not empty of human activities or influence, although many features such as former shielings and bothies are small in scale and their effect on the overall wilderness of an area is limited.

That made my blood boil.

My support team noticed that when you superimpose the sites of evictions gathered in my Highland Clearances guide, in its most expanded form in 2006, and placed them on the core wild land map there was an uncanny, if unscientific, overlap. Far from being wild land, I call it Clearances Country. Reactions from the outdoor lobby would only admit to a superficial overlap. Indeed, one JMT official told me that developments in the glens were not their target in the wild land quest. Yet, the small, highly vocal, band of anti-wind farms campaigners backed by the JMT want bigger and bigger buffer areas around so-called wild land areas. Is their real intention to smother all the land in aspic?

I believe CLS must insist that there has to be another way. After all,

Frank Fraser Darling explained in 1947 that we are seeing a manmade wilderness not wild land. Even so SNH has described 'a lack of continuity of occupation to present times' as just a cultural link of the past to wild land areas. Surely the abnormal landscape of the shooting estates and sheep clearances of the past 200 years are the cause of that lack of continuity?

Meanwhile on the north coast, around Bettyhill and Strathy, the local people describe themselves as the most endangered species. This was their response to suggestions that the Scottish and Southern Energy (SSE) proposal for Strathy South wind project was a danger to birds and or deep peat. I added my two pence worth saying that the breeding pairs of humans were more endangered than birds! It's another case of conservation by command by the RSPB and similar NGOs who feel entitled to dictate the future of wide swathes of Scotland as of right.

Ioan Bowen Rees noted that his family were brought up on the edge of the Snowdonia National Park and were part of its fauna. That's why I believe we need to apply the 'social nature' concept Fiona Mackenzie describes in a major reappraisal of all natural heritage designations. These reach over 50% of the hinterland of Strathy compared to 14% on average across Scotland. The need for the proper use of land was summed up by Schumacher:

> In the simple question of how we treat the land, next to people our most precious resource, our entire way of life is involved, and before our policies with regard to the land will really be changed, there will have to be a great deal of philosophical, not to say religious, change.

For community empowerment and land reform to be effective today we need that holistic outlook among all stakeholders. It is abundantly clear from my sources 40 years ago, and more recently, that the land revolution will start to succeed with an honest embrace of social nature and community control.

The lesson for all of Scotland's aspiring communities is to take that control and take on clear responsibility for all aspects of land management and related conservation issues. CLS is in the vanguard of revitalising Scotland from the ground up. It is a vital part of land reform to energise communal and co-operative action – not just for crofters but all small communities who aim for health, beauty and permanence.[221]

Wide-ranging lessons learned

My background comments in my speech on the context of land use and land reform prompted considerable debate on the day and subsequently. The long gestation of ideas and responses which link social, economic and environmental elements all played their interlocked part in the Land Reform Bill debate to come.

In the 2011–16 session, the RACCE committee scrutinised the Scottish Government commissioned reviews of both land reform and agricultural holdings, crofting, community empowerment and RTB changes and long leases... The committee therefore began its scrutiny of the Land Reform Bill with extensive background knowledge of many of the issues involved and a well-informed understanding of the problems that needed to be resolved.[222]

221. Rob Gibson, speech to Community Land Scotland, 22 May 2015
222. Rural Affairs, Climate Change and Environment Committee, 'Stage 1 Report on the Land Reform (Scotland) Bill', 4 December 2015, www.parliament.scot/S4_RuralAffairsClimateChangeandEnvironmentCommittee/Reports/RACCES042015R10Rev.pdf

l :. :   *6. 2393*

State Subsidies for Private Tyrannies--
The Lesson of Knoydart

By Dr R. D. McIntyre,
Chairman, Scottish National Party.

The action of the men of Knoydart has resulted in a singular and important exhibition by the British Government of its true political position. That the estate of Knoydart has been grossly mismanaged for more than ten years under the ownership of Lord Brockett has been amply established. In accepting the Cameron Report the Government does the following:—

1. Condones the mismanagement of the estate and the waste of potential food supplies.

2. Intimates to all similar Highland estate owners that so long as they neglect their estates, tyrannise over their people and generally pursue a policy calculated to destroy social life and encourage depopulation they will be backed by the London Socialist Government against any just demands from the people.

3. Puts the ' rights ' of large scale alien property ownership over the human and social rights of the people whose moral claim to the land is incontestable.

4. Shows the Government's willingness to spend public funds in the form of large subsidies to private enterprise of an immoral and inefficient kind against the interests of the people.

5. Demonstrates that it is the policy of the Government to discourage the settling of a free community on their own land in security.

Ideological Prejudice

The fact that the Cameron Report is superficial and inadequate should not blind us to the fact that it reveals an ideological prejudice of the greatest danger not only to the Highlands but to Scotland as a whole. If the point of view of the report were taken to its logical conclusion the Highlands would be entirely evacuated. Its narrow materialism finally leads to economic disaster by not considering human and social values.

The fundamental trouble in Knoydart is the way in which the people there can have no protection against the whims of estate management and have no independent security. When it is realised that the place is, for practical purposes, an island entirely owned by one man, it can be seen how irksome and impossible the situation can become if arbitrary action and personal victimisation are practised by the management. No community can develop in a healthy way in such conditions. The recent raids were an attempt to find some security for the local community on a free and stable basis. The men of Knoydart were staking their claim to survive as a community without having to have the prior consent of Lord

✗

Brockett or any other such chance incomer. A similar situation exists in many other places (e.g. Rhum), and the law is not yet on the statute book in Scotland giving proper rights on the land to those living and working on it.

Central Direction

The one feature on which the Cameron Report insists is the maintenance of central direction of the vast Knoydart area. Even if the land were to be taken over by the State the position of the local community would be no better. There would be no more guarantee against arbitrary tyranny. The Government, which is Socialist, is quite prepared to uphold the rights of personal property of Lord Brockett in the power it gives him over the people in Knoydart. At the same time the Government prevent the people of Knoydart from acquiring rights to private property of a very limited kind in crofts and houses. It is this limited property which would give the freedom and stability required to develop a healthy community and which cannot be used to exploit others.

Socialist meets Tory

Like Lord Brockett and his kind the Socialist Government prefer the people to be defenceless and without independence. They must be employed by some agency under central control. The materialism of Victorian Capitalism of which the Brockett Estates provide a working example is upheld by the materialism of the newer central state power. The action of the men of Knoydart is symbolic of the need for free people to fight against both evils if they are to survive. It is encouraging that the people of Scotland wherever they are informed are behind the Knoydart men. One should perhaps remark in passing on the sheer hypocrisy of the Communist Party in trying to cash in on the Knoydart affair.

Woodburn's acceptance on behalf of the Government in London of the Cameron Report is not the end of the case. We now know where the Socialist Government stands in relation to all the similar problems which are arising and will arise. It stands along with Tory centralist reaction in opposition to the development of free communities in Scotland.

A Scottish Parliament could not have accepted the Cameron Report.

VOTE NATIONALIST

Join the Scottish National Party

THE PARTY OF THE PEOPLE OF SCOTLAND

HEAD OFFICE—59 ELMBANK STREET, GLASGOW, C.2.
Phone: Douglas 2287.

Read the "SCOTS INDEPENDENT," from which this article is reprinted.

S.N.P. Leaflet—New Series. No. 10. · 8/49.

Published by The Scottish National Party and Printed by The Reiver Press, Ltd., 39 High Street, Galashiels.

Strollamus crofters and FSN students protesting against Horace Martin the new laird who raised many local objections and court cases. I'm holding placard right of centre behind the speaker's pointing finger, Sept.1972.

Rally at Croick Church, Strathcarron, Ardgay summer 1980 recalling the Clearance of Glen Calvie. Dr Iain Glen, speaking on trailer. Willie McRae waiting to speak to SNP members and friends. (A. Allan)

1995, Iain Quinn, son of a Knoydart land raider, looks on as Archie Mac-Dougall makes the final adjustment to the second plaque I helped produce, and Duncan Stalker who built the memorial cairn in 1991. (W Morrison)

SNP formed Land Commission meeting in Aberdeen 1995. Clerk, Stephen Noon, legal adviser, Donald Ferguson with members Dot Jessieman, Douglas MacMillan and chair, Prof. Allan MacInnes.

Outrage on Ben Braggie? Revisited in October 2016 with Cameron McNeish filming for Roads Less Travelled, BBC Scotland. The saga of the Duke's statue resonates still.

Glen Diobhan, Arran 2003. Evidence of unfinished repairs on broken fence set to protect rare Arran Whitebeam, sorbus arranensis.

Rob and Eleanor surveying deer damage to 'protected'
young Arran Whitebeams.

Rural Development and Environment Committee members en route by rib
to Lamlash Bay from Brodick to view proposed no-take zone. (S Blackley)

Blackley with Howard Wood of COAST having dived onto the maerl bed to show MSPs the potential breeding ground.

Attending Coigach and Assynt Living Landscape project launch at Glen Canisp Lodge. 2011 along with representatives of the estates involved and curated by Scottish Wildlife Trust CEO Johnny Hughes.

MSP information gathering on the Isle of Bute, May 2012. Apparently prosperous tenant farms on Mountstuart Estate.

Muirburn on the killing grounds –
Upper River Gairn, Deeside, RACCE enquiry on Aquaculture Bill.

With John Randall, the event organiser of Recovering from the Clearances
at Balallan School, Isle of Lewis 2012. My talk covered the school board
sacking of Donald MacRae, the 'Alness Martyr' who then led the
Great Pairc Deer Raid in 1887.

August 2013 searching for tree seedlings on Ardvar land overgrazed by herbivores to the detriment of protected native tree. This led to the RACCE deer management enquiry and ministerial orders to toughen deer management plans.

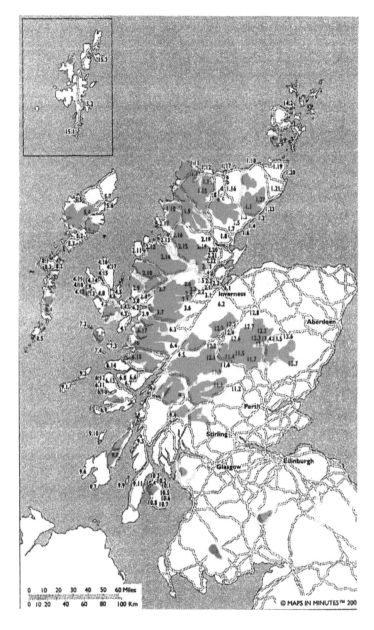

A composite map of 42 core 'wild land' areas superimposed on the map of my book *The Highland Clearances Trail*. The controversy was dubbed 'Clearances Country'. Repopulation is now beginning. (N MacDonald)

RACCE committee final membership 2015 who tackled the land reform bill process. (Permission granted by Scottish Parliament – photograph by Andrew Cowan.)

View of Craighouse, Isle of Jura, the morning after convening a public meeting of residents in the local hall during RACCE members' land reform fact finding September 2015. (T Edwards)

Surveying the Daily Telegraph commentary of the land reform
bill process. (N MacDonald)

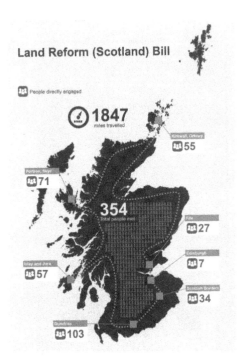

Infographics of RACCE
scrutiny of Land Reform
Bill 2015

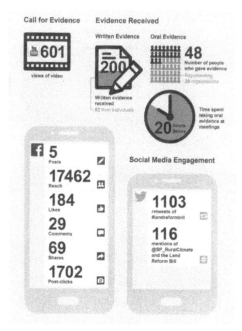

11. Consulting on the future of Scottish land reform

The big asks – diversity, transparency and supportive land tax
  – Scottish Government consultation (2 December 2014 – 10
  February 2015) results.

Which topics from the LRRG Final Report would the Scottish Government choose to include in its draft Land Reform Bill? When an independent analysis was conducted, after the required consultation that closed in February 2015, and a creditable 1,165 responses were sifted: 82% of these were by individuals while the remaining 18% were from organisations. The LRRG Final Report had made 62 recommendations. The scale of their survey could potentially take several parliamentary sessions, each of five years duration, to make the required laws. As it was, 11 topics were chosen in December 2014's consultative document.

Following an opening question concerning the value of a Land Rights and Responsibilities Statement, a clear pattern emerged. Out of those who responded, 87% agreed with the need for such a vision statement. Those objecting felt it was unnecessary, or likely to delay business decisions or be another bureaucratic hurdle to business and interfere with the free market. These would be recurring themes.

Respondents indicated three clear priorities:

a) transparency of ownership and control;
b) diversity of land ownership; and
c) a supportive land tax regime.

Thereafter various topics obtained majority support in varying degrees. Of those responding:

- 75% were for establishing a Land Commission;

- 79% were for a limiting legal entities which could own land;

- 88% saw the need for clear up to date and accessible land information;

- 72% were in favour of public interest powers to apply tests to overcome barriers to sustainable development;

- 79% wanted a more proactive role for public land management;

- 76% agreed that land owning charities must engage with communities affected by their plans;

- 64% wanted proposals from the Agricultural Holdings Legislative Reform Group (AHLRG) included in the Land Reform Bill;

- 71% wanted an end to the exemption from deer shooting rates;

- 71% saw a new legal definition of common good land as essential;

- 69% wanted more regulation of wild deer;

and finally, most agreed that core path planning required simpler, more direct revision.[223]

On the other hand:

---

223. Nicholson, 'A Consultation on the Future of Land Reform, 2015

- 93% of landlords and their organisations opposed sustainable development tests and suggested legal challenges would be likely;

- 50 out of 51 organisations were opposed to the return of shooting rates while 52% of organisations disagreed with tougher deer management;

- 65% of organisations responding to the question disagreed that AHLRG recommendations had any place in the proposed Land Reform Bill.

The cleavage between pro and anti-land reform sentiments was stark. What would the Scottish Government include in a draft Bill?

Orkney opinions sampled on the Bill consultation

Hearing the views of tenant farmers in Orkney, Islay, Dumfries and the Scottish Borders prepared RACCE members for tenancy questions ahead of other sessions with owner-occupiers and landlords, which were organised in Orkney, Jura and Islay, Dumfries and on Roxburghe Estate in the Scottish Borders. Our committee programme of evidence taking on the Land Reform Bill process transported us on 7 June 2015 to a hearing as part of a Parliament Day event in Kirkwall, the Orkney county capital. RACCE members made several visits around the isles ahead of the formal roundtable hearing, which had been timed to precede the conclusion of the Scottish Government consultation. By and large, Orkney is farmed by owner-occupiers who may, additionally, rent or own crofts. Only one landlord who had tenants was drawn to our attention and some committee members visited one of those tenants that day. It reinforced for us that tenancy relationships can be very strained and take years to work out changes as simple as building a modern dwelling.

The formal committee meeting that evening, in the ambiance of Kirkwall Grammar School, brought forth hostile views from Paul Ross, the NFUS Orkney branch chairman, that land reform was irrelevant to Orkney practices. However, the committee was determined to sample a wide range of views on the likely contents of the Bill and decided to seek written submissions from interested parties with an early August deadline.[224]

Return to Skara Brae

The Parliament Day in Orkney allowed RACCE committee members to survey island and farming issues. Then they held land reform discussions with local representatives later that day. MSPs split up into groups to cover various topics. In fine, dry weather, only slightly chilled by the ever-present Atlantic wind, we arranged a guided tour of the ancient village at Skara Brae. It is Europe's most complete Neolithic village, a UNESCO World Heritage site hidden by the swirling sands of time for millennia till a storm in the Bay of Skaill blew away its earthen duvet in 1850. Historic Environment Scotland (HES) are its current custodians, fearful that climate change accompanied by rising sea levels could obliterate the ancient homesteads for good. Our visit flagged up rising sea levels, higher wave action and threats to such low-lying places.

Some years previously, as a Regional MSP, I had been asked by Orkney tour guide Bob Miller, an old friend of my partner Eleanor, to help him lift a veto by HES on altering their timeline interpretation on the path to Skara Brae. Bob had been guiding a Russian journalist, Alexander Korobko, who was to make a film of his visit to Orkney in search of one strand of his DNA that included elements from the Donbass and Rumania as well as far-flung Orkney. The travels of northern Europeans as far back as the Neolithic is well-documented. Bob and Alexander visited Skara Brae in their research where they saw the series of sandstone blocks placed by the path from the visitor centre that takes you back in time from the present to 3,000 years BC. Mr Korobko was puzzled why the first block announced, 'man lands on the moon'. The next, the 'invention of the telephone' and so on. Hadn't the Russians been first in space? Why was there no acknowledgement of that pioneering epic journey beyond the Earth's atmosphere by dogs and later Yuri Gagarin and his fellow cosmonauts?

HES bosses in Edinburgh were unmoved by a request from the tour

---

224. RACCE visit to Orkney, June 2015

guide to remedy this. What if a case was made for a whole lot of other prominent world events to feature on their tablets of stone? So, Miller asked me to weigh in, which I did. Brushing off HES's initial rebuff, I warned them I'd be visiting Orkney in the summer recess tour in 2008 and would make a very public call for a change of heart, even if embarrassing the heritage body was entailed. Surprisingly, HES agreed! A new block would be fashioned, local primary school children and a Russian cosmonaut would unveil the new tablet and I would join them on a blustery and showery morning on 10 April 2008.

HES insisted on running the show. In attendance were several Russian TV teams that filmed the scene. The HES organiser refused to change the timetable to avoid an incoming shower and so, along with Georgi Grechko and local children, Alexander Korobko and the Russian consul general in Scotland, I played my part in the plinth's unveiling. Grechko recited part of Robert Burns' universal anthem 'A Man's A Man for A' That' to honour Scottish and Russian friendship after the Saltire and Russian flags were pulled away to reveal the missing tribute to man's first orbit of the Earth.[225]

I was delighted to return to the Skara Brae path in 2015 with other MSPs and point to its special stone. My colleague, Jim Hume MSP, kindly took my picture at the plinth and I regaled colleagues with a quiet conversation I had back in April 2008. I had asked one of the local guides, 'Did they forget any other significant stone on the path?' 'Yes,' replied my informant, 'the birth of Christ.'

Critics round on 'modest Land Reform Bill'

After the publication of the draft Land Reform Bill, the BBC reported on opposition to the proposals:

> David Johnstone, chairman of Scottish Land and Estates, which speaks for private landowners, had previously said that sporting estates were 'too readily singled out in a negative light', when in fact 'they were businesses that made

---

225. Return to Scara Brae, www.youtube.com/watch?v=hAzE9IY1kbI and photos.orkneycommunities.co.uk/picture/number10626.asp

a key contribution to rural tourism, local employment and the environment.'[226]

And the Scottish Conservatives had criticised the government's proposed reforms as 'a Big Brother-style land grab'. Landowners underlined these views ahead of the Stage 1 hearings at Holyrood of our first evidence session on 2 September 2015.

From the opposite standpoint, Lesley Riddoch laid out her critique of the draft Bill for radical reform. Her remarks were couched in deeply pessimistic terms. To her thinking, the Scottish Government seemed

> to find the business of reforming the 'most concentrated, most inequitable and most undemocratic land ownership system in the entire developed world' to quote Professor Jim Hunter in 2013 – fiendishly difficult.[227]

She went on to deplore the

> hysterical accusations of a Mugabe-style land raid and assertions that change is too complex, risky and unnecessary,

which was the landlord position. It bore echoes of scaremongering against a Yes vote in 2014, she opined, while

> for the majority (of voters) the debate will likely go right over their heads – couched as it is in language that is now as remote as the prospect of ever owning a tiny bit of Scottish land.[228]

Following her call to end a tax exemption on non-domestic rates for derelict and vacant land, Riddoch excoriated the

---

226. '"Radical" Scottish Land Reform Plan Unveiled', BBC News, 23 June 2015, www.bbc.co.uk/news/uk-scotland-scotland-politics-33226303
227. Lesley Riddoch, 'Where Do You Stand on Land Reform?' *The Scotsman*, 30 August 2015, www.scotsman.com/news/opinion/columnists/lesley-riddoch-where-do-you-stand-land-reform-1496454
228. ibid.

nervous Scottish Government lawyers [who] blocked the even more modest proposal to require all landowning trusts and companies to register in member states of the EU.

She claimed this would have stopped landowners from using offshore tax havens to avoid their details of ownership becoming public. If, Riddoch stated, this measure was not reinstated,

the public will conclude that ministers and MSPs are running scared of lawyers who in turn are running scared of landowner pressure.[229]

Transparency of ownership would lead our committee deliberations towards a radical set of proposals that Riddoch hadn't dreamed possible when she posed her article's concluding question – how much land reform is enough? That would be one trigger for an outburst of debate at the SNP Annual Conference held in Aberdeen six weeks later.[230]

In scrutinising the Bill, the committee had continued to hear from, and engage with, as many people as possible across the country, and embarked on an extensive evidence-gathering and engagement exercise.

---

229. ibid.
230. RACCE, 'Stage 1 Report on the Land Reform (Scotland) Bill', 4 December 2015

12. Urban land reform

Scotland had the most rapid urbanisation of any European nation in the industrial revolution of the 19th century. Its workers, its poor, its middle classes all lived in tenements while the rich alone could build suburban and rural mansions. All were built on feus from great land-owners, and by the end of the century waves of immigrants, such as the Irish, added to the pressure on one and two apartment dwellings, most often served by common toilets and no baths.

The problems of urban land reform centred around town planning, housing and sanitation. Halfway through the 20th century, less than a third of all families lived in houses larger than two rooms – this was down from a half of families in 1911. Again in 1951, 43% of all households lacked a fixed bath, while a third of households still shared a WC.[231]

The biggest house owners, by 1951, were the city, town and county councils. Government subsidies had been applied serially since 1919 to council housing. This was to alleviate the dire Victorian heritage where rapid industrialisation and lower wages had propelled Scotland to the forefront of the world economy for steel and iron, ships, railway engines and associated engineering products. Private renting shrank as slum clearance, new towns and peripheral housing estates kept the social classes apart in a modern variant of feudal society.

In the 19th century, trade unions in Scotland remained weak and local,

---

231.   TM Devine, *The Scottish Nation*, Viking, 1999

unlike their English counterparts where higher wages were the norm. This had encouraged investment in Scottish heavy industries. However, the arrival of new socialist ideas began to take root in the 1870s. Irish political connections opened a new strand of thinking following the success of the Irish Land League (ILL), founded in 1879, and with branches among the Irish diaspora in Glasgow. Michael Davitt, 'Father of the Land League', became deeply impatient with the conservatism of Irish small farmers who welcomed the three Fs (fair rent, fixity of tenure and freedom of sale) enshrined in Gladstone's Land Law (Ireland) Act of 1881.

Davitt was a frequent visitor to Glasgow and he also visited crofting areas of the Highlands in 1882 and 1887. On these visits he broadened his land reform arguments thanks to the work of the American radical, Henry George, whose book, *Progress and Poverty*, urged the introduction of the single tax on land. It transpired that his message had the greatest traction in the overcrowded cities, while the crofters, like their Irish cousins were content with a Scottish version of the three Fs.

Land nationalisation was Davitt's take on the Land League slogan, 'The Land for the People'. He saw this as a catalyst for more widespread social and political reform. While the landless cottars of Ireland and the Scottish Highlands continued to resist evictions and mount land raids, the Scottish Land Restoration League became a short-lived political party, based on the Georgist theory, around Glasgow in the mid-1880s.[232]

Land values, and site value rating was to become a radical strand in UK political thinking, especially associated with the Liberal chancellor of the exchequer, Lloyd George, in his 1911 budget which led to official survey completed in 1915 of all landowners in Britain. With the Bolshevik Revolution in 1917, the idea of land nationalisation took on an entirely different slant of expropriation, amalgamation and collective ownership by the state. Such was the fear felt by the British landowning class that the modest Lloyd George proposals were scrapped by the overwhelming Tory dominated coalition government of 1919. Thereafter, in UK politics LVT was a fringe concern, except for a strand of Labour Party thinking

---

232. Andrew Newby, *History Scotland*, July/August 2003 and Dr Brian Casey, *History Scotland*, July/August 2019

exemplified by chancellor of the exchequer, Philip Snowden, and among the Liberals.

The main thrust of urban land use change, from the 1930s, centred on housing and developments in shopping and manufacture. Gradually, the old centres of our towns were transformed by the vast clearance of overcrowded slums into council-controlled peripheral housing estates. Manufacturing developed in newly created industrial estates from the later 1930s onwards.

The annexation of agricultural land into urban spaces played host to the sprawl of built up areas. One interesting designation arising from the 1947 Town and Country Planning Act was the green space concept in attempts to limit ribbon development. The main tenet was to be detailed town and country planning and planning gain accruing from existing use prices of land as they acquired enhanced value when readied for development. Successive UK Labour-controlled Governments in 1945, 1964 and 1974 wrestled with the means to capture this development value for the community, only to see their work quashed by a succession of incoming Tory regimes culminating with the Thatcher Government in 1979.

To that date, 75% of all housing in Scotland had been owned by local authorities, the Scottish Special Housing Association or New Town Corporations. Radicalised Tory individualism ordered an end to council-controlled house building. It ushered in the RTB at deep discounts for council house tenants but also favoured the creation and development of the housing associations in which local tenanted property would be managed more locally than at, often Labour, council level. This had the effect of energising a new cadre of local people to make decisions about their neighbourhood with professional services provided by a new breed of housing officers to construct the plans and supervise the delivery of renovations and new build.

Housing still is the *sine qua non* of urban land use. The tenurial revolution in the 1980s tended to privatise the norms, moving Scots from being predominantly tenants to 60% owner-occupiers by 2015.[233]

---

233. Douglas Robertson, 'Housing Policy: Exposing the Limits of Devolution and Ambition', in Gerry Hassan and Simon Barrow (eds.), *Scotland the Brave? Twenty Years of Change and the Future of the Nation*, Luath Press, 2019

Urban land slowly addressed in Scottish Parliament

Scottish Office minister Lord Sewell introduced UK Labour's LRPG consultation in February 1998 with the statement:

> The land area of Scotland is about 2% urban and 98% rural. Land reform issues relate primarily to rural land.[234]

This set the direction of policy development despite submissions to the consultation which stressed the need for urban land reform. I reflected on these proposals amidst the overall land reform picture in April 1998:

> Scotland's land resources belong to the whole community of Scotland therefore the SNP is committed to the long-term rejuvenation of this most basic physical resource by ending the ossification of both rural and urban landscapes which has occurred under successive Unionist Governments.[235]

When the LRPG solutions paper was published ahead of the Scottish Parliament election in May 1999 the trend was set to focus on rural reforms.

Of course, abolition of the feudal system applied to urban and rural alike, but CRTB, a key plank of future legislation, followed the trend set by Assynt, Eigg and Knoydart. Indeed, Calum MacDonald MP had helicoptered to Knoydart to celebrate its liberation day in March 1999. Rural rights to buy could include communities up to 3,000 inhabitants. It was in August 2003, after the landmark Land Reform Act had been passed, that First Minister Jack McConnell sought to include urban land of 10,000 residents.[236] Speculation arose about a deal with his Lib Dem partners which would have benefitted 500,000 more small town residents. This would have suited their voters, even if the

---

234. Scottish Office Land Reform Policy Group, 'Identifying the Problems', February 1998
235. Rob Gibson, submission to Scottish Office consultation, April 1998
236. Jack McConnell, BBC Scotland, 19 August 2003

secondary instrument was not laid when the Labour/Lib Dem coalition lost office to the incoming minority SNP administration in May 2007.

Urban land reform as such had years to wait. The existing RTB for communities beyond the crofting areas relied on a willing seller. Court cases showed the procedures to register and ballot were cumbersome. Indeed, the idea of urban communities demanding more local control would possibly finger largely Labour-controlled councils with their inbuilt belief that they knew best how to develop urban spaces. Previous to the 1999 return of the Scottish Parliament, the SNP had pointed to the need for land reform in towns but without working out the best way to proceed, save the election of community land councils to meet and discuss with landowners as to an agreed approach to development or an end to urban decay. The party was well aware of the work of local housing associations as many party activists had sought that work in the 1980s.

It took the LRRG reporting in 2014 to suggest ways to legislate. New reasons for community rights to buy were incorporated in both the Community Empowerment (Scotland) Act of 2015 and the Land Reform (Scotland) Act of 2016. These were chosen to break the logjam and were the grounds for buyouts being extended to include the triggers of neglected and abandoned land, the imperative to promote local economic development and grounds for concern regarding the environmental detriment on land in question.

Much of the debate about urban land occupied the Local Government and Regeneration committee at Holyrood while RACCE concentrated on rural transformation. Not enough has been made of the locally controlled Housing Association movement which flourished from area regeneration in the 1970s, and matured in the 1980s, as a model for resident controlled places seeking to climb out of deprivation and neglect. Since the bulk of these are still functioning today, it suggests that alongside community owned estates created by land reform laws that their urban equivalent must be recognised and included in revisioning urban and rural housing delivery.

Such a package to create four homes in Helmsdale, in my constituency, was achieved by a local development trust with multi-agency support. I played a part in helping achieve an affordable energy package from SSE. These were the first public homes built in the East Sutherland village for 35 years. Their unveiling and allocation were a model for other small communities.[237]

The LRRG had suggested a form of Compulsory Sale Order to push reluctant landowners to sell, in order to trigger quicker transfers of such properties. This has been taken up by the Scottish Land Commission to develop a policy approach in 2019. It's a consideration, like many other moves to interfere with property rights, that needs to be ECHR proof.[238]

As I review the legacy of house building in towns, it appears to me that devolution seemed to offer the chance to break free from the dominance of Thatcherite private housing markets. However, that has still proved elusive; the huge imbalance of house building still relies on private sector speculative building.

A full analysis by the LRRG argued, in Section 20 of its final report, that a public body, once again, is needed to lead the urban and rural housing renewal. A Housing Land Corporation (HLC) could meet Scottish Government placemaking aspirations. It could be charged with acquiring and developing sufficient land to meet all affordable housing need. Given the history of housing policy since devolution, such a corporation would re-establish a national housing leader to replace Communities Scotland. The latter had been abolished by the Scottish Government in 2007 and was the last in a line over 70 years of government-led agencies to lead the nation's house building efforts.[239] I will address the rural housing crisis in discussion of the RACCE committee report on the Land Reform (Scotland) Bill in December 2015 in a later chapter. However, the HLC could supervise rural housing provision too. It must address the inadequacy of the Scottish Index of Multiple Deprivation because this is incapable of revealing poor

---

237. 'Helmsdale & District Development Trust', Community Land Scotland, www.communitylandscotland.org.uk/members/ helmsdale-district-development-trust/
238. Scottish Land Commission consultation, 2019
239. Robertson, 'Housing Policy', 2019

housing next door to luxury dwellings that can occur in rural Scotland. Remembering that a lead housing agency is once again required would be the first step to revisioning the repair, renovation, replacement and new build homes fit for a climate change aware era.

13. Formal Bill process

*Don't be satisfied with half measures of change, but to go in for
what is your just and your natural right.*
  – Michael Davitt, Portree 1887.

*And when the sky darkens and the prospect is war
Who's given a gun and then pushed to the fore
And expected to die for the land of our birth
Though we've never owned one handful of earth?*
  – Workers' Song.

As I, and my fellow MSPs, returned from the 2015 summer recess, raring to go, we were disturbed to hear that the Bill team leader, a civil servant, Stephen Pathirana, had been moved to a key job in the housing division. Until July 2015, Pathirana had been part of the Scottish Government Short Life Working Group (SLWG) which was working on achieving the target of one million acres in community ownership by 2020. It would report in December when we completed Stage 1 scrutiny. This key staff move was triggered within the Civil Service itself. It is a UK-wide structure with procedures immune to political interference. In other words, transfers are triggered regularly by arcane Civil Service appraisals and promotions which are not in the gift of Scottish Government. It was a mystery to us on the brink of a major Bill to see this experienced hand removed from the tiller and two others replaced to guide the Bill team in short succession during the parliamentary stages.

Stephen Sadler who had led another Bill team, on votes at 16 before the independence referendum, took over Pathirana's role on the SLWG and by the end of the year of the Land Reform Bill 2015 team. He appeared on 2 November at RACCE under the title of Head of Land Reform and Tenancy Unit along with minister Dr Aileen McLeod.

Extensive public engagement planned

For me, engagement with public opinion is a key part of MSP activity. After Kirkwall in June, we had agreed on a public call for evidence to scope out the range of possible visits for sampling views on the Bill's proposals. We sought snapshots and moods in as many places as possible. That said, the few weeks from 7 September to 2 November, which excluded time off for the October recess and SNP Annual Conference, was logistically, tight for groups of committee members to travel to far-flung spots over weekends and outside the normal Tuesday to Thursday parliamentary schedule.

We plumped for two formal committee meetings outside Holyrood, namely in Portree on 7 September to begin the public evidence sifting and in Dumfries on 2 November, to hear some more detailed answers from Dr Aileen McLeod MSP and her Bill team. In between we made fact-finding visits to Fife, Jura and Islay, the Scottish Borders and the Registers of Scotland HQ in Edinburgh. Public meetings were held in Jura and Dumfries with large and often quite critical audiences.[240] As well as briefings from SPICe, the indispensable parliament information service, we all received a fat ring binder full of written submissions on the Bill. A systematic read through of the 200 separate responses covered the breadth of the Bill.

A large tranche concerned the agricultural holdings proposals. In my rough calculation, 37% were supportive, 37% firmly opposed and 26% had searching questions and suggestions for improvements on all aspects of the Bill. Some respondents had previously given their views to the LRRG who had gleaned 484 submissions in 2012 and to the Scottish Government Bill consultation earlier in 2015 which had previously attracted nearly four times that amount.[241]

Two examples from written submissions to the call for evidence by RACCE in August 2015 show the extensive range of views we received. Both were made by residents of the Isle of Arran. First, Henry Murdo:

---

240. RACCE, 'Stage 1 Report', 2015
241. Independent Analysis of Consultation Results for the Scottish Government

Having worked for the Duke of Buccleuch, Lord Bute, and Arran Estate as a gamekeeper when I was a young man, land reform has been my passion ever since! I have been bitterly disappointed by the timidity of the SNP Government and fear I will end my days still living in a feudal society. The propaganda from the landowners is very slick and accepted by a largely urban population who do not understand how they have been deceived and robbed for generations.

Huge areas of Scotland are held down by this small number of people who stop any improvement or development and actively denude the country of its people. My own home island, and all the neighbouring ones are the same, are unable to develop anything without owning the land and the present reform Bill will do nothing to help. We need to do the same as was done in Eire and dissolve the estates. It was the present Duke of Buccleuch's grandfather that I worked for and the royals and the Tory party grandees came for the grouse shooting on what is laughably called the glorious 12 August. I can think of few other less glorious events as the toffs slaughter hundreds of grouse just for fun! However, it was the treatment of the working men that was sickening and I learned what it was to be a serf. Dissolve the estates! Follow the European example and limit land ownership to hundreds, rather than thousands, of acres.[242]

I feel his pain personally. For a lifelong friend feeling so badly of our fledgling land reform powers is heart wrenching.

To understand the deep cleavage of land views, read the thoughts of the laird of Arran Estates, Charles Fforde whose own written submission 188 shows his utter contempt for the land reform process.

---

242. Henry Murdo, Submission 33, RACCE call for evidence, Land Reform (Scotland) Bill

Fforde called proposed Land Commissioners 'commisars' at the public expense; his use of the word 'insane' 16 times, in the submission, as Mike Russell reminded him in an email exchange, is extraordinary. Fforde's conclusion that the Scottish Government was aping Zimbabwe went like this:

> The Leninist notion of proletarian utopia has not worked in Russia, Zimbabwe, North Korea, China or anywhere else. It is insane to think it will work in Scotland. A good deal more common sense and less bigotry are called for on this occasion.
>
> In the words of the Roman Emperor Marcus Aurelius (AD 121-180), 'The object in life is not to be on the side of the majority, but to escape finding oneself in the ranks of the insane.'[243]

I can only note that two of the LP farm tenancies out of seven in the final complex court cases were on Arran Estate.

Also, the attempt in 2006 by the Rural Development and Environment committee to offer a route for Arran smallholders to become crofters and escape the thrall of Arran Estate had been contested from the outset by Charles Fforde. The smallholders still seek a means of escape today. Charles Fforde is intransigent and Henry Murdo's wishes unfulfilled.

Who were the RACCE committee members in 2015?

During the deer management inquiry late in 2013, Alan Cochrane, columnist for the *Daily Telegraph* and *Scottish Field*, quipped that we were all a bunch of townies, or words to that effect. Membership of committees change, but even then, I retorted that three of the committee members were farmers and from farming backgrounds while four of the nine represented rural constituencies. We were small town

---

and country dwellers and in close touch with the issues in hand.

Following the 2014 change of ministerial posts with the Nicola Sturgeon reshuffle we gained a former Labour minister and a more recently former Cabinet Secretary. My colleagues had a wide range of experience in land issues. Three represented the south of Scotland, three, the Highlands and Islands and one each from Lothians, Falkirk and Angus. We spanned the country and several of us had seen service in three sessions of parliament and two with four terms' experience. That gave us a depth of knowledge of the important empowerment and Land Reform Bills we were to shepherd forward.

Claudia Beamish, a Labour Regional MSP for South of Scotland had been a primary school teacher and had a keen interest in environmental issues.

Sarah Boyack was a Labour Regional MSP for the Lothians, having formerly sat for Edinburgh Central. She was an Environment and Transport Minister in Donald Dewar's first administration. Her background as a town planner brought precision as to acceptable proposals that would stand the test of ministerial scrutiny.

Graeme Dey SNP MSP for Angus South had been a journalist by profession before arriving at Holyrood in 2011. His role as my Deputy Convener was invaluable as he could concentrate on important details and advice while I kept the show on the road from the chair.

The Rt Hon. Alex Fergusson, Conservative and Unionist MSP For Galloway and West Dumfries, had been elected in 1999. His sheep farming background gave him considerable rural questioning skills and his chairing of the Rural Development committee in Session 1 of the Parliament included his stewardship of the Agricultural Holdings (Scotland) Act of 2003. He was elevated to Presiding Officer in Session 3 from 2007-11 which added new insights and gravitas to his 'one nation' Tory perspective. Unfortunately, he died in the summer of 2018.

Jim Hume was elected as a Lib Dem Regional MSP for South of Scotland in 2007. His policy briefs had been widespread in what had become a small party group. His family background in farming and experience as an NFUS officer brought very useful skills to the table.

Angus MacDonald was elected SNP MSP for Falkirk East in 2011. Originally brought up in the Isle of Lewis, he had been a Falkirk councillor from 2004–11. With his farming and butcher's business background he was well acquainted with land and crofting issues.

Mike Russell was elected SNP MSP for Argyll and Bute in 2011 where he lives. He had two previous spells in 1999 and 2007 as a Regional MSP for South of Scotland. His background in politics as SNP chief executive in 1990s and in cultural roles previously gave him a hugely articulate grasp of Scottish political issues. His ministerial role included environment in 2007 and culture and international relations in 2009 followed by cabinet membership for education until 2014. Resuming a backbench role in RACCE allowed his ministerial experience full scope to probe and develop many aspects of human rights and land use issues.

Dave Thompson was first elected an SNP Regional Member for Highlands and Islands in 2007 and then in 2011 as constituency MSP for Skye, Lochaber and Badenoch. His earlier career in consumer and trading standards took place in the Western Isles and Highland council areas. His attention to detail was essential to his election in 2007 during a miscounting of the regional votes. As an MSP for a vast rural and island seat he brought persistence and forensic skills to the committee's work.

Stage 1 began appropriately in Portree, Isle of Skye

In 2006 a plaque was unveiled at the front door of Portree Hotel and a re-enactment was made of the speech in 1887 by Michael Davitt, the ILL leader, from the hotel balcony. A few words from Davitt's speech strike a chord:

> my advice to the people of Portree and the people of this island is, not to be satisfied with half measures of change, but to go in for what is your just and your natural right, the ownership of the land of Skye for its people.[244]

It was fitting that RACCE should meet in Portree to start the Bill scrutiny.

On a fine early autumn morning mists rose to reveal the Cuillin

---

244. Michael Davitt, speech in Portree, 1887

Hills to our modern day land reformers who could be excused for not recollecting land struggles in the 1880s, as I did. These widespread acts of civil disobedience in Skye had produced such compelling testimony that Liberal Prime Minister William Gladstone agreed to curb the powers of croft land proprietors on behalf of the newly enfranchised male crofters by introducing the mould-breaking 1886 Crofters Holdings (Scotland) Act. An echo of those pioneering land reform days was in my mind for two reasons. Firstly, the Napier Commission heard its opening evidence session in May 1883 six miles from Portree in the schoolhouse at Braes. Secondly, the Crofters MPs voted against the subsequent 1886 Act because it did not return the land to the people from whom it had been taken.

Our witnesses would include academics, sceptics and naysayers, but also advocates of comprehensive land reform and campaigners from the Our Land campaign. When the first witness came before Lord Napier he asked to give evidence in Gaelic. This was granted and marked a breakthrough for the identity and dignity of the witnesses before a Royal Commission. In a present-day echo RACCE would ensure that the Land Reform Bill 2015 included a clause ensuring that one of the new Land Commissioners would be a Gaelic speaker, as had the Land Court, furthering the spirit of the Gaelic Language (Scotland) Act of 2005.

I gladly dashed indoors after a midge-infested interview outside the Aros Centre where Mark Steven and Euan McIlwraith quizzed me for BBC Scotland's *Out of Doors* programme which was to fully chronicle the Bill's progress over the coming months. I was also delighted that the Official Report of the day's evidence was heard by around 70 members of the public in the hall. Cuillin FM presenter Andy Mitchell recorded the proceedings for later transmission through the local radio for Skye and Lochalsh.[245]

After the hearings in the late afternoon, Graeme Dey MSP, my Deputy Convener, who had driven to Skye the previous day, gave me a lift back to Edinburgh with our colleague Angus MacDonald. I had arrived in Skye by train and bus from my home in Easter Ross. Under clear blue

---

245. RACCE OR, 7 September 2015

skies on the return journey I had the leisure to look at many hills I had climbed years before. I could see how empty so much of our country was all the way through Kintail, Lochaber, Rannoch, Glen Dochart and on to Callander.

Our political task was to address such resource issues and try to turn around that sad outflow of people and find ways for more of us to live sustainably across the length and breadth of Scotland. I was truly awed by the size of the task that our journey reminded me of.

Fact-finding across Scotland

RACCE members had taken in a significant slice of Scottish life in the rural communities we visited throughout the session from 2011 and on the fact-finding visits planned specifically to explore aspects of the Bill. Groups of members had been to Gigha, Bute (as mentioned above), Flanders Moss, Glenlivet, Deeside, Montrose and Lochaber in previous years. Matters of concern in many of these areas were germane to aspects of the draft Bill.[246]

Our visit to Falkland took in the concepts of land stewardship as practiced by Ninian Stuart and at the Kinghorn Community Land Association and its Ecology Centre developing the local potential of the land around Kinghorn Loch.[247] Two focused visits on tenant farming exposed the diversity of conditions, and the similarities of relationship problems, shared by farmers in Islay and the Scottish Borders. The outlook of Lord Margadale and the Duke of Roxburghe respectively, the major landowners, provided us with first-hand accounts of the divergent views of tenants and lairds on the need for greater clarity in the Bill as published. Bute, Islay and the Scottish Borders are landscapes dominated by tenant farming. Tenant farmers were the backbone of these communities and anything which strengthened their rights would have a direct bearing on sustaining populations there.

We had previously received details of the precarious condition of tenant farming on the four Islay estates. Frustrations with the estate management left us certain of the current imbalance of power between

---

246. RACCE, 'Stage 1 Report', 2015
247. ibid.

landlords and tenants. It was a theme that would be amplified in discussions that autumn on human rights to land, food and housing. On Jura and on the Roxburghe Estate major criticisms were voiced over the planned clauses to end the exemption from sporting rates which had been in force since 1995.[248] Initial evidence received at the Skye hearing stressed the need to speed up and deepen the map-based registration of our land. Our visit to Registers of Scotland HQ in Edinburgh led to searching questions in some members' minds as to the need for a much-enhanced section on transparency in the Bill.

Our last fact-finding mission took us, on 2 November, to Dumfries with a Q&A session between RACCE members and a far from sympathetic audience of over a hundred people. Many of them stayed on to hear the formal committee session with the land reform minister Dr Aileen McLeod MSP. These informal, and later formal, committee events raised some tetchy issues for several farmers over the possible fate of their holdings if the CRTB policy was to be applied. I reflected, on the return journey to Edinburgh, that there were many apparently contradictory implications of this huge Bill that would require great patience and sound judgement by MSPs if we were to influence its final shape.

Seven evidence sessions grappled with the substance of the Bill. The largest section, Part 10 on agricultural holdings reform follows below.

In committee – Agricultural holdings accentuated a deeply divided industry

From the outset, the Tory member of RACCE, Alex Fergusson made it plain that he would oppose Part 10 on agricultural holdings. Alex had attended several of the committee fact-finding visits around the country. This did not prevent him from probing witnesses to justify his party's position before and after Stage 1 evidence sessions started on 2 September 2015.

In RACCE's Stage 1 Report published on 4 December 2015 salient points on agricultural holdings were made clear. Extracts from paragraphs 402 to 406 are as follows:

---

248. ibid.

402. Over half of the Bill relates to changes to agricultural holdings law... The changes are largely proposed because of the work of the Agricultural Holdings Legislation Review Group (AHLRG)... which reported to the Scottish Government on 27 January 2015.

403. Scrutiny of agricultural holdings issues has been a central theme of the Committee's work in this session. The Committee has scrutinised primary and secondary legislation on the issue; held many evidence sessions with stakeholders and the Scottish Government; and carried out a significant number of fact-finding visits to meet tenants and landlords across the country. In that time the Committee has developed a greater understanding of the views of both tenants and landlords from different parts of the country, and the various challenges facing the tenant farming sector in Scotland.

404. The Committee therefore approached its scrutiny of the provisions in the Bill by assessing them against its fundamental desire to see a healthy, thriving tenant farming sector in Scotland which delivers real public benefits... The key question is: will the provisions in the Bill help to deliver that desired outcome?...

405. The Committee also examined the provisions from the perspective of compatibility with ECHR and other human rights instruments. The fact that the Committee scrutinised this Bill at the same time as it continued to deal with the very unfortunate aftermath of the Salvesen v Riddell judgement by the UK Supreme Court, which found that a specific section of the Agricultural Holdings Act 2003 was not compatible with ECHR and therefore out with the Parliament's legislative competence, was not lost on the Committee. It would not serve anyone well if provisions were passed in this Bill which went on to be successfully challenged in the courts.

406. It was clear... that the issue of human rights is being very keenly felt by all sides of the debate and that many stakeholders feel that ECHR issues are overshadowing the process and causing nervousness and tension.[249]

Of land in farming at the time, a slight increase in acreage was noted, but the LRRG also provided a clear picture of the owner/tenant divide. Taking figures for 1990 and 2013, the land in farming rose from 5,622,323.0 to 5,670,391.0 acres in use. In tenure terms, 62.09% had risen to 75.91% owner occupied over the 23 years surveyed while the land tenanted fell from 37.91% to 24.09%. No amount of special pleading by landowners could disguise the steady increase in land owned and the decline of land under all types of tenancy to a ratio of 4:1. That had seen land re-let as less secure tenancies and land farmed in hand when a tenant retired without a successor. These were contributory to the feelings of desperation voiced by the STFA on behalf of its beleaguered members. Threats to landlords' rights were given as perennial reasons why this was so and the SLaE spokespeople talked up the idea of a 'healthy tenanted sector' but refused to see any reduction in the rights of landlords to repossess their property from a dwindling number of secure tenanted holdings.

An example of SLaE tactics had been a call in June 2012 by board member Andrew Howard, the factor of Forres-based Moray Estates, for each farming sector to take a step back and look at the bigger picture and 'stop trench digging'.[250] An SLaE survey of 20 of Scotland's largest landowning businesses stated that let farmland showed 70% under agricultural holdings laws. The remainder was farmed in hand or under contract. Of the 449,445 acres they surveyed, SLaE had 'no information on how that (balance) had changed in recent years'. The lairds claimed that this contradicted recent political and industry views that big landowners had surplus land to let. Although Mr Howard admitted that there were estates, at the extreme end of the spectrum, that may not have been letting land this would amount to about 10% of the all let holdings. If land were to be made available for

---

249. RACCE, 'Stage 1 Report', 2015
250. *Press & Journal*, 14 June 2012

let, then these large land owners would have to offer land they farmed in hand, said Howard. Additionally, senior SLaE policy officer, Andrew Midgley, stated 'there is no evidence of their land sitting there being underused'. In contrast to the vast majority in Scotland's Parliament he argued that landowners were being 'implored to do something that is not in their interests'.

The most potent example of that age-old landowner stance was the move to widen the range of assignees and successors to 1991 secure tenancies now contained in the Land Reform Bill 2015, Part 10, Chapter 5. Andrew Howard gave oral evidence at Stage 1:

> What the Bill needs to aspire to is ensuring that the agricultural holdings framework is seen as a perfectly viable and attractive option for someone who does not want to farm the land themselves at that time, whether they are a large landowner or someone who is currently an owner-occupier farmer. At the moment, the option of creating a tenancy is not being taken up, even if, in all other circumstances, it might suit that individual, and other structures such as contract farming or share farming are being used because of concerns over the politicisation of the agricultural holdings system.

I felt I had to respond as convener:

> Well, it is politicising the agricultural holdings system to suggest that we should consider contract farming when it has been rejected as an approach in Scotland. We can use the word 'politicisation' in lots of ways, and we should be careful about doing so. We have been trying to find a way through this maze and are trying not to be too partisan in our language, but the word 'politicisation' is quite partisan. I can assure you that we are aware of what is being said.[251]

---

251. RACCE OR, 16 September 2015

As already noted, the widening of the list of those entitled to assignation or succession was a flash point.

SLaE objected... claiming it was an unwarranted and unjustified extension which would be disadvantageous to landlords and represent a significant loss of their rights. It was felt by some that widening assignation and succession rights would also be a disincentive to investment and counterproductive to the aim of encouraging the letting of land...

Andrew Howard [who] said the Bill was trying to force land to remain in out-date tenure rather than looking to create a flexible, modern tenanted sector and that landlords would be deprived of land they previously thought they would get back at some stage. He also said that this would not help new entrants as it would lock land into permanent tenure, regardless of productivity.

He added that, if passed, these provisions were likely to be challenged, and said there was a lack of acceptance that sometimes a tenancy should be able to end, even if a tenant does not want it to.[252]

SNP grassroots revolt

Issue by issue the RACCE committee explored responses on agriculture, sporting rates, deer management and human rights before the recess when SNP members gathered in Aberdeen for the party's annual conference on 15 to 17 October which included a land reform resolution on the agenda and on the unofficial fringe as well. A huge attendance was expected and the vote on Resolution 15, 'Empowering communities and the road to radical land reform', on Friday 16 October was to engage 1,010 delegates in a card vote on the subject.

The mood of delegates was restive following a previous card vote to uphold the moratorium on fracking. Leith branch's proposals were seen, by some, to be too timid. An outright ban was called for from the floor. However, the Scottish Government view prevailed in the card vote. The timing of the land reform debate which followed immediately could not have been worse for a rational appraisal of its contents. Lodged in the names of land reform minister Dr Aileen McLeod and local government minister Marco Biagi, it read:

---

252. RACCE, 'Stage 1 Report', 2015

As we continue to make significant progress towards our target of one million acres of land in community owner-ship by 2020, Conference welcomes the passing of the Community Empowerment Act and the introduction of the Land Reform Bill.

Conference notes that the Community Empowerment Act represents a momentous step in the drive to decen-tralise decision and give people a stronger voice in their communities; notes the Act will give communities more powers to take ownership of land and buildings, in both urban and rural areas, and to actively shape and influence how their services are delivered.

Conference also welcomes the introduction of the Land Reform Bill which aims to ensure the issues of fairness and social justice connected to the ownership of, access to and use of land in Scotland are given permanent footing with the creation of a Scottish Land Commission.

Conference believes that, when people have greater control of their own future, they are more engaged and are able to tackle barriers to making their communities more resilient, sustainable and therefore wealthier and fairer.[253]

In the debate that followed, the mood of discontent became im-mediately apparent. Loud applause followed the first speaker's charge that the Bill lacked radical content. The previous evening, Channel 4 News had aired critical examples of land grievances. The item high-lighted lack of tenancies and housing on Islay. It also featured LP tenant Andrew Stoddart whose East Lothian holding was due to be reclaimed by his landlord the following month.

After the minister, Dr Aileen McLeod, the next person called to speak was highly critical of the motion. Nicky Lowden MacCrimmon

---

253. SNP Annual Conference, 15–17 October 2015

of Carse of Gowrie branch pointed to the 750,000 acres held in tax havens and tenant farmers without a RTB as glaring examples of what was missing from the Bill. He concluded his call to remit the resolution back to its proposers with a clarion call that garnered huge applause from delegates:

> I don't think as a party we are being as radical as we have the powers to be. When you [offer] radical land reform then we'll sign up to it.

Despite pleas from RACCE member Mike Russell and the Minister Aileen McLeod a card vote delivered a defeat for the government view by 570 votes to 440.

The BBC reported that a number of delegates to the SNP conference said they wanted to see a strengthening of the Bill. In response to those calls, Dr MacLeod told the BBC:

> I welcome the very strong contributions made in the debate and the passion and commitment that they have been delivered. I am listening to all the comments and evidence made thus far to the Rural Affairs Committee [at the Scottish Parliament].

> This Bill is not an end in itself and as a government we are committed to taking forward the recommendations of the land reform group.

The Bill will put to an end the stop-start nature of historic land reform.

> I want to give you my reassurance that I am listening as to ways in which we can strengthen the Bill further.[254]

Lesley Riddoch questioned why the media had not probed deeper.

---

254. 'SNP Conference 2015: Delegates Vote for More Radical Land Reform Plans', BBC News, 16 October 2015, www.bbc.co.uk/news/uk-scotland-scotland-politics-34555773

She had joined up with land campaigner Andy Wightman to hire the Aberdeen Arts Centre for an unofficial fringe meeting to which it was said several hundred delegates attended. Riddoch and Wightman claimed that an official fringe venue was too expensive and by that vehicle promoted their views defining radical land reform to many SNP members who attended.

The Scottish Government was, indeed, shocked. Though it would not derail the Bill, it did give campaigners extra leverage to claim that a grassroot SNP member revolt was a 'new force in Scottish politics'. MacCrimmon told Riddoch:

> I take it very personally when the SNP is characterised as feart or bottling it on radical land reform. I know this isn't how people feel in my branch or on social media. What I stood up and said was what other members had been saying to me.[255]

In my view, as the RACCE convener, the tenor of the criticism of the Land Reform Bill was more complex. As the vote was being counted laboriously, I was angry that the spirit and letter of the resolution had been ignored in favour of calls for so-called radical action. I was aware that the fracking debate had set up a hostile mood in the conference hall. Both subjects are a good deal more complex to deliver than through sloganising but the delegates' mood was for delivery of radical proposals. Time would show that the SNP Government's tactic of further study and an extended fracking moratorium would lead to an effective ban within the limited powers of the devolved administration taking an anti-fossil fuel stance. The SNP's renewable energy policy which Scottish planning powers had allowed to be deployed were indeed radical but not such a flash point for delegates as fracking or land.

The social media focus of dissent on land reform by party members opposed to the SNP leadership's stance hid the failure of those keen

---

255. Lesley Riddoch, 'SNP Must Get Radical on Land Reform', *The Scotsman*, 18 October 2015, www.scotsman.com/news/opinion/columnists/lesley-riddoch-snp-must-get-radical-land-reform-1492368

on change to digest the limits of legal powers available to the Scottish Government. Compelling owners of land held anonymously in offshore tax havens was complex. Offering tenant farmers security of tenure was fraught with memories of the recent use of ECHR by landlords. In contrast, the Andy Wightman advocacy of a thorough-going land reform programme as set out repeatedly in his books had big traction for activists. The Our Land campaign that summer had exampled derelict land in Granton, Edinburgh and raptor killings associated with grouse moor management. The plight of a small but vocal group of LP tenant farmers piled up grievances in the summer of 2015. Stung by the narrow No vote in 2014, many Yes supporters sought ways to change Scotland's glaring land ownership as an instalment towards their hoped for, free and fair Scotland.

There was a second strand which Lesley Riddoch touched on internally for the SNP. As she put it,

> an influx of members [since the 2014 No vote] has encouraged a 'loosening of the stays' at grassroots level which is democratising and challenging the top-down style of leadership in the SNP.[256]

I saw this in two associated aspects of the debate. It was true that the party's mechanisms to discuss policy development had been in abeyance. The party constitution made provision for National Assemblies to be led by the Deputy Leader. Interested party members should debate policies and recommend how National Council and Conference should adopt and vote on new policy proposals. Even so, party members could not instruct the Scottish Government but it could make clear the direction SNP activists expected to see. I have little doubt this policy vacuum led directly to the inchoate cry for more radical land reform that I saw in the remitted land reform resolution in Aberdeen.

I use the word inchoate advisedly because my second strand of argument is this. Try as I might I could not find evidence of SNP members contacting their MSPs to demand more specific radical actions. I asked my SNP colleagues on RACCE, had they been approached? They

---

256. Riddoch, 'SNP Must Get Radical on Land Reform', 18 October 2015

could not identify calls by aggrieved SNP members with proposals to 'beef up' the Land Reform Bill. It leads me to question how our much-heralded, openly accessible, Scottish Parliament engages the voters. This seems to be mainly the preserve of those interested individuals and groups who respond to consultations. Of course, specific matters contained in public petitions do reach subject committees like RACCE, but no such petitions were lodged for MSP scrutiny on specific land reform issues at that time. Don't get me wrong. I was not happy with the, alleged, slow progress. The lack of real local powers of decision in the Community Empowerment (Scotland) Act 2015 is only a fraction of the democratic deficit which Holyrood must address. The rhetoric of community empowerment and far-reaching change could spark engagement by local people. Certainly, policies for radical change have to be made law, but the wider media debate has seldom encouraged a real grasp of the intricacies. Mainstream media focuses on sound bites in news schedules. These tend to preclude enough time to cover complex issues adequately, such as land reform.

Subsequent interpretation by land campaigners on the Bill's progress tended to hark back to that conference blow to SNP leaders and claimed that the remit back vote had been the primary spur to action for my MSP colleagues. Did it push us to strengthen an already radical measure, a measure that sought to put land reform on a permanent footing in Scottish political discourse?

Shooting rates to return

As part of the Bill, introduced by Richard Lochhead and supported by Aileen McLeod on 22 June 2015, Part 6 provided for the valuation of shootings and deer forests by the assessors to levying non-domestic rates. Part 8 proposed further functions for deer panels which advise SNH. Regarding DMPs, it was intended to give SNH new powers to enforce these and increased the maximum fine for the offence of failing to comply with a control scheme. The increase was to level 4 on the standard scale to £40,000. This sent a clear signal of a toughening attitude by government to deer managers and other shooting proprietors.[257]

---

257. Land Reform (Scotland) Bill, 'Explanatory Notes', 23 June 2015

In consulting the Bill, 71% of those who answered agreed with rein-troducing shooting rates while 50 of 51 landowning organisation were opposed.[258] Regarding further deer management regulation, of 883 respondents, 76% responded to this question and 69% agreed. Again, individuals supported tougher deer plans while landowners and pro-fessional bodies such as land agents were heavily opposed.[259]

In its Stage 1 Report, RACCE commented on the lack of clarity of the approach to reintroduction of shooting rates; it sought 'thorough, robust and evidence-based analysis' and felt the need for these before it could support Part 6 at Stage 2. The committee sought possible im-provements to the tax that might allow rates relief to those who could demonstrate effective deer management in the public interest.[260] Such clarity could perhaps have helped end the stalemate in Assynt.

Regarding the Bill's Part 8, RACCE noted the proposals happily took the line of the committee's 2014 Inquiry. The Bill highlighted lack of progress to deliver DMPs and their negative effect on the 2020 Scottish Government biodiversity target. If the 2016 date for producing working DMPs was not met, then the Scottish Government must quickly replace 'the failing voluntary system'. RACCE sought amendments to enable SNH to set cull targets for individual DMGs; to require landowners to apply to SNH for licences to cull; and, to enable SNH to take over culling responsibilities. Additionally, an urgent need was raised to build a DMG structure to tackle Lowland deer issues and for the proposed Scottish Land Commission to provide the necessary leadership.[261]

The in-depth work on deer management by RACCE in 2013–14 had given considerable weight to our recommendations, and the Scottish Government response to the Stage 1 Report, which was published early in 2016, acknowledged this. More information on shooting rates was promised in time for Stage 2. The voluntary deer management system, with the 2016 deadline for DMPs, would be underpinned by a commit-ment to enact Part 8 clauses during 2016, ahead of the deadline, not

258. Land Reform (Scotland) Bill, consultation
259. ibid.
260. RACCE, 'Stage 1 Report', 2015
261. ibid.

thereafter. Members of RACCE were well satisfied, in the main, with these responses.[262]

At Stage 2 of the Bill hearings in Scottish Parliament committees, amendments are tabled by individual MSPs and by the Scottish Government. In Parts 6 and 8 some debates ended due to government assurances without a division. Others were voted on. True to form, Alex Fergusson tried to remove the reintroduction of shooting rates and was rebuffed by seven SNP and Labour members with only the Lib Dem member, Jim Hume, joining the Tory member. Mike Russell withdrew a probing amendment when he was assured that normal application of rates relief could reward good deer management in the public interest.

Labour's Claudia Beamish sought to introduce a power for SNH to serve notice on a landowner not complying with the Code of Practice on Sustainable Deer Management. The amendment was disagreed to by two votes to six with one abstention. Whereas Mike Russell's amendment for SNH to request details of the number of deer landowners planned to cull in the following year gained eight votes in favour with one abstention.

As for DMPs, Mike Russell withdrew his amendment that had proposed SNH should keep a public register of DMPs thus allowing local input before plans were finalised. When his amendment was debated to allow SNH to modify DMPs with the increased fines for non-compliance with DMPs to fall on the landowner who defaulted not on all other members of the DMG, it was agreed to by eight votes in favour with one abstention.[263]

On 16 March 2016 the Land Reform (Scotland) Bill would reach Stage 3. Amendments passed by the parliament clarified matters given the assurances by ministers at Stage 2. Among them was leeway for assessors to have regard to such factors relating to deer management as these assessors considered appropriate, in other words Mike Russell's suggestion that rates relief could reward good deer management practices. Regarding Part 8, details were firmed up to review compliance

262. Scottish Government response to RACCE, 'Stage 1 Report', 5 January 2016
263. Mike Russell and Claudia Beamish, Stage 2 debate, RACCE, 2016

with the Code of Practice on deer management. Also, powers to require returns on numbers of deer planned to be killed and powers for SNH to require returns of these numbers planned to be killed were included in the final Bill.[264]

Speaking in the Land Reform Scotland Bill at Stage 2 in the RACCE committee I made the following points on deer management as convener:

> The last report (in 1963) of the Red Deer Commission complained that lack of co-operation from farmers and landowners could cripple it in its task, which is to reduce the red deer population of the Highlands to manageable proportions.
>
> The matter is even more pressing today, as there is a much wider range of landowners. Some of them, such as community land trusts, are small; some are non-governmental organisations; and some are shooting organisations. It seems that deer management could, in areas of crisis such as Assynt in my constituency, bear down on a community trust, which has need of a small income, rather than on people who shoot for pleasure and therefore have no likely pecuniary interest in carrying out the culls that are necessary, or on an NGO such as the John Muir Trust, which has a stated national policy of not allowing fencing and so on in areas in which there are threats to trees.
>
> I understand that, in the circumstances of this debate, we must take into account the realities on the ground, but the view of Major Crichton-Stuart in 1963 suggests to us today that we cannot wait any longer for action to take place.[265]

Most members agreed to the return of shooting rates and that deer

---

264. Scottish Parliament OR, 16 March 2016
265. RACCE OR, 3 March 2016

managers were on notice that tougher action would be taken if non-compliance with statute could be proved. This produced the usual divided response between conservationists on the one hand and land-owners and land agents on the other. A solicitor told me he was looking forward to the appeals by landowners against assessors' valuations for shootings. He recalled that these hearings had been of considerable entertainment value before Michael Forsyth abolished shooting rates in 1996. The smell of tweeds and labradors was alluring.

The reintroduction of shooting rates was a popular matter for many across the country who were determined that land taxation would not stop there. As for the actual regulation of local deer management, as in Assynt, that was yet to be tackled successfully but FES has helped fund fencing for small blocks of threatened trees.

This was a small step in reclaiming revenue from landed assets which affected all sizes of land holdings. However, Martin Birse, who manages Pitganeny Farms near Elgin and at the time was Highland Regional chair of NFUS, told the *P&J*, when he had received his shooting rates notice,

This is yet another cost to be borne by the farmers and landowners – where will it end?[266]

The sense of entitlement seems to know no bounds.

Human rights debate rivets MSPs

Probably the most fascinating evidence session of Stage 1 of the Land Reform Bill 2015 was held on 7 October 2015 when five witnesses contributed to a high level debate over the impact of human rights in the proposed Bill. The witnesses were Eleanor Deeming, Legal Officer of the SHRC; Kirsteen Shields, a lecturer at the University of Dundee; Megan MacInnes an adviser at Land, Global Witness; Charles Living-stone, a partner at the law firm Brodies; and Mungo Bovey QC, Faculty of Advocates. On rereading the Official Report I still see it as the most incisive and cogently argued evidence session we conducted in the Bill process.[267]

---

266. *Press & Journal*, 21 October 2017
267. RACCE OR, 7 October 2015

The direction of debate broadened the base for land reform from ECHR to internationally adopted human rights covenants. Proportionality is key to using Article 1 Protocol 1 and Article 8 of ECHR. This was teased out to explore the tests that the courts would apply. Later in that two-hour session the full worth of ICESCR (International Covenant on Economic, Social and Cultural Rights) and VGRGTLFF were explored. There was a palpable sense that these United Nations measures would have a growing importance for more radical land reform in future.

As we shall see in the next chapter, the committee believed that the Bill should be bold in its ambition and clear in its purpose, in order for these issues, which undermined confidence and trust that people in Scotland have in the ownership, and use of land, could be settled for a good long time.[268]

Land Value Tax investigated

At the same time as our Land Reform Bill scrutiny, investigations on applying LVT had progressed from the LRRG report via the Scottish Government Commission on Local Tax Reform which reported in December 2015. According to its website the Commission brought together local and national politicians from different political parties and a range of expertise from across Scotland to look at ways of developing a fairer system of local taxation:

> The Commission highlights that its very membership – encompassing four political parties, local and central government, and experts in public finance, law, housing, welfare and equalities – is a unique and bold statement of intent, creating an opportunity not to be missed.

> The Commission does not advocate any single alternative to the present system, highlighting that 'There is no one ideal local tax.' In making the case for change, the Commission's report shows that local taxation can be fairer and more progressive.

---

268. RACCE, 'Stage 1 Report', 2015

They examined three alternative types of tax system that could be applied at the local level to replace the present council tax – taxes on property, taxes on land and taxes on income. Their analysis extends to the potential impact of each on different households and how the tax might be administered. They also considered the impacts each would have on the financial accountability of local government, concluding that 'A well-designed local tax system drawing revenue from multiple sources would provide more options for local democracy, delivering greater financial accountability and autonomy to local government.'

The intention was to aid the preparation of party manifestos for the 2016 Scottish Election. It was also clear that local income tax would be hard to collect and easily avoided. The conclusions on LVT stated:

The geographical impacts of a LVT would be largely similar to a property based tax, although our analysis has found a likelihood of higher tax bills per square metre of land in valuable city centre locations and lower liabilities in outlying and rural areas. The actual liability for a household will depend on the amount of land owned and the planning permissions that exist on that land, as well as eligibility for any discounts, reductions or exemptions.[269]

This remains to be fleshed out, but as a departure from the unpopular council tax it is an increasingly popular focus. Indeed, the SNP Annual Conference in October 2017 was told by the Finance Minister, Derek Mackay, that LVT would be investigated in-depth by the Scottish Land Commission. It could cost farms and estates more than council tax at present, but at last taxation of land was placed firmly in government discussions. Since no one likes paying more taxes the sales pitch for any conclusions will need to be seen to be fair, in the public interest and for the common good.

---

269. Scottish Government Commission on Local Tax Reform

RACCE deliberate

RACCE took a month of meetings to deliberate into early December 2015 to agree our Stage 1 Report on the Land Reform Bill of 2015. It contained 575 closely argued paragraphs. The Scottish Government response was awaited but deemed too complex to be tabled ahead of the Stage 1 debate in the Holyrood chamber on 15 December.

14. Land Reform Bill Stage 1 Report
Launched, debated and approved in principle

We cannot roll back hundreds of years of history overnight and nor can we fix all problems in one easy step. However, we can and must focus on taking the next step in our journey.
  – Dr Aileen McLeod, Minister for Land Reform

It was a great moment in my tenure as convener of RACCE; at 10am on 4 December 2015 I launched the Stage 1 Report on the Land Reform (Scotland) Bill at Registers of Scotland headquarters in Meadowbank House, Edinburgh. Our report ran to 141 pages and 575 paragraphs. It was detailed, complex and certainly not geared to sound bites.

Scottish Parliament communications staff had trailed details of the launch to the media and immediately BBC Radio Scotland sought a sound bite from me as RACCE convener to suit their news schedule before 8am on the day. I refused to budge from the planned event at 10 am held in front of a case holding the ancient Register of Sasines in RoS HQ. No BBC reporter attended the launch, unlike STV which sent a camera team. The BBC website, as predicted, later contained bullet points and minimal reaction that day. It stated:

> The Scottish Government's Land Reform Bill needs to be 'enhanced and strengthened' to deliver the 'radical changes needed', MSPs have declared.

> A report from the Rural Affairs and Environment committee said the land management proposals need 'more work'.

The Bill was also rejected by delegates at the SNP conference in October, who argued it should be strengthened.

Landowners say the Bill as it stands would have 'far-reaching and detrimental consequences for business.'[270]

Take your pick, both sides in the land reform debate either praised or
condemned our work. The October SNP Conference rebuff to ministers
remained a repeated theme. The BBC, *Daily Telegraph*, *CommonSpace*
and *The National* each included the delegate dissatisfaction with the
Bill. Lesley Riddoch ran with an old refrain:

The committee backed SNP conference demands to give
tenant farmers greater protection and end offshore tax
havens and secrecy designations which mask the identity
of Scottish landowners.[271]

It was necessarily a complex report which was not easily summarised.
As previously highlighted, in consultations that preceded the Bill, the
most common asks of land reform included transparency, diversity
of ownership and a supportive tax system. The RACCE conclusions
aided certainty of delivery and progress to reach these asks in a more
radical measure than any previous Land Reform Act. Arch-critics of
the SNP Government, such as the editor of the *West Highland Free
Press* failed completely to acknowledge this. Instead their crusty editor
questioned whether the SNP Government was 'really serious about
land reform'. He suggested that the SNP's aim was a 'step back' from
the 2003 Act passed by Labour and the Lib Dems (with, lest we forget,
SNP support):

---

270. 'Land Reform Proposals Need Word, Says Holyrood Committee',
BBC News, 4 December 2015, www.bbc.co.uk/news/uk-scotland-scotland-
politics-35005602
271. Lesley Riddoch, 'Land Reform a Step in Right Direction', *The
Scotsman*, 7 December 2015, www.scotsman.com/news/opinion/columnists/
lesley-riddoch-land-reform-step-right-direction-1997510

Instead of progressing land reform and giving the process new impetus, it could bog it down in qualifications intended to mollify all parties, not least our powerful landowning lobby.

In fact, many proposed clauses were set to strengthen parts of the 2003 Act and build on them. There's no getting away from the contrary nature of such a Free Press editorial![272]

On the very day of that editorial, the report 'One Million Acres by 2020' was published, following the work of the Scottish Government One Million Acre SLWG established in January 2015 which had operated in four work streams. They identified actions to raise awareness of the opportunities of land purchase; what support services were required; how engagement with communities should develop; they underlined Scottish Government must co-ordinate the process proactively; they suggested ways to increase the supply of eligible land; and offered means to measure and evaluate progress.[273] Surely this was the exact opposite of backing away from radical development?

Our committee was forensic in dissecting the Bill and pointed to strengthening parts of it we deemed essential. Lesley Riddoch, from a campaigner's stance did get closer to this fact:

> Real change in Scotland's concentrated and unequal pattern of land ownership moved a step closer.

She argued this, not just because of RACCE's measured critique, but because some of the themes of the Bill did chime with 'SNP conference demands'.[274] Lobbying of MSPs ahead of the Stage 1 chamber debate on 16 December produced the usual diverse advice. For example, more clarity was needed as community buyout concerns lacked details, was

---

272. *West Highland Free Press*, 11 December 2015
273. 1 Million Acre Short Life Working Group, 'One Million Acres by 2020, Strategy Report and Recommendations', Scottish Government, 11 December 2015, www.gov.scot/publications/one-million-acres-2020-strategy-report-recommendations-1-million-acre/pages/1/
274. Riddoch, 'Land Reform A Step in the Right Direction', 7 December 2015

the NFUS critique. On the other hand, Scottish Environment Link broadly supported the principles of the Bill and much of the RACCE Stage 1 Report. They concluded,

> We hope to see a strengthening, in line with our Stage 1 evidence, of many parts of the Bill amendments brought forward at Stage 2.[275]

RACCE had shared the Devolved Powers & Law Reform committee's views that far too much detail was consigned to regulations to be passed after the Bill was enacted. Previous experience such as over the 2003 Acts showed that far-reaching measures would require dozens of secondary instruments to apply the principles set out in workable and detailed form.

Another concern was raised by some opposition MSPs. This was the failure of the ministers to respond to the Stage 1 Report ahead of the chamber debate; a point raised repeatedly before and during the chamber debate on the principles of the Bill.[276] The land reform minister Dr Aileen McLeod opened by acknowledging the difficulties of responding to such a detailed report in a short 12 days. It would receive a full government response in good time for amendments to be lodged for Stage 2 by both government and MSPs. She then underlined the centrality of land reform to the Scottish Government's programme:

> We started this process with a good Bill, and I know that we can make it an excellent Bill. As the First Minister said last week at the human rights innovation forum, we in the Government 'welcome the growing interest in the role that human rights... can play in achieving' a 'wealthier and fairer society'.
>
> Land reform is a vital part of the Government's aspirations for a fairer, more equal and socially just Scotland.

---

275. NFUS and SWT briefings, December 2015
276. Scottish Parliament OR, 16 December 2015

Underpinning the Land Reform (Scotland) Bill is an ambition to fundamentally change the framework of legal and social rights and responsibilities that determine how our land is used and governed, to address inequalities and to ensure that our land delivers the greatest benefits to our economy and all our communities.

She concluded by stressing the radical intent of the Bill but the constraints of tackling huge problems. This would be a big step towards wider goals:

We cannot roll back hundreds of years of history overnight and nor can we fix all problems in one easy step. However, we can and must focus on taking the next step in our journey. The Bill will make a series of key changes to the way in which land is governed to ensure that responsible and diverse land ownership is encouraged and supported; that transparency of land ownership in Scotland is increased; that communities are helped to have a say in how land in their area is used; that a thriving tenant farming sector in Scotland is supported; and that issues of fairness, equality and social justice that are connected to the ownership of, access to and use of land in Scotland are addressed.[277]

My own speech on behalf of the committee followed the Minister's. I covered as many points from our report as I could in the allocated time. These timings depend on the length of debates which are agreed by the Business Bureau of the Scottish Parliament. Afternoons often see constrained timings even if the subject is complex. I had to cover the ground, so to speak, in a tight ten minutes:

---

277. Scottish Parliament OR, 16 December 2015

Rob Gibson (Caithness, Sutherland and Ross) (SNP): The Land Reform (Scotland) Bill has generated a huge debate across Scotland about the very land that we stand on. The RACCE committee's extensive programme of engagement ensured that the report that we are debating today was informed by as many views and experiences as possible. The huge response to that engagement is testament to how much the Bill means to so many people.

The committee received 200 written submissions, held formal external meetings in Orkney, Skye and Dumfries and travelled to Islay, Jura, the Borders and Fife to hold public meetings to hear people's views. Following that wide consultation, we have produced a constructive report that clearly sets out how to ensure that the Bill fulfils its radical potential in practice. Supportive comments included those of Dr Calum Macleod at the University of Edinburgh, who wrote that the committee's scrutiny and report 'have provided a valuable public service in anchoring the Bill to land reform as "the art of the possible".'

The Bill is bold in its ambition and must be made clear in its detail. We share the Government's vision for land reform in Scotland and support many of the measures in the Bill and the principles behind them, but the Bill needs to be strengthened and clarified to fully deliver the ambitious and radical change that many people want.

Before I go into details, I ask members to note that Alex Fergusson dissented from our conclusions on Part 10, relating to agricultural holdings, and on some specific issues in Part 5, on a new Community Right to Buy, and that Jim Hume dissented from our conclusions on a right to buy for 1991 Act tenants. Those members will no doubt speak for themselves.

Many parts of the Bill have our full support, subject to recommended improvements, including Part 1 on the establishment of a land rights and responsibilities statement and Part 2 on the establishment of a Scottish Land Commission. Those are the most radical departures from previous Land Reform Bills.

A land rights and responsibilities statement must focus on land as a national asset for the benefit of all Scotland's people. It must underpin the process by clearly setting out a fundamental vision for land reform that is rooted in international human rights obligations. The statement will underpin the Land Commission's work on guiding Scotland forward on the land reform journey, year by year. However, the Bill must be amended to ensure that the statement and the commission's strategic plan and work programme are debated in and endorsed by this Parliament.

We want at least one of the commissioners to be a Gaelic speaker, as is the case with organisations such as the Crofting Commission and the Scottish Land Court.

We strongly support in principle, subject to recommended amendments, those parts of the Bill on engaging with communities and giving them a right to buy land to further sustainable development.

To improve engagement between communities and landowners, which the Bill seeks to do in Part 4, much more than guidance is required. Local people need to know who a person of significant control on behalf of landowners is. In addition, the consequences of non-adherence to the guidance must be spelled out.

Part 5 will introduce a right to buy to further sustainable development, but the Government must clarify whether that is intended to empower communities or to deter landowners. The proposed tests for communities are set at such a high level that amendments are needed to sections, such as section 47, to replace 'the only practicable way' with 'the only or most practicable way'. In addition, the definition of harm must be broadened to include potential impacts on the community's sustainable development objectives.

All committee members agreed that access to information is essential.

For many people, access to information is at the heart of our land problem. Evidence shows us that the proposals in Part 3 will fail unless they improve transparency and unmask some of the murky ownership models that exist in the world of shell companies, tax havens and trusts. Knowing who owns, controls and benefits from Scotland's land is a basic human right.

The evidence underlined the fact that the Bill does not go far enough to solve the problem. The Bill must be strengthened so that information can be required rather than requested, and so that anyone in Scotland can ask for that information, as people in other European countries can. However, we need to go even further. We have asked the Government to consider several options, including requiring those who want to buy land to be entities registered in the European Union, requiring them to provide a Scottish contact point and requiring them to name those who will benefit from the ownership of the land.

Part 6, which seeks to reintroduce sporting rates, needs far more work. It is fair in principle to tax sporting estates and enterprises but, as the detail of the provision emerged, the Government's case to see this as a money-raising exercise to boost the land fund was unclear. To convince us, the Government must provide a thorough, robust and evidence-based analysis before the start of Stage 2.

The deer management practices in Part 8 are deficient in many areas. It is in the public interest for the Bill to strengthen SNH's powers to ensure that it can take early action, if found necessary by mid-2016 review, without it having to wait for further legislation to be passed.

Provisions on agricultural holdings account for around half the Bill and try to address hotly-debated issues and tenancy disputes that have existed in many communities for many years. Everyone agrees that we want a thriving tenant farming sector in Scotland, the big question is how we get there.

We support the Bill's aims of: removing barriers to 1991 Act tenants buying farms; providing for forced sale of a farm if a landlord is in breach of the lease; introducing an amnesty for tenants, to note improvements that they have made; and tightening rules in cases in which landlords are seeking to make improvements to a farm.

However, other proposals are too often left to secondary legislation, such as changes to the way in which rent is set and measures to allow tenants to retire with dignity and to enable new entrants and young blood to come into the sector. We must have more detail on those provisions before Stage 2, because the annual drain on secure 1991 Act tenants and the move towards limited duration tenancies fail to ensure tenancy security and sustainable agriculture.

The majority of RACCE committee members support giving 1991 Act tenants a conditional right to buy their holdings, so that we can finally resolve a recurrent problem and move on. As ever, European Convention on Human Rights issues need to be applied proportionately, because the long-term reduction in tenancy security is detrimental to human rights.

Other issues, which are not in the Bill, should be considered at the amending stages, such as the future for small landholders, the often poor condition of tenant farmers' houses and the lack of affordable rural housing more widely. We must resolve such issues, which are intrinsic to a sustainable rural Scotland in which people can live and work.

Many eyes are on this Parliament. People want to see whether we can deliver the land reform that they want. I hope that we can match the ambition of the Scottish people and change our relationship with land, so that everyone can feel connected to it, be involved in how it is managed and benefit from its use.

The Bill is a good start and we hope that it passes Stage 1 today. However, members of all parties should realise the scale of the work that lies ahead and the role of international human rights in underpinning land reform.

We cannot ignore the warning by Scottish Land & Estates of huge financial penalties should land reform laws interfere with entrenched property rights. Is that landowner view legitimate? One witness, Kirsteen Shields, a human rights lecturer, thinks that it is not legitimate. The thrust of this radical Bill and the temper of the committee's report champion the interests of a fairer Scotland.

Ms Shields put it succinctly when she said: 'the question should not be "Is it legitimate to disturb property rights?" but "Is it legitimate not to?"'[278]

---

278. Kirsteen Shields, 'A Tale of Two Kingdoms', *New Statesman*, 14 December 2015, www.newstatesman.com/politics/staggers/2015/12/tale-two-kingdoms

My speech had been drafted and discussed with the RACCE committee clerks to cover the all ten parts of the Bill. I had little space to spice up the content. But in places I gave emphasis where I could. Thereafter 14 speeches ranged across the parties' views both from committee members and other MSPs. Some who spoke were there to make up the numbers and had little knowledge of the subject. A precis of these contributions gives glimpses of good ideas, wishful thinking and in a few cases downright opposition to any such land reform.

Sarah Boyack sought compulsory purchase orders for the creation of affordable housing as the LRRG had suggested.

Alex Fergusson believed that saving tenant farming would be a major goal with a 'glorious prize to be won' – the renewal of trust between landlords and tenants.

Nigel Donn, convener of the DPLR which had questioned why so much of the Bill would rely on regulations after it was enacted. 'Too much regulation too little detail', and such powers in secondary legislation he described in waspish tones as 'a substitute for thorough policy development'.

Graeme Dey emphasised that all parties agreed on the need for transparency of ownership, to be developed by amendments at Stage 2. Horror stories about the behaviour of land agents, he argued, would also require new powers for the Tenant Farming Commissioner to intervene.

Johann Lamont welcomed the aims of the Bill but sought as little added bureaucracy as possible.

Angus MacDonald welcomed the Minister's assurance that an amendment would ensure the appointment of at least one Gaelic speaker to the Land Commission as was the case in the Land Court.

Tavish Scott remarked that scrutinising such detailed work was extremely difficult at the tail end of a parliamentary session.

Dave Thompson emphasises that the Bill was about bad landlords, not good ones. He took biblical, literary and historical quotes to back his case, including a riposte to the editor of the *West Highland Free Press*:

> The editor of one of my local papers, the *West Highland Free Press*, seemed to doubt that the Scottish Government

was committed to any kind of radical land reform. Well, the Bill is radical. Once the Land Commission is created, it will consider land issues day in, day out, week in, week out and month in, month out for evermore.

John Lamont spoke as a true Borders Tory doubting the rules proposed for the sale of land which had been misused would be fair to existing landlords. Also, he opposed the reintroduction of shooting rates as a possible hit on local businesses.

Rhoda Grant welcomed the Bill and concluded:

I hope that it will be greatly strengthened at Stage 2. If it is, parts of the country that have been ignored for far too long will be empowered to build their own futures, which will be of benefit not only to them but to all of us.

Interestingly Alison Johnstone pressed for the most rigorous transparency of ownership. She also quoted the Scottish Affairs committee report from Westminster in seeking an end to rating exemptions for forestry and agricultural holdings to add to reintroduced shooting rates, which Andy Wightman had been calling for.

Mike Russell ranged over the deer management mess, the human rights imperative, tenancy proposals that still gave too much power to the landlord and too little to the tenants and the continued plight of small landholders such as those on the Isle of Arran but he concluded:

The issues that the Bill addresses are certainly emotive for some people, but they are emotive because they are about not only how people earn their living but how they live and have lived.

Scotland will be the richer if we engage more and more people in the issue of land and its relationship to our future. We will also be the stronger if we ensure that our legislation recognises that rights are about more than money and that equality and equity need to be embedded.

Jamie McGrigor pointed out that landlords contributed significantly to the rural economy and investment therein.

Hanzala Malik said he had

> experienced land issues and land reform in different countries. It is a minefield, with so much confusion. In particular, land that has shareholders must be clearly defined in terms of ownership as well as value, because there is nothing worse than land disputes destroying families as well as businesses.

Jean Urquhart said:

> There are many wrongs to be righted, and this Bill is to be welcomed as the first step on that long road.

Christian Allard hoped, as a committee substitute member, that he could take part in the further development of the Bill:

> I think that we need such radical reform to update where we are and to bring us to where our European neighbours already are with land use and land reform. It is very important that the eventual legislation is seen as something that brings Scotland up to date and into the 21st century.

In the summing up speeches Murdo Fraser for the Tories gave his party's predictable verdict:

> At best, the Bill will be a distraction from the real issues that face rural Scotland: depopulation, lack of connectivity, poor-quality jobs and the continuing loss of local services. Although there are some measures in the Bill that we would support, overall, we think that it is more likely to damage than to assist rural communities. For that reason, we will not support the Bill in the Stage 1 vote today.

For Labour, RACCE committee member Claudia Beamish offered strong support for the Bill's intentions. She said:

> Let there not be a reason for the Scottish Government to run scared of the fairness that the Bill will produce, but let us make it a clarion call to test and test and test the Bill and its aims before and during the Bill process so that we do not have problems with ECHR compliance afterwards. Let us not forget – as Mike Russell, Sarah Boyack and others have stressed – the other international human rights obligations that the committee examined in oral evidence.

Cabinet Secretary Richard Lochhead showed the Scottish Government''s commitment to radical change and development:

> We are in the midst of a momentous groundswell in support for action on land reform. Our proposals are about ensuring that one of our greatest assets benefits the many, not the few. The Bill is not a one-off, and it is not a quick fix. It does not have all the answers, but it will implement effective and radical land reform. It will knock down some of the obstacles that communities and our citizens face in fulfilling their potential and controlling more of their own destiny.

> Good landowners should have nothing to fear, but bad landowners – there are bad landowners in Scotland – will know that the law has empowered communities and individuals.

> Of course, we need to know who the landowners are in the first place. We need to know who owns Scotland and people who own land need to know that they have not only rights but responsibilities. People and communities need to be empowered to act when those responsibilities are not fulfilled.

The Bill and the committee's report are milestones on Scotland's land reform journey – a journey that started with feudalism but will take us to fairness. Those milestones will help to make Scotland a better country.

I urge Parliament to support the Land Reform (Scotland) Bill at Stage 1.

At decision time, a few minutes later at 5pm, the Scottish Parliament agreed to the general principles of the Land Reform (Scotland) Bill by 100 votes to 15 votes with no abstentions.

15. Opinions differ

More radical reform emerges

The Scottish Government has repeatedly stated that 'good landowners' have nothing to fear from the Land Reform Bill but I fear for tenant farming
 – Earl of Seafield, *The Press & Journal*, 16 Janurary 2016

When the mask begins to slip with our SNP masters it really does hit the floor with a thud.
 – Alan Cochrane, *The Telegraph*, 20 January 2016

The Roxburghe Estate, has only, apart from one hill farm, let small and poorer farms, some of which they themselves have previously farmed at a considerable loss.
 – Email sent to the author, 26 January 2016

Richard Lochhead does not seem to be listening. If his proposed measure goes ahead he will go down in history as the Cabinet Secretary who heralded the demise of the tenant farming sector in Scotland.
 – David Johnstone, SLaE press release, 1 February 2016

Whitehall links with Highland lairds

I arrived in Inverness on the morning of Friday 27 November. I had been invited to address the committee members of the Highland branch of SLaE to outline the Land Reform Bill. At this time, the final shape of the RACCE Stage 1 Report was nearing completion. I duly travelled to the old *Inverness Courier* building which was now the offices of land agents

Strutt & Parker. Their top-floor conference room hosted my Q&A on salient points of interest to landlords.

Some desultory debate and polite disagreement followed this Q&A and, over sandwiches, I chatted with various members of SLaE who were present, some of whom I had already met in the line of duty. One person who I had not previously met was Joanna MacPherson. She had taken over the management of Attadale Estate from her father in. Unbeknown to me at the, was that, for the previous 12 months – when MSPs were immersed in preparations for the Land Reform Bill – BBC Scotland had been filming a series on 'The Lady Lairds'. It was to chronicle a year in the lives of four women who, unusually in the hoary domain of primogeniture, managed estates in Scotland. Joanna MacPherson was one of these women.

By 2015, the actions of the MacPhersons had already affected my constituents in the communities of south-west Ross. In the 1960s, Ross and Cromarty County Council attempted to open a road (which was to replace the ferry across the narrows from Lochcarron to Strome) on the A890 road from Lochcarron to Kyle of Lochalsh. The Attadale Estate seemed to offer the perfect inland route to do so. The 30,000 acres had been in the family since Joanna MacPherson's grandfather purchased them from another financier and blood sports enthusiast, Baron Schroder, in 1952. They had since maintained the sanctity of a private estate – except for hosting the local Highland Games and opening their prize-winning gardens, originally laid out by the Schroders, to summer visitors. The MacPherson family thus vetoed the inland route through Attadale. As a result, the A890 that opened in 1970 runs alongside the Kyle railway line for several miles below unstable cliffs.

These cliffs, long wired and scoured for loose debris have often crumbled and blocked the road, costing local authorities millions of pounds in repairs over the decades. A severe rockfall in the winter of 2011 closed the road for three months. School pupils travelling to Plockton High School from Lochcarron had passed by only 40 minutes before the 20 tonnes of rock fell onto the road. Parents were horrified, but local opinion was still divided about a solution: some wanted a bridge and some wanted a tidal barrage at the Strome Ferry narrows. As local MSPs, Dave Thompson and I championed a potential new route inland through Attadale land, and through Glen Udalain, leading to Forestry Commission tracks, as a less expensive option. The Highland Council, as the successor local authority, also costed various routes. Yet, even today, the issue is unresolved.

Regular maintenance and mounting costs to the taxpayer followed these road closures. Huge detours have been necessary on several occasions. Recently, the Highlands and Islands Transport Partnership (HITRANS), the integrated transport body, suggested a road straddling the railway line as a permanent solution. Otherwise, bringing the Attadale land into use would need a compulsory purchase order. This would, no doubt, become a very lengthy and costly process for the Highland Council to even consider; Joanna MacPherson and her family would most likely vigorously resist it in court. So, as I introduced myself to Joanna at the SLaE meeting in 2015 this was all in the back of my mind. But there was a more recent connection between us too.

Links between major landed families in the Highlands and high government positions in London are nothing new. However, Sir Nick MacPherson, Joanna's brother was, at that time, Permanent Secretary at the UK Treasury and had served three consecutive Chancellors. This Eton- and Oxford-educated high official had little interest in his parental domain, we were told. Nevertheless, his very vocal and partisan role in the Scottish independence referendum (he publicly advised Tory Chancellor George Osborne against any agreement to share the pound sterling with a would-be independent Scotland) drew Alex Salmond's ire. The former First Minister's later described MacPherson's comments as a 'rant'. With this intervention, Sir Nick had fundamentally altered the relationship of civil servants and politicians. MacPherson told The Strand Group, a London policy seminar, in January 2015, that

> where people are seeking to destroy the fabric of the state... the normal rules of Civil Service impartiality do not apply.

He was in post as head of the Treasury till he retired in March 2016 and was soon ennobled as Lord MacPherson of Earl's Court.[279]

---

279. Alex Salmond, *The Dream Shall Never Die: 100 Days that Changed Scotland Forever*, William Collins, 2015, pp.20–21

In late 2015, I had been probing the transfer of management powers over the Crown Estate assets in Scotland as mooted by the Smith Commission. A Treasury transfer scheme had been concocted and, to Scottish annoyance, this would preclude the lucrative partnership of the City of Edinburgh Council and Gibraltar Holdings which controlled the Fort Kinaird shopping centre situated in the south-east of Edinburgh. The Fort Kinaird LP had been set up using an English law of 1907, the Limited Partnerships Act. And this was the Treasury's excuse to exclude it from the Scottish assets list.[280] This was much argued over in the Devolution Further Powers committee of which I was also a member. RACCE and the Scottish Government were furious at this sleight of hand. So I wrote to the UK Government, in my capacity as convener of RACCE, to seek clarification on this decision not long before I met Joanna MacPherson at the SLaE meeting in Inverness. When I introduced myself at this meeting and quipped that I had recently written to her brother, she replied, 'he's only a civil servant'...

Land grab rebels speak up

An opinion piece, 'The Highland Clearances and Land Reform in Scotland: The Country's Semi-Feudal Great Estates Face Reform', originally written by Ben Judah for *Standpoint* magazine, appeared in a shortened form in *The Independent* on 15 December, the day before the Stage 1 Land Reform Bill debate in Holyrood. Published, no doubt, with the debate in mind.[281] I was alerted to its content of differing Highland attitudes to the Land Reform Bill, but I kept my focus on the upcoming debate .

In the article, Judah opened with the historical perspective of the Clearances; particularly the sight of the Mannie, that huge statue of the

---

280. Devolution (Further Powers) Committee, 'New Powers for Scotland: Final Report on the Scotland Bill', Third Report, 2016
281. Ben Judah, 'The Highland Clearances and Land Reform in Scotland: The Country's Semi-Feudal Great Estates Face Reform', *The Independent*, 15 December 2015, www.independent.co.uk/news/uk/politics/the-highland-clear-ances-and-land-reform-in-scotland-the-countrys-semi-feudal-great-estates-face-a6774631.html

1st Duke of Sutherland which towers over Golspie. He also cited the independence referendum result and the surge in SNP support as the prompt for frustrated Yes supporters to demand radical land reform as a step on the road to Scottish freedom. This had been highlighted by some SNP members at the October annual conference six weeks beforehand.

I read Judah's views on the 17 December as I headed home to Ross-shire. The genuine strength of feeling he heard on his travels struck me. Having set the scene around the Mannie and the 'SNP' reply of the emigrants statue at Helmsdale, funded by Dennis Macleod, he reported on the forthright views of a Yes activist from the vicinity of Aviemore. His second interviewee was a reluctant gamekeeper near Rannoch. And his third was a landlord-in-waiting, Donald Cameron, the Younger of Locheil, heir to 72,000 acres in Lochaber. The first two were anonymised, Donald Cameron was not. He came over as moderation personified. Six months later he would be elected as a Tory Regional MSP for Highlands and Islands in the Conservative ranks swelled by their opposition to further independence referendum.

The first interviewee, the 'land grab rebel' in Badenoch, Judah dubbed as 'Alex'. 'Alex' duly spoke, in graphic detail, of rural communities at the mercy of lairdly whims. Alex had seen the referendum effects on several local estates and the subsequent uncertainty for tenants created by changes of landowner:

> That old laird, from the estate, we remember him, back in the referendum, he had his huge big poster: 'Delighted to be united', or whatever. But then six months later, he sold up. There were families living and farming there, and one day to the next, the new owner, some billionaire, went 'Leave'. I tell you, it was like a new Highland Clearances for them, it was.

Second, Judah interviewed the gamekeeper near Rannoch who was 'unwilling to make eye contact' but confirmed that many people he knew had sympathy with what he called the 'SNP message', ie 'against the English landowners'. The ghillie continued:

But now we know they are going to interfere with our way of doing things, those of us up the hill don't like them at all.

Finally, an emollient Donald Cameron told Ben Judah:

Various people have set up this, I think, false argument: it's not private land equals bad, community landowners equals good. I feel part of my local community. I don't feel separate from them. These simplistic divides are not there in real life. When you get to an estate you see a vibrant business that is employing local people and attracting them to the area. And were they not all tarnished with the brush of landowners, the SNP would be hailing them for their enterprise.

Cameron eventually referred to the Clearances, which he said, were a 'great stain on our history and reputation', but that we can't be shackled by it. 'We are in 2015. And life goes on.'

It is understandable that Judah linked the 2014 referendum with the history of the enforced evictions and British government reprisals after Culloden (which Donald Cameron explained away as land myths). Even so, Judah, an experienced international correspondent, tellingly concluded that the Scots'

role in the conquest of India, and the Protestant mission, are not glorious stories anymore. And in that absence, the Clearances loom largest.

Ben Judah's work covered the likes of the war between Russia and Georgia and other flashpoints. His books on Russia and London little prepare us for this international reporter's sally up north. Yet his background research was thorough, and his two interviewees quotes cannot be brushed aside as sensationalist metropolitan hype. They hold up yet another mirror of distinctive attitudes to Scotland's land issues from opposing points at a crucial time in the parliamentary progress of the Land Reform Bill.

Tough deer controls 'political prejudice'
Three days after reading Judah's article, another shot was fired at the deer management proposals in the Land Reform Bill. The *Sunday Times'* (Scotland) reporter Mark Macaskill's claimed that

> a parliamentary committee dominated by SNP MSPs has 'misrepresented' the environmental threat from red deer to suit the Scottish Government's 'prejudice' against wealthy landowners.

In his article, Macaskill rehashed figures mustered by Richard Cooke on behalf of the Association of Deer Management Groups as evidence to prove his hypothesis. Cooke purportedly showed that data his group had shared with SNH had been ignored by RACCE, describing our report's conclusions on deer management as 'prejudicial and unjustified'.

Mid Scotland and Fife Tory MSP Murdo Fraser opined,

> people are very sceptical when they see the workings of a parliament that is supposed to be balanced.

Would he ever get over the SNP elected victory in 2011 as a majority government? After all it was achieved despite the Scottish Parliament's explicit use of the D'Hondt voting system specifically to stop SNP progress. It followed that committee convenerships under D'Hondt would give government appointees many of these. In RACCE's case, to Fraser's chagrin, I was voted to be that SNP convener.

Mark Macaskill's piece then quoted Richard Seaman, an Edinburgh-based chartered surveyor of Goldsmith & Co (Estates):

> The recommendations by the committee are clearly based on political prejudice rather than fact.

Macaskill noted at the end, he had been unable to contact me for comment.

On reading the story, I assumed that my mobile phone had failed to pick up Macaskill's message in good time; phone signals are notoriously poor in many parts of the Highlands. Since several parties are represented on the committee, and had voted for this section of our Stage 1 Report, the prattling of the lairds and their Tory supporters to *The Sunday Times* was predictable.[282]

There were to be no recess weeks for the Scottish Government's Land Reform Bill team and lawyers until Richard Lochhead and Aileen McLeod were satisfied that their response to the committee's report was comprehensive and offered to strengthen the Bill. That response was published on 5 January in time for amendments to be lodged for the Stage 2 hearings.

---

282. Mark Macaskill, 'Deer Threat Claims Fuelled by "Prejudice"', *The Sunday Times*, 20 December 2015, www.thetimes.co.uk/article/deer-threat-claims-fuelled-by-prejudice-gxq2d6qqxpf

16. An exciting New Year
Lairds fulminate while ministers formulate

Does it lie within the mischief of the Bill?
– Ross Finnie

*Crucial amendments over the last few weeks mean the Land
Reform Bill is a feistier beast than it would otherwise have been
and much of that's down to public pressure.*
– Lesley Riddoch, *The National*, 11 February 2016

The process to develop the transparency section of the Land Reform
Bill requires to be told in one sequence; there was widespread approval
across the political spectrum of the mission to know who owned Scotland. But the New Year of 2016 promised a continuation of hostilities
from critics of the Bill. The coordinated critiques by the lairds and land
agents raised their fears about the viability of the spread of community
ownership. These groups also criticised proposals from the Cabinet
Secretary to offer rights for secure tenants to assign their tenancies to
other secure tenants. But were the interests of property owners being
seriously threatened?

Transparency breakthrough
The spark for the demand for more precise use of human rights was
ignited with the Scottish Government response to the RACCE Stage 1
Report. This response finally arrived on 5 January after many hours of
Civil Service overtime spent during the festive recess. The document
suggested that incorporating international covenants was assured by
the Scottish Government's duty to include them in keeping with clauses
of Scotland Act 1998. The Bill team argued that explicit mention of

every likely UN document would not be helpful. But. they would try to include amendments that underlined the international commitments which was RACCE's stated wish[283]

Taking powers to find out who owns Scotland – The inside story

Information on the control of land in Part 3 of the Bill proved to be a practical means to utilise international obligations, standards and practices. This was curated by five-sided talks that would reach a more thorough delivery of transparency over land ownership to be placed on the face of the Bill.

Between 4 December 2015, the launch date of the RACCE Stage 1 Report, and 16 March 2016, the Stage 3 debate on the Bill, the SHRC, led by Professor Alan Miller; Megan MacInnes of Global Witness; Peter Peacock of CLS, a former MSP and minister; Graeme Dey MSP of RACCE; and the Minister Dr Aileen McLeod and her Bill Team embarked on a series of multilateral debates in private to reach a final agreement. This is testament to the extended civic engagement in the parliamentary process and of the willingness of an SNP Government to reach a commonly agreed and much more advanced outcome.

Public engagement with each phase of the land reform process had drawn hundreds of responses and many were from individuals, according to the analysis produced for the Scottish Government.[284] When RACCE made a call for written evidence over 200 submissions were received. These required analysis before the committee could decide on the range of witnesses that were to give oral evidence. As this was conducted, three main priorities kept appearing. First, calls for transparency as to who owns Scotland; second, the need for more diversity of land ownership; and third, a supportive tax system to ensure all who could pay did so. I would add that, on our extensive committee tour of Scotland from Kirkwall to Dumfries where we met 354 people, the subject of affordable housing was also a heartfelt and repeated theme.

The transparency debate stemmed from a Scottish Government view

---

283. Scottish Government response to RACCE, 'Stage 1 Report', 5 Jan 2016
284. Independent Analysis of Consultation Results for the Scottish Government

that, although transparency was a prominent demand, the RoS's primary task was to give legal certainty of ownership via a map-based register. This, in December 2015, contained 58% of Scottish properties covering 26% of the total landmass. The venerable Register of Sasines, with its far from accurate written entries deposited over the past four centuries, was slowly, far too slowly, being replaced by a map-based system. The Land Registration etc. (Scotland) Act 2012 expected public land to be mapped by 2019 and private land to follow on.[285] It should be noted that two of the best European examples of multi-layered digitised and map-based land registration systems are found in Switzerland and Spain. These have taken several decades to achieve completion. Scotland only has one layer, that of title, and a cash-strapped devolved government with strong intent but limited means.[286]

Another pertinent register was the Register of Crofts. It was set up by the Crofting Reform (Scotland) Act 2010 and its dominant characteristics are:

> It is a free-to-search, public register of crofts, common grazings, and land held in runrig... Like the Land Register, the Crofting Register is map-based. It shows defined extents of land and property on the Ordnance Survey map. It also contains information on the tenant or owner-occupier crofter on the land, as well as the landlord and/or the landowner of the registered land... the registration of crofts, now falls to the Keeper of the Registers of Scotland. Registration in the Crofting Register is compulsory on the occurrence of certain events which mainly relate to actions that need a regulatory application to the Crofting Commission for approval to change some aspect of the croft land (for example, the assignation or division of a croft).[287]

---

285. Land Registration etc. (Scotland) Act, 2012
286. Ethan Webster, 'Scottish Land Reform 2015: Land Registry and Ownership'
287. Registers of Scotland, www.ros.gov.uk

If crofters had to enter the map-based register, why not all other land owners? Why not decide an accelerated and compulsory approach for both private and public land? In 2012, the minister Fergus Ewing was conscious of the limited resources and personnel at the Registers and the size of the task being asked of them; there were years of work to follow.[288] Thanks to Alasdair Reid and Samantha Pollock of the Scottish Parliament's invaluable information service, SPICe, we have evidence as to why this process takes time, here and abroad, and that map-based land mapping can have many purposes. Also, it is 'free-to-search' in other countries as is the Crofting Register in Scotland.[289]

My intern, Ethan Webster, from Edinburgh University's Academy of Governance programme, gathered a wide range of information on land registry and ownership in December 2015 – the time when RACCE published our Stage 1 Report on the Land Reform Bill 2015. He delved into the restrictive rules of Denmark and Norway which protected local ownership of land. He noted the important opt-out in Denmark that was agreed in 1973, on its accession to the EEC, the same year as the UK. These rules prohibited the purchase of land by non-Danish owners (eg of holiday homes); Government permission was required in special cases. It's an example I will return to later[290]

The debate about how to achieve transparency of ownership had been skewed into a European context by LRRG recommendation 11 in its final report of May 2014:

> The Review Group recommends that the Scottish Government should make it incompetent for any legal entity not registered in a Member State of the European Union to register title to land in the Land Register of Scotland, to improve traceability and accountability in the public interest.[291]

---

288. SPICe briefing, 2016
289. Webster, 'Scottish Land Reform 2015'
290. LRRG, 'The Land of Scotland and the Common Good', 2014
291. Scottish Government response to LRRG, 'The Land of Scotland and the Common Good', 2014

We should remember the wording of the land reform consultation which followed:

> The Scottish Government understands that occasionally it can be difficult to trace and contact landowners, leading to practical difficulties for those seeking to engage with them or for enforcers of fiscal or environmental obligations.

> The Review Group recommended that the Scottish Government should make it incompetent for any legal entity not registered in a Member State of the European Union (EU) to register title to land in the Land Register of Scotland, in order to improve traceability and accountability.

> The Scottish Government supports the aims of this recommendation and is considering how any potential measures could work in practice while taking into consideration relevant policy and legal issues.[292]

While individual respondents were overwhelmingly in favour of an EU based approach, landowners and land agents were less impressed. So, the Bill looked carefully at the 'relevant policy and legal issues' and, when the Bill as published, it was dubbed a climb down by campaigners. When it came to the Scottish Government response, in January 2016, to RACCE's Stage 1 Report it was made plain why the EU approach would not work. Minister Dr Aileen McLeod called it beyond the competence of the Scottish Parliament. The notion had been proposed by Andy Wightman to the LRRG and pursued by Scottish Green MSP Patrick Harvie in Parliament. On 5 January 2016, the Scottish Government promised to strengthen Part 3 of the Bill but, bearing in mind the costs and who had a need to know on ownership details, their answer was still not convincing to MSPs and human rights activists.[293] On 11 January, Megan MacInnes of Global Witness reached her third draft of 'Key points on improving transparency and information disclosure in

292. ibid.
293. Scottish Government strengthen Part 3

the LRSB [Land Reform (Scotland) Bill]'. With the help of independent legal opinion, she presented her detailed and cogent arguments to replace Sections 35 and 36 of the Bill with further changes to the Land Registration etc. Act 2012.[294]

The public interest argument for disclosure had been flagged up by the UK Small Business, Enterprise and Employment Act 2015. This included the impetus for the disclosure of beneficial owners of companies to be held in a public register. The Act appears to have motives that go far beyond tackling money laundering and terrorism and its provisions are fundamental to open government. This Act had responded to the fourth EU money laundering Directive and so applies to Scottish Government policies.[295] Indeed, SLaE had given evidence to RACCE at the Land Reform Bill Stage 1, Doug McAdam stated:

> It's crucial there is a clear point of contact and face of the trust or company is identified and ideally also the beneficial owner, if there is one behind that.[296]

Furthermore, we heard that the Voluntary Guidelines on Tenure (VGGT) recommends such disclosure to all states.

Megan explored the limitations made by ECHR Articles 6, 8, 14 and Article 1 Protocol 1 to encourage the intent of the Scottish Government for as much transparency as could be justified in law. Undoubtedly, parallel legal consultations by government lawyers arrived at similar conclusions. Thus, the exchange of ideas between campaigners and officials bore fruit. Dr Aileen McLeod MSP, Minister for Land Reform, announced on 11 January 2016:

> I am pleased to confirm that the Government plans to create a public register of who controls land in Scotland and to enable this we will amend the Land Reform Bill at stage three to give the powers required to create a public

---

294. Megan MacInnes, private papers
295. Small Business, Enterprise and Employment Act, 2015
296. RACCE OR, Doug Adam, October 2015

register which will contain the information needed to give greater transparency about who controls our land.

> More work is required on complex legal issues, such as what information should be disclosed and how to protect the privacy of individuals. So, I will put in place the necessary powers to allow further work to be done and ensure that this Bill delivers a framework that gives, subject to parliamentary scrutiny, detailed information about who controls land in Scotland.[297]

Briefing RACCE members, Aileen confirmed that EU issues such as the free movement of capital between member states and with third countries made an EU based registry plan *ultra vires*. Also, tax evasion and other such matters were reserved to Westminster. Trusts could keep the issue of beneficial ownership secret so that communities or individuals could still fail to find the identity of a person with significant control over land.

The way forward was to involve new tasks for RoS. Powers were planned to provide for a public register of persons that have a controlling interest in land. Measures to take forward the registration of public land by 2019 and private land by 2024 required clear and accessible information. RoS, it was announced, was committed to Scotland's Land Information System so that issues relating to an area of land could be disclosed in a single enquiry. The same day CLS announced on its website:

> Today's announcement is clearly a breakthrough and obviously a significant step in the right direction... it is good to see a clear intention to act on this.[298]

On 14 of January, the very next day, Megan MacInnes concurred in a blog and added:

---

297. RACCE OR, Aileen McLeod, 11 January 2016
298. Community Land Scotland, 13 January 2016

This announcement has completely changed the terms of the debate about transparency in land ownership in Scotland and this can only be good.[299]

On 20 January 2016 RACCE began consideration of Stage 2. On transparency Graeme Dey MSP lodged an amendment based on full disclosure of ownership in the registration process. He said:

I welcome the Scottish Government's commitment on transparency of ownership, which the committee received in the formal response to our Stage 1 report. The fact that the minister has indicated an intention to lodge amendments in that regard at Stage 3 represents progress on reaching the goal – which is shared by stakeholders, the committee, the wider public and the Government – of us as a nation having a far clearer idea of who owns and controls land in Scotland.

Given the complex nature of the issue and the fact that my amendments may have flaws – despite the considerable work that Megan MacInnes of Global Witness and Peter Peacock of Community Land Scotland did on them – I recognise that the minister may not be entirely comfortable with accepting them, not least because the Government has had only a week to consider them. However, I lodged them in the spirit of common purpose on the principles of transparency and because I believe that they point to a possible and implementable way forward.[300]

Patrick Harvie MSP appeared at the committee to lodge amendments that pursued the registration under the EU approach. The minister

---

299. Megan MacInnes, 'Sunlight or Shadow: Will the Government's New Public Register of Land Ownership be Effective in Improving Transparency', Land Matters, 14 January 2016, www.andywightman.com/page/9?pa
300. RACCE OR, 11 January 2016

rehearsed the difficulties of inconsistent records in each EU Member State and in the event only the two Labour members voted for his stance. All parties agreed that the greatest transparency was essential and Graeme Dey's amendment was passed unanimously.

This was welcomed in press comment with optimism that radical land reform measures would now be possible in a Bill that had seemed to some commentators too limp. Transparency was widely supported across the land ownership divide, but journalist and Our Land campaigner Lesley Riddoch and Common Space preferred the Green Party's amendment on registration in the EU. She echoed hopes that it too could be incorporated in the Bill. Riddoch admitted that that many land reform supporters were 'astonished and chuffed' that Graeme Dey's amendment had been met with support from the minister who had not opposed the amendment and then undertook to bring in a watertight wording to be debated at Stage 3.[301] Riddoch was at pains to suggest even Scottish Government lawyers and policymakers had given long overdue recognition that the current Bill 'really is unacceptably limp in key parts'. She praised campaigners for effecting this welcome climbdown. They had ensured in Riddoch's words that they had 'turned land reform into a litmus test of the SNP's capacity to deliver radical change'. Nevertheless, she concluded 'this week, the chances of a radical Land Reform Bill got a whole lot better.'[302]

RACCE members who had absorbed the impact of the legal advice on what was achievable, and listened to the minister, realised that the LRRG recommendation and its preference for a Europe-wide solution, was not well founded in legal terms. Radical MSPs inside parliament had worked with well-informed NGOs and provided the breakthrough which the wider public was demanding.[303] In the event, criticism of

---

301. Lesley Riddoch, 'The Land Reform Bill is a Win But There's Still Ground to be Gained', *The National*, 21 January 2016, www.thenational.scot/comment/14861480.Lesley_Riddoch_The_Land_Reform_Bill_is_a_win_but_there_s_still_ground_to_be_gained/

302. ibid.

303. Scottish Parliament OR, Land Reform (Scotland) Bill Stage 3, 16 March 2016

the Stage 2 process that took place over four Wednesday mornings (and early afternoons) from 20 January to 10 February was much more agitated about Part 10 on agricultural holdings and moves by the Scottish Government to introduce new clauses that widened the scope for assignation and succession of farm tenancies.

At Stage 3, on 16 March, the Harvie EU based transparency amendments were again rejected and the minister's revised amendments to Sections 35 and 36 were passed when, as promised, they took the spirit of Graeme Dey's work and made it legally defensible. Such was the outcome of an excellent collaboration by the NGOs, MSPs and government to achieve a new and enhanced role for RoS that was set to include questions in the land registration process that would establish 'persons with a controlling interest' in the same entry as the confirmation of who had a 'real interest' in the property as in the ancient Register of Sasines under an enhanced map-based system.[304]

Scottish Government responds to Stage 1 Report on Land Reform Bill

A 76-page ministerial response to the RACCE report appeared on 5 January 2016. Consisting of 296 paragraphs it was a detailed and measured document. Readers could see a range of ideas for progress, many of which acknowledged the committee's views. Others, with the ghostly imprint of lawyers' advice avoided ECHR and similarly fraught litigious traps.[305]We pored over the details, as did many others. Some of them took aim within a very few days.

On 10 January, I received an email from Ewen MacPherson of Attadale noting my discussion at the SLaE meeting before Christmas with his daughter Joanna and my letter to his son Sir Nicholas. MacPherson raised concerns about the costs to taxpayers of many existing land buyouts, he mentioned Eigg and Gigha, that would, in his words, 'need further public funding'. He went on:

What will occur in the future if it is decided that one of

---

304. ibid.
305. Scottish Government response to RACCE, 'Stage 1 Report', 5 Janurary 2016

the buyouts is not viable and that no further public money is available. Will it be put up for auction? The history of governments messing about with property rights is not encouraging.[306]

Curiously, land agents Bidwells, in their winter newsletter *News from Scotland*, asked very similar questions. An article described as 'Expert Advice' by Raymond Henderson under the headline, 'Clarity required on land reform vision', claimed that there was no over-riding vision by the Scottish Government:

> It seems illogical to produce a Bill when there is no clarity in what it intends to achieve.

As if to ignore this stricture, Mr Henderson then claimed a, 'lack of transparency in relation to funding of community ownership'. Presumably the same sources of funding tapped so successfully by private estates was what he meant? And again, from Bidwells:

> We believe it is appropriate that before embarking on a much accelerated, tremendously ambitious programme of further transfer, there should be a process of proper checks and balances – a serious look at the real costs and liabilities that go with land ownership and levels of ongoing public funding that may be required in many cases. As taxpayers, the people of Scotland have a right to see the full picture.[307]

SLaE research suggested that large tracts of hill land under deer and grouse often make a loss and that many landlords subsidise their private kingdoms in the hills from non-land-based income. Ewen MacPherson clearly confirmed this.

In the Farming Supplement of the *P&J* on 16 January, the Earl of

---

306. Email – E MacPherson to R Gibson, 10 January 2016
307. Bidwells, *News from Scotland*, Winter 2015

Seafield called for the conversion of secure farm tenancies to Modern Limited Duration Tenancies. This would reduce the security of tenant farmers and suit the lairds, allowing them to get more leverage on their land holdings. The Earl objected strongly to Mr Lochhead's intention to propose that a retiring farmer with a 1991 tenancy could assign his lease to a new entrant or improving farmer with continued security of tenure. Seafield amplified the longstanding SLaE view that this 'could have a detrimental impact on landlords'. Proprietors seeking to claw back control of their farmland had been featured prominently in the evidence received by MSPs up and down the country. The lairds always assured us of their full support for a vibrant tenanted sector, but only if the tenants were subject to their wishes and, of course, to their own business plans.[308] The Earl of Stair also wrote to me on very similar lines at that time. He claimed Mr Lochhead's proposal would 'perpetuate the stalemate and tie in disputes and legal challenge for another decade'.[309]

I decided, as a result of this heavy lobbying by landlords, that a personal statement was required ahead of Stage 2's deliberations. The lairds had complained about bias and about the negative angles of the Bill's proposals to landlords letting land. The return of shooting rates came a close second. On 17 January, I released a personal statement to sympathetic media outlets and awaited the inevitable reaction.

News Release: Amending stage of the Land Reform Bil – A time for sustainable development!

I read the press and pressure group comments about how amending the Land Reform Bill is down to hardy campaigners. Yes, but many of these operate inside Holyrood and indeed inside the RACCE committee charged with the Bill's scrutiny and development.

You would think the oft repeated tale of grassroots SNP members demanding a more radical Land Reform Bill was like a cattle prod to the

---

308. The Earl of Seafield, *Press & Journal*, 16 January 2016
309. Letter – The Earl of Stair to R Gibson, undated

Scottish Government to apply the Land Reform Review Group report to the letter. In fact, the quiet work of dialogue and debate inside the Parliament has focused minds on ways to enhance the original proposals. Giving them a cutting edge that campaigners outside Holyrood would wish also requires knowledge of various lobbyists' perspectives and of MSPs' own engagement to influence the Bill team's response.

Happily, the SHRC and specific human rights lawyers along with CLS have engaged in the substance of evolving the aims of sections of the Bill. A variety of MSP and Land Reform Minister proposed amendments have appeared for the first six parts of the Bill. More amendments will follow for parts seven to ten.

I can see that the landowners and their organisations have been hyper-active, applying various tactics. I have never heard from so many Lords, Earls, and Dukes in my life. Take the Earl of Seafield, who wrote in the *P&J* farming section on 16 January. Discussing a proposed government amendment said to allow secure 1991 tenant farmers to assign their tenancies to new secure tenants, Lord Seafield says this 'will clearly impact on the property rights of landlords…'

That view has been echoed by other noble lords as proprietors of agricultural tenanted estates. Yet no heed is paid by SLaE and its members to the shrinking of tenants' rights since the 1948 Act. On the contrary, SLaE spokesperson Stuart Young from Dunecht Estates warned RACCE last March that their senior counsel's opinion saw an ECHR breach on open assignation proposals that could 'ultimately leave the Government with the prospect of a hefty £600 million for paying compensation to landlords'. So, no pressure then?

Peter Hetherington in his recent book, *Whose Land Is Our Land*, interviewed the Duke of Northumberland and his cousin the Duke of Buccleuch, who with many of their noble friends he dubs 'property developers'.

Their interests are in letting land to maximise income while allegedly offering minimum security for their tenants. Feeding the nation appears to be a poor second, argues Hetherington, to keeping a grasp of every acre of Scotland's soil where so very few own so very much.

While these tenancy matters will come at the end of this five-week cycle of amendments to the Bill, the landed interest is getting in a polite lather. Alex Fergusson MSP speaking for them called the Bill 'rushed'. According to their logic it should be a separate Bill in the next parliament, not now – not ever?

Clearly the lobbying gets intense as the committee reaches Stage 2. I welcome the arguments and the government's responses. Press comments have rarely analysed the detail but merely cut and pasted the various press releases. Pressure from commentators should not be mistaken for radical opinions that have grasped the complexities of making ECHR compliance work for the common good. However, the general thrust of serious and often collaborative amendments will show that an overwhelming majority of MSPs support the radical thrust of the Land Reform Bill that puts human rights, rather than solely property rights, as the driving force of the public interest.

Richard Lochhead and Aileen McLeod wrote to the RACCE committee in early January:

> Considering the Stage 1 report, and the Stage 1 debate, the Scottish Government will work to strengthen the Bill where possible to ensure that it will contribute to our core objectives for land reform:
>
> - Encourage and support responsible and diverse land ownership;
> - Increase transparency of land ownership in Scotland;
> - Help ensure communities have a say in how land in their area is used;
> - Address issues of fairness, equality and social justice connected to the ownership of, access to and use of land in Scotland; and
> - Help to underpin a thriving tenant farming sector in Scotland.

I believe the Scottish Parliament will see this Bill gets to be as substantially radical as humanly possible at this time.

– *Rob Gibson MSP*[310]

(I write this as an individual but conscious of my role as RACCE convener for this crucial stage in the land reform journey) 17.1.16

The expected retorts by landlords duly arrived. They opposed key sections of the Bill despite it being based on lengthy consultation and in the case of agricultural tenancies following years of prolonged debate. My inbox filled up as critics decrying my 'bias' vented their spleen. David Johnstone SLaE chairman questioned my position regards his organisation.

> Of course, landowners have their own commercial interests but I am sorry that you felt obliged to portray us as people with only our own interests at heart. I would suggest that in 21st century Scotland we are business people who hold rural Scotland dear and strive to make it a better place for all.[311]

Alan Cochrane wrote, in the *Daily Telegraph* on 20 January, that 'behind the moderate mask we can see the true face of Nationalism'. He also referred to the RACCE scrutiny of the Bill as a 'polite fiction'. And he went on:

> As far as Mr Gibson and the SNP members on the committee are concerned its job is not to scrutinise the Bill but to radicalise its proposals as far as they can, thereby, changing forever the nature of land ownership in Scotland.

310. Rob Gibson, 17 January 2016
311. Letter – D Johnstone to R Gibson, 26 January 2016

Alan Cochrane poured more spleen on my motives and partiality ahead of Stage 2 debates:

> Given the way all Holyrood committees are stuffed with Nats there was never any chance of a balanced view on this or any other legislation from the SNP Government.[312]

What a pity his remarks blithely ignored the biggest section of Scots voters who elected a majority SNP Government? That's something no Tories can ever stomach. Cochrane made that plain. He ignored the Lib Dem, Labour, Green and SNP votes for each stage of the Bill making the measure a reflection of the broad wishes of Scottish voters. Why let such facts get in the way of his right-wing polemic? The well-documented anti-land reform campaign by landowning interests makes Mr Cochrane's remarks unfit for serious consideration. But then the language of politics in the Farage era has been coarsening and the *Daily Telegraph* has not been slow to join in.

The landlords had attempted to stop a wider range of persons entitled to succeed to a secure farm tenancy. They failed. Unfortunately, the Lib Dem member Jim Hume often joined Alex Fergusson to press the lairds' case. SNP and Labour members saw the amendments through. So, the committee wasn't just 'stuffed with Nats'.

The SPICe briefing which was published on 7 March 2016, ahead of Stage 3 of the Bill, and compiled by Tom Edwards, Wendy Kenyon and Alasdair Reid, explains the key changes voted through at Stage 2:

> The Land Reform (Scotland) Bill (the Bill) was introduced to the Scottish Parliament on 22 June 2015. Stage 2 of the Bill took place at our meetings of the Rural Affairs, Climate Change and Environment Committee between 20 January and 10 February 2016, where the committee considered over 300 amendments.
>
> Significant amendments include a change in approach to Part 3 – Information on About the Control of Land, where

---

312. Alan Cochrane, *Daily Telegraph*, 20 January 2016

the Government is expected to bring forward broad regulation making powers at Stage 3 which will provide for the creation of a public register which requires the disclosure of information about persons who control land. A significant change was also made to Part 10 of the Bill in relation to farm tenancies. As introduced the Bill provided a regulation making power for Scottish Ministers to allow 1991 Act tenancies to be converted into the new form of Minimum Limited Duration Tenancy, also created by Part 10. Government amendments passed during Stage 2 would now allow a 1991 Act tenant to sell or assign their tenancy to an individual who is either a 'new entrant' or 'progressing in farming' (terms to be defined in subordinate legislation) having first given the landlord the opportunity to buy the lease back at a price fixed by an independent valuation. The tenancy would remain a 1991 Act tenancy, with the same rights eg of security of tenure.[313]

Other changes mentioned had included specifying the International Covenant on Economic, Social and Cultural Rights, and the Voluntary Guidelines on the Responsible Governance of Tenure of Land, Fisheries and Forests as relevant human rights that Ministers must have regard to.

As described above, the significance of the transparency amendment was seen as a signal by campaigners that the Bill was being beefed-up. To members of RACCE we were seeing the fruits of quiet persuasion based on what was legally valid being endorsed by government following MSP and NGO ground work. As per parliamentary rules, the Stage 2 Report was published on 18 February so that Stage 3 amendments could be lodged in good time.[314]

---

313. Tom Edwards, Wendy Kenyon and Alasdair Reid, 'SPICe Briefing: Land Reform (Scotland) Bill: Stage 3', SPICe, 7 March 2016, www.parliament. scot/ResearchBriefingsAndFactsheets/S4/SB_16-24_Land_Reform_Scotland_Bill_Stage_3.pdf
314. Scottish Parliament, Stage 2 call for amendments, 18 February 2016

17. Stage 3 concluded successfully

Amendments at Stage 3 usually fall into three types. First, there is the tidying up done by the government of the day along with member's amendments discussed and sympathetic to the government aims for the Bill. Second, there are probing amendments to draw out a sympathetic government response. Third, failed amendments from Stage 2 that members wish to pursue to a vote to make a political point that are usually agreed for debate by the Presiding Officer.

In a large Bill, such as this was, the range of concerns took several hours to debate and vote on. Contentious matters raised included attempts by Tory and Lib Dem members in Section 47 to curtail the range of discretion of government, both in the letter of the law and in regulations to follow, over CRTB issues which affected existing farm tenants. These were rebuffed by ministers and voted down by SNP, Labour and Green MSPs.

Sarah Boyack and Patrick Harvie pursued ideas of giving compulsory purchase powers to local authorities to provide land for allotments. Ministers agreed to consult on the matter if the forthcoming election in May returned an SNP Government.

Patrick Harvie led on taxing vacant and derelict land by having these registered amongst other landed property owners. Again, the government offered to consult after the election on the subject as conflicts could arise between local authorities and central government concerning the appropriate rates to levy. He also pressed his proposal to have all property owners registered in an EU jurisdiction to promote openness of ownership. As was previously debated at Stage 2 this was likely to be beyond the competence of the Scottish Parliament's powers. Despite vocal backing from land reform campaigners the proposal, that was first mooted by the LRRG, was deemed incompetent and voted down despite Green and Labour support.

After Stage 3 amendments were completed the wrap up debate offered members a final chance to air their verdicts. Disappointment, approval and various degrees of approbation flowed across the chamber. The main protagonists had their say on aspects of the previous years of preparation and nine months of actual scrutiny of the Bill. Unfortunately, Dr Aileen McLeod was too ill to conclude her responses, so Paul Wheelhouse took over her role. But the final words went to Richard Lochhead, the Cabinet Secretary for RAE and the longest serving minister in that portfolio. He concluded:

> The Government will continue to do everything possible to support Scotland's land reform programme. The Parliament will continue to hold us to account to ensure that the Bill is as effective as we all want it to be.

> Like all legislation, however, the Bill can only ever provide the tools and mechanisms for democratic accountability. Ultimately, the Bill is about empowering communities and individuals to take control and giving them new opportunities to shape their future and their lives.

> Every time we debate land reform in the Parliament there is a sense of history. We can all be confident today that the Parliament is making history and building a better Scotland. I urge all members to support the Land Reform (Scotland) Bill this evening.

In the vote, Holyrood overwhelming passed the Land Reform (Scotland) Bill 102 votes to 14.[315] This passage provoked favourable com-

---

315. Scottish Parliament OR, Land Reform (Scotland) Bill Stage 3, 16 March 2016

ments from many commentators and campaigners. This was welcome reading to the MSPs and ministers closely involved. Of course, the Tories and landowning interests decried these radical measures. Here's a flavour of some views.

The Scottish Farmer reported on 17 March 2016:

> Now, 17 months and a whole lot of talking later, legislation that will enact that 'vision' – or at least, its supporters hope so – was voted into law by MSPs, with a margin of 102 to 14. Scottish Labour backed the SNP over the proposals, while the Conservatives voted against them.

It also reported that SLaE chairman David Johnstone declared that an 'incessant clamour for radicalism' from land reform activists had led to landowners' contribution to the countryside being ignored by lawmakers.[316]

Lesley Riddoch also summed up her views in *The National* on 17 March:

> So yes, the Land Reform Bill which passed its Stage 3 debate in Holyrood yesterday was feistier than the Scottish Government originally proposed, but less far-reaching than the Land Reform Review Group (LRRG) recommended back in 2014.[317]

Andy Wightman commented at length in the same issue of *The National*. He saw it as a historic step forward after what he said had been too long a hiatus:

> The commitment to establishing a Land Rights and Responsibilities Statement and a Scottish Land Commission

---

316. David Johnstone, *The Scottish Farmer*, 17 March 2016
317. Lesley Riddoch, 'Massively Rushed Land Reform Bill is Note Perfect – But It's a Good Start', *The National*, 17 March 2016, www.thenational.scot/news/14863166.lesley-riddoch-massively-rushed-land-reform-bill-is-not-perfect-but-its-a-good-start/

will do nothing directly to change the pattern of landownership. But it is an important move to ensure that land reform remains on the political agenda in future. This in itself may well turn out to be the most enduring legacy of the Bill.

Then he repeated his charge:

One of the reasons this legislation has taken so long to arrive is because the Scottish Government abandoned land reform in 2007 and didn't get going on the topic again until 2012. Land reform will not happen without sustained, determined and vigorous effort...

Other measures in the Bill, such as bringing shooting estates and deer forests back in to the non-domestic rating system are welcome, but only serve to highlight the fact that amendments to do the same for vacant and derelict land were defeated. Transparency has been one of the topics in the Bill that has attracted greatest public attention. Again, proposals to bar ownership of land by companies registered in British Overseas Territories and Crown Dependencies were defeated and, instead, regulations are to be introduced in the next parliament.

Tenant farmers emerge as one group who can sleep easier at night, thanks to a substantial strengthening of their rights and the Scottish Government is to be commended on the manner in which it stood up to sustained lobbying from landed interests. Smallholders, however remain the poor relation of the tenanted class, with none of the rights that have been granted to crofters and tenants since 1999.

Communities, too, have a new suite of rights to acquire land that they need for sustainable development.

Adding to a growing body of rights, the legislative land-scape is now rather complicated for voluntary community groups to navigate and ensuring that people have the knowledge and capacity to exercise these new rights remains a significant challenge.

Altogether, this is a historic piece of legislation.

Land reform is back and the opportunities and challenges for the next Parliament are to enact the voluminous secondary legislation to make the Bill work and to bring forward further reform on the wide range of land reform topics not captured in this Bill such as inheritance law land taxation, land information, housing, compulsory purchase and Crown land governance.

The level of engagement with the legislative process has been encouraging and MSPs such as Sarah Boyack, Patrick Harvie and Mike Russell [what about Graeme Dey?] have all worked hard to strengthen what started as a much-less-ambitious Bill. Land reform is a generational project.

Wightman had raised two cheers, concluding:

Much remains to be done over the next 20 years, but this is as good a start as could have been hoped for.[318]

Nicky (Lowden) MacCrimmon, who was thrust into the limelight of the SNP grassroots 'rebellion' at the 2015 SNP conference, told *The Guardian* on the night of Wednesday 16th March:

I'm pleased we are having this debate and welcome every

---

318. Andy Wightman, 'Historic Bill Will Keep Land Reform on Agenda, *The National*, 17 March 2016, www.thenational.scot/news/14863177. andy-wightman-historic-bill-will-keep-land-reform-on-agenda/

part of the Bill that is being passed and will eventually become the Act. I'm less pleased about what has not made it, particularly the amendment calling for a ban on land being owned by companies in tax havens.

What is doubly disappointing is that there may well be a very good reason that this amendment was not supported by the Scottish Government but as their legal advice is to remain private we have no way of having an informed debate on the topic.[319]

---

319. Libby Brooks, 'A New Dawn for Land Reform in Scotland', *The Guardian*, 17 March 2016, www.theguardian.com/uk-news/scotland-blog/2016/mar/17/a-new-dawn-for-land-reform-in-scotland

18. What did the Land Reform (Scotland) Bill 2016 do for us?

The people may not have lawyers, they do have a government.
 – Alastair McIntosh explaining the possibilities for the Ulva buyout, Bella Caledonia, November 2017

In the past you had no powers to do anything – now we can!
 – BBC Radio Scotland, Out of Doors, reporting the Ulva buyout June 2018

From my viewpoint, as RACCE convener, I have mulled over some of these responses. First, the praise for public pressure as the catalyst for a more radical Bill; second, the canard of land reform being abandoned by the SNP between 2007 and 2012; and third, another contention that the LRRG's final report in 2014 was a cast iron template from which the Scottish Government wilfully deviated. Specifically, the registration of landowners in the EU became a chosen option by the Greens and Labour for promoting transparency and dominated comment from the 'left'.

Repeated references to the 'rebellion' at the SNP conference in October 2015 as a game changer was cited as pushing the Scottish Government's Bill in a more radical direction. Where's the evidence? Coincidentally, there had been, until then, little recognition of the part played by MSPs, until a mention by prospective MSP, Andy Wightman after the Bill's conclusion. He noted that MSPs, particularly in the RACCE committee, working every day on the Bill, had explored ways to strengthen several key clauses such as transparency. Seen from the perspective of the RACCE committee, there was a deafening silence from any specific lobby by SNP members after the October 2015 're-bellion'. I've asked many colleagues if they were approached and have drawn a big blank. Did SNP delegates consider a vague call for more radicalism in conference debate to be enough of a signal to ministers?

Undoubtedly, the Cabinet had been shocked to see a land reform resolution remitted back by the conference; land reform is a touch-stone of the SNP's ethos. Starting in the 1940s examples of campaigns and policy documents testify to that, such as the SNP pamphlet on Knoydart (see illustrations) In 1974, the SNP Annual Conference called out 'the abuse of power by some landowners'. It went on to vote for a Land Commission with powers to identify land not being used or developed in ways most appropriate for the benefit of local communities or of the nation. They proposed that all such land should be subject to taxation to compel owners to comply with publicly agreed uses or convey the land to the nation at existing use value.[320] That was long before the SNP even dreamed of a real Scottish Parliament or forming a government. Also, it was long before the constraints of human rights laws meant a more cautious approach would be taken by successive Scottish governments.

Regarding the period of minority SNP Government from 2007 to 2011, the effects of the 2003 Acts were still bedding in and lottery funding for land purchase had come to an end in 2006. For example, Responsible Right of Access passed in 2003 only became active in 2005. Experience of how it would work was scanty but hopeful. The SNP Government, newly arrived in power, for the very first time, required great skills just to survive. Many tasks lay before it and land reform was part of a long list. The banking crash of 2008 had been a big hit on policy development, cutting budgets year on year, but the mess left by the Labour and Lib Dem coalition over crofting law reform required further action. Tweaks to make the Land Reform (Scotland) Act 2003 more workable, and a courageous thumbs up by Roseanna Cunning-hame to the Pairc buy out in the face of the ECHR threat, proved a breakthrough for the crofting RTB against an unwilling seller.

In the face of such evidence, Andy Wightman's impatience with the Scottish Parliament was an ingrained response of a single-issue campaigner. However, more positively, his painstaking research, extensive and sustained reviews of necessary policies required to achieve

---

320. SNP Annual Conference, resolution 29, 1 June 1974

thorough-going land reform were welcome. He and others have often listed the programmes they required to modernise Scotland land laws. But his polemic style takes no prisoners. From the claims made in his book, *The Poor Had No Lawyers*, all setbacks to progress, or alleged back-sliding were always decried in stinging terms.

In the summer of 2013, once the SNP had a majority in Holyrood, and behind the scenes in the second phase of the LRRG, Andy's close collaborator, Robin Callander, had a key role in steering the conclusions of the final report. There emerged the demand for landowners to be registered in the EU, and not in tax haven jurisdictions. What would it take for Andy Wightman to ever agree that his proposal would be found unworkable? As previously described, Global Witness, CLS, Graeme Dey MSP and then Minister Dr Aileen McLeod MSP all poured over several sources of legal advice that, at best, saw EU registration as beyond the powers of the Scottish Parliament but crucially that they were unworkable. Such was the apparently radical intent in EU transparency registration that Wightman's ally, Lesley Riddoch, continued to push it via Patrick Harvie's Green Party amendment in committee and chamber. Also, Nicky MacCrimmon, SNP land radical, believed Wightman was correct even on 16 March. This was despite the Official Report of the RACCE meeting which explored the issue in depth on 20 January 2016. Who with any interest had read and digested these debates?

Holyrood's politicians should be recognised for being as radical as was practical. Even so, debates will always rage as to what is radical in land reform terms. Constraints over legislative competence on these issues as well as the will of ministers to deliver their practical best for Scotland will be questioned, and rightly so.

Here's a pertinent and cautionary reminder. In 2014, ministers and RACCE had to correct the ECHR breach handed down by the Supreme Court following Ross Finnie's well-meaning moves at Stage 3 in the 2003 Agricultural Holdings Bill. He sought, at the time, a route to security and the end threats of eviction to hundreds of LPTs. If ever there was a douche of cold water on last-minute amendments, that was it. This has not stopped Andy Wightman declaring recently that we should not be scared to challenge ECHR, after all, Salvesen v Riddell was the only set-back so far. What I would say is, choose your ground to fight as an essential first step.

Who can forget the seven LPTs caught in the toils of the Supreme Court judgement. This provoked a 19,000-signature petition lodged at Holyrood on 10 November 2015, in the middle of RACCE deliberations on the contents of our Stage 1 Report.[321] Along with Sarah Boyack I accepted it from the protesters on behalf of the Parliament in an extremely heated atmosphere. Meanwhile, the stalemate had been prolonged by claims and counter claims in the Court of Session between aggrieved tenants and the Scottish Government. Richard Lochhead had offered mediation but was acutely aware that each case required different levels of compensation.

Altogether, it was an unholy mess, created by well-meaning decisions in 2003, made after the best legal advice at the time to protect hundreds of tenants under threat of eviction by landlords. Let's not forget that, much later, Lochhead tried, successfully, to ease the exit arrangements for tenant farmer Andrew Stoddart from Coulston Mains.

* * *

The parliamentary processes at Holyrood have always been based on Westminster practise. This process, for the Land Reform Act 2016, followed through from manifesto pledges to green paper, to white paper including a draft Bill with each stage widely consulted and finally to the Bill process itself which, in the Scottish Parliament, can and did take nine months.

I've discussed the rounds of evidence of hundreds of submissions at each stage where interested parties were keen to express their diverse views. It certainly suggests that a five-year parliamentary cycle was required for both the LRRG and AHLRG to reach their conclusions and the Bill to pick up what was deemed deliverable. Governments require time to digest and draw up credible draft Bills. The decision, in this case, to put land reform and agricultural holdings in the same Bill differed from the approach in 2003. During the process other

---

321. Stoddart petition lodged outside Holyrood, 10 November 2015

members may wish to put forward new clauses to add to the proposed Bill. This happened previously, and it did again with this Land Reform Bill.

Again, a cautionary note. I was taken to task, at a debate on crofting reform in Assynt in July 2018. It concerned the clauses passed in the 2010 Crofting (Scotland) Bill seeking five-yearly reports by grazings committees on the physical condition of their townships. Three related amendments at Stage 3 were proposed by Elaine Murray, John Scott and me were voted into the final Act. The lack of consultation with those affected, before being proposed, caused no end of anger about 'snooping on neighbours' and other criticisms by crofters. The new Crofting Commission consulted on a form of report but drew little comfort from responses received.

The catalyst had been a comprehensive township survey at Camus Croise in Skye. Its authors admitted that there had been opposition to the report's contents from some families in the township. Yet my intent was to see where 'abandoned and neglected' crofts were being made available to willing tenants. It was a lesson to me well-learned. You should take the people with you when you offer big changes as in the 2016 Land Reform Bill.

Iain MacKinnon from Coventry University, himself a native of Camus Croise, opposed the motion being proposed by Peter Peacock at the Scottish Crofting Federation sponsored debate. Peter favoured more radical action to effect much needed change. Iain argued that social justice cannot be forced, it must be discovered and nurtured. He ended his case with the slogan, land reform's role in supporting greater social justice in Scotland is, 'go slow, go further'.[322] Impatience with progress to date is obvious but the function of parliament is to reflect people's wishes and empower their lives. The balance must be carefully struck, as I can surely testify.

Another view of the parliamentary process is that propositions can be made by any party on a subject that is relevant. But should these be accepted by the governing party? Circumstances dictate the response and it signifies a system that isn't perfect; however, it does reach out to

322. *Am Bratach*, August 2018

many citizens. The 'mischief' of the Bill in question is confirmed by the Presiding Officer who agrees or disallows any late amendments.

* * *

The asks and expectations of the public on land law reform are less clear cut and more varied in detail than can be adequately addressed by the parliament in a five-year session. In our recent process the LRRG recommendations were the key database.

Taking the three-part grid proposed by Robin Callander in 1998, namely property law, administrative law, regulations and incentives, we can judge that a strong start has been made. Firstly, feudal abolition, increased rights for tenant farmers and community land ownership are in hand. Secondly, public bodies such as the Scottish Land Commission, the enhanced RoS and community empowerment structures are operative. Thirdly, the Land Rights and Responsibilities Statement was agreed and various aspects of Crown Estate property management are feeding funds into coastal communities. But much more is now needed for further reform.

I have made my own list of items from the LRRG final report that are still to be tackled. Briefly they include:

- Succession law;
- A register of ownerless land;
- Modernising CPO rules;
- Extending the State forests;
- A fuller development of community land rights;
- Meeting community acquisition costs;
- Focusing urban renewal on local government-led partnerships;
- Building new affordable housing with special focus on self-builds and remote rural needs;
- A comprehensive land use survey;
- Developing a National Land Policy;
- Scoping out a new law on maximum size for holdings;
- LVT;

- Giving crofting trusts rights buy at less than market price;
- RTB for small land holders;
- Statutory rights of access;
- Freshwater resources and management reform.[323]

As we all acknowledge there's plenty to do in the next 20 years.

Adapting land policy to modern conditions and pressures must be made to work in practice. Experience suggests we have a way to go in the delivery of policies through government agencies. Think on these: the Raasay Deer Lease issue; FES set to market forests such the one in Sutherland inadvertently included the protected site of the clearance village of Rossal in the forest sale document; SNH's prolonged and frustrating handling of tougher deer management rules; FES employment of land agents who have been private estate factors during divestment and leasing out of public land. Again, FES outsourcing legal work for land leasing and sales which is costly and time-consuming. I could go on. There are many necessary correctives to deliver 'joined-up' government. Since community empowerment is a key priority, delivering community proofing must be the guarantee of good practice.

Another critic, Gerry Hassan, assessed SNP Government land reform in his book, *Scotland the Brave?*, describing the SNP as having 'little appetite or feel for the subject'. He emphasised the rebellion at SNP conference in November 2015 claiming it 'defeated' the 'tepid' land reform proposals on offer in the Bill. The facts I've laid out refute this.[324]

Reflecting on the progressive land reform agenda in Scotland, two contrasting pictures from Norway and England emerged during the Land Reform Bill deliberations in 2015. *Northern Neighbours: Scotland and Norway since 1800* was compiled and edited before the outcome of the 2014 independence referendum by John Bryden, Ottar Brox and Lesley Riddoch. It surveyed many aspects of the divergent development

323. Rob Gibson, 'Community Proofing', *Bella Caledonia*, June 2018
324. Gerry Hassan, *Scotland the Brave?*, p.147

of the two northern European nations. It particularly explained how the franchise was obtained by many farmers after Danish control was removed from Norway in 1814. This progressively led to a deep-rooted democracy and state backing for land rights. By contrast, Scots gained only in small part 100 years later. The links to national democratic self-government built from scattered tiny communes along the vast Norwegian coast lies in stark contrast to Scotland's experience of early modern land grabs on a massive scale.[325]

In England, stirrings of interest about Scottish land reform prompted former *Guardian* journalist Peter Hetherington to write *Whose Land Is Our Land: The Use and Abuse of Britain's Forgotten Acres* for the Policy Press Insights series. He contrasts land reform proposals in Scotland and inaction in England, combined with searching interviews which included those with the Scottish Duke of Buccleuch and the English Duke of Northumberland who are cousins. Comparisons between Scots and English land questions offer a critical contrast. A worked-out manifesto published in 2019 by Guy Shrubsole builds on his painstaking work to find out who owns his native Berkshire. Thanks to the Labour Land Campaign launched in 2015 by John McDonnell MP, the secrecy of English and Welsh landownership, the extremely narrow rights to access open countryside, the need to tax landowners and free up land at lower prices for affordable housing have struck a chord. Both Hetherington and Shrubsole see aspects of the Scottish reforms as a guide to action down south. Jeremy Corbyn embraced a land reform policy in the hope that Labour could be elected in Westminster. Meanwhile, in Scotland, far higher expectations require an assessment of our progress.[326]

* * *

---

325. John Bryden, Ottar Brox and Lesley Riddoch (eds.), *Northern Neighbours: Scotland and Norway Since 1800*, Edinburgh University Press, 2015
326. Peter Hetherington, *Whose Land is Our Land? The Use and Abuse of Britain's Forgotten*, Policy Press, 2015; Guy Shrubsole, *Who Owns England: How We Lost Our Green and Pleasant Land, and How to Take it Back*, William Collins, 2019; Labour Land Campaign

I want, now, to look at the limits and opportunities of our land reform journey. Earlier in this book I pointed out how the powers of devolution constrain all matters related to company law and trusts which are reserved to Westminster. Of course, tax powers are far too limited to apply other than local tax charges which I hope will be the mode to introduce LVT. However, secondary legislation flowing from Land Reform (Scotland) Act 2016 is making good progress. The way in which the consultation on the Statement of Rights and Responsibilities brought many helpful suggestions showing that those who are interested continued to be engaged. The Scottish Land Commission has been very active. Its blogs and recommendations will inform new government action.

Among local authorities where the SNP leads, such as in Glasgow and Edinburgh, the thrust of urban land reform is promising a much more imaginative way to identify and release assets that have often been moribund. It is particularly gratifying to see Glasgow's first SNP-led Council taking very serious steps to identify and secure for use land on the banks of the Clyde to bring the heart of the city waterfront to life.

I discussed the potential of local activists who are busy identifying abandoned and neglected land in Springburn and Maryhill in anticipation of possible purchase for community uses. Again, it shows that it takes years for primary legislation to kick in and before any thorough assessment can be made of its benefits and pitfalls by government and public alike.

It reminds me that even in the city of my birth it will take not just direction from City Chambers but a real push for much more community democracy. The full benefits of land reform can raise confidence, improve the local environment, encourage new small enterprises and begin to build more social housing. Then urban dwellers can begin to emulate the repopulation, job diversification and clean energy projects of the best examples from our islands such as Eigg, Gigha, West and North Harris and Galson.

Back in 2003 in my first speech as MSP I argued for appropriate ways to build affordable and badly needed, rural housing. We are not there yet. In the RACCE Stage 1 Report we added a section on the subject. Ministers replied that housing policy and budgets were the appropriate vehicle, not land reform. In my final speech as MSP in March 2016 I continued to call for democratic local control as the way to finally solve the crucial housing deficit and control the uses of our land.

Motion debated: That the Parliament welcomes what it sees as the growing means to promote local control in communities through the Community Empowerment (Scotland) Act 2015 and various land reform measures to effect land purchase and access to natural resources; believes that this has been benchmarked in the recent Scottish Government report, Impact Evaluation of the Community Right to Buy; considers that the Scottish Government target of one million acres being in community control by 2020 is both achievable and necessary; notes the view that, the closer to communities the decision taking processes over matters such as affordable housing, environmental designations, cultural life and health provision are, the more there is a requirement for a fundamental review of local government and the powers to raise local taxes and to answer widespread and increasing calls for localism, including in Caithness, Sutherland and Ross, which has a land area that is equivalent to that of Northern Ireland, and further notes the view that subsidiarity, sustainability and social justice should be applied to all community life, the length and breadth of Scotland.

Rob Gibson (Caithness, Sutherland and Ross) (SNP): For my final speech as the member of the Scottish Parliament for Caithness, Sutherland and Ross since 2011, I will explore bringing more local control to the people whom I have had the immense privilege to represent. I will reflect on how the Highlands and Islands region, which I represented from 2003 to 2011, and my huge mainland constituency, which is the size of Northern Ireland, have suffered without enough say in their affairs. I hope that I will point out how decisions that affect local lives can be sustainable and socially just and how, by applying subsidiarity, all our communities around Scotland can, I believe, thrive.

First, I will recall some of the pressures that have shaken our land and shaken out its people. The so-called improvements by lairds in the early 19th century evicted the age-old, cattle-raising Gaelic communities from the most fertile land and brought in sheep farming, deer shooting and salmon angling for personal gain and the pleasure of the rich few. The results have been stark. Since around 1810, the exodus of surplus population to the industrial areas and to the ends of the earth has been augmented by losses in war after war, which has undoubtedly made the area clearances country.

I whole-heartedly welcome the Community Empowerment (Scotland) Act 2015, as it can pave the way to build on the Land Reform (Scotland) Act 2003, which has enabled 500,000 acres to come into community ownership. The cause has a long back story. Early protest against individual clearances led to the major victory of the 1880s in the crofters' war for secure rented tenure. In the 1920s, the Stornoway Trust gained local control, but it was the 1992 fight by the Assynt crofters in my constituency to win their land that ignited the modern debate.

Professor James Hunter talked of 'new lights shining in the glens' when the crofters won. In praise of their 20,000-acre purchase, my old friend the singer-songwriter Andy Mitchell told it like this:

> No love nor commitment those past lairds did display,
> A playground for the wealthy always was their way,
> This land they once stole from us, they've now been
>   forced to sell,
> Since we've paid for what we own we'll try to keep it well.

Our Scottish Parliament will leave its teenage years behind and reach adulthood before the 2021 election. As discussed in the strategy report on having one million acres under community control, there is a new mood of hope for more diverse land ownership that is ready to roll.

That opens wider questions about the democratic deficit in local government, as well as the need to build confidence and capacity and to use every possible resource to maintain and, we hope, repopulate more of our land beyond the crofting communities, create more smallholdings and create 1,000 huts and allotments across the land. We must apply human rights under the United Nations International Covenant on Economic, Social and Cultural Rights to ensure that local people have the right to decide how to provide affordable housing, safeguard their most cherished environmental features, supervise local health provision and develop a vibrant local cultural life.

When I was a district councillor in Ross and Cromarty from 1988 to 1996, our policy had to cope with a steep downturn in economic activity, such as the then oil slump. Ross and Cromarty District Council promoted quality of life at the core of its work. Fèis Rois and arts provision were created alongside environmental adaptation and modern affordable house building.

In 2010, as an MSP, I consulted on decentralising services in local government and argued that small works. Today, the urgent need to develop local control could not be clearer. Local management of the Crown Estate coastal funds is looming and strategic planning of considerable community benefit funds from renewables is urgently needed.

The need to break up Highland Council, which covers an area the size of Belgium, is widely discussed. How can 80 councillors meet local needs in an area of that size? Caithness has always wanted its council back and deserves to have it. Other areas should have that, too.

In Highland, the democratic deficit shows as one elected councillor per 4,000 voters. Germany has one to 500 and representatives have full planning and service powers in thousands of communes. In Scotland, we must gain the right for local communes around groups of secondary schools and their catchments to decide local taxes to meet local needs. That is urgent business because, as the Parliament grows up, so should local democracy.

On the environment, my constituency has been heavily subject to conservation by command. All manner of designations hamstring scattered communities. We have a quarter of the high-profile core wild land areas. Our hinterland is criss-crossed by restrictive designations. We need conservation by consent.

We are caught between the zealots of the John Muir Trust, who want no wind power and who fail to manage deer culls acceptably, and some retirees and the rich, who often object to renewables or other developments in sight of their properties. Dougie MacLean described the latter in his song *Homeland (Duthaich mo Chridhe)*:

> You sold your house in the city
> You put it on the market and you did so good
> Now you've bought a little piece of something
> That you don't understand, and you've misunderstood.

Despite the growing constraints, I have witnessed many leaders emerging over the years—even from the smallest communities – to make a difference. Open debate and the ability to spend taxes will bring out many more local voters if we have more local elections.

Those who have led communities to own their own land include the late Allan MacRae of Assynt; Maggie Fyffe in Eigg; Willie McSporran on Gigha; and the real David Cameron, of North Harris. They have made their own lands places of possibility, aided immeasurably by the late Simon Fraser of Carloway – at last, the poor had gained a lawyer.

I have so many folk in my constituency to thank for advice and support, including my staff over the years, two of whom are now members of Parliament. I thank my current staff: Niall MacDonald, Maureen Forbes and Councillor Gail Ross. They call me the moss boss—I will not explain why, but some members will know. My sincere thanks go to the clerks of the Rural Affairs, Climate Change and Environment Committee; the Scottish Parliament information centre; my MSP colleagues, not least the RACCE members; and most of all my family and my partner, Eleanor Scott, who is my rock.

We live in a better land thanks to the huge support for this Scottish Parliament, which will soon reach adulthood. I will be cheering it on in helping to make our land fit for a sustainable future.

A dozen miles from where I stay on Easter Ross, at Kildermorie, in the winter of 1921, Christopher Murray Grieve taught the children of the estate gamekeeper, whose then laird Dyson Perrins – of Worcester sauce fame – was philanthropic at least in the village of Alness near his private kingdom. Much later, Grieve, who was the founder of the Scottish literary renaissance, having adopted the nom de guerre Hugh

MacDiarmid, reflected in his long poem *Direadh III* on the act of surmounting difficulties. Thinking of the rugged Cuillins of Skye, he wrote:

> Let what can be shaken, be shaken,
> And the unshakeable remain.
> The Inaccessible Pinnacle is not inaccessible.

My case for deepening local decision taking is unshakeable and rests on the solid ground of an increasingly confident Scotland where full powers are not inaccessible.[327]

As it turned out my final MSP contribution was on the final day of sitting of Session 4 in the Scottish Parliament on 23 March 2016. This came with a supplementary question to the First Minister:

> *Rob Gibson (Caithness, Sutherland and Ross) (SNP):* Will the First Minister ensure that the current review of the Scottish planning system helps and does not hinder the much more diverse pattern of land ownership that will assuredly flow from the Community Empowerment (Scotland) Act 2015 and the Land Reform (Scotland) Bill?

> *The First Minister:* The Community Empowerment (Scotland) Act 2015 and the Land Reform (Scotland) Bill have increased opportunities for communities across Scotland to own land. The planning review is being undertaken by an independent panel, which will make recommendations in due course, and we will respond to the panel's recommendations when we have them. I assure members that land reform and community empowerment will be key drivers in any further planning reform that we undertake. The Scottish Government will continue to do all that we

---

327. Rob Gibson, Scottish Parliament OR, 22 March 2016

can to encourage and support responsible and diverse land ownership. We have a target of 1 million acres in community ownership by 2020.

It is appropriate that Rob Gibson's final question in this Parliament was on land reform, which is an issue that he has championed for decades. Our new Land Reform (Scotland) Bill is, in large part, testament to his campaigning. I thank him for his work and I think that he will be a great loss to this Parliament.[328]

Thus, lively debate flourishes today.

By increments we can see changes dawning and aspirations rising. To my mind the Land Reform Acts of the Scottish Parliament from its inception to the present show a continuity of self-belief tempered by the perennial, healthy trait of argumentative Scottish haggling over who has done what best. The evidence speaks volumes for concerted action. Land Reform Bills have been passed by overwhelming majorities from 2000 to 2016. Now community landowners are widely seen as a beacon of local self-government. Self-belief drives wider shared belief among many who call Scotland home. We seek a fairer, more sustainable nation. Both urban and rural land reform is a key component to reclaim our land and a permanent feature of our political discourse. The linkage with universal human rights has been most welcome and overdue step to challenge the entrenched power of the landowning elite. In future, Scotland will thank us for our efforts but keep demanding more land reform until our people enjoy a modern decentralised democracy with which the clear majority can be proud.

---

328. Rob Gibson, Scottish Parliament OR, 23 March 2016

19. Four years on

It has taken four years to put into law the details of the Community Empowerment and Land Reform Acts of 2015 and 2016. The final piece of secondary legislation to give communities the right to buy for sustainable economy development was passed in April 2020. The time taken for consultations and parliamentary scrutiny and has lasted a similar time span to the implementation of the 2003 Act. The latter received post-legislative scrutiny in 2010.

A commitment to a review of land reform had been included in the 2011 SNP manifesto. This led to the appointment of the Land Reform Review Group from 2012 to 2014 which offered a raft of proposals that would take many more than a five year of parliamentary time to enact. The SNP government in late 2014 consulted on as a draft Bill and the results were published in June 2015. Thereafter the three stages of parliamentary scrutiny were completed in March 2016.

Roseanna Cunningham, Cabinet Secretary for Environment, Climate Change and Land Reform from 2016 to 2021 has answered critics who say 'get it done quicker' to heed the processes that have taken ten years to reach this stage. There will follow a period of bedding in and assessment of the complex steps taken forward as the laws are put into practice. Institutional changes have been set in place. The Statement of Land Rights and Responsibilities and the creation of the Scottish Land Commission (SLC), chaired by Andrew Thin, have each produced three years of positive guidance, research, and proposals for the next government to make into law post May 2021.

The SLC aims in their three-year plan, *Making More of Scotland's Land - Our Progress So Far* were assessed in September 2020. They were to investigate land for housing and development; modernising land ownership; land use decision-making; and agricultural holdings. Their impressive work rate was guided by three strategic objectives: productivity, diversity, and accountability.[329] This embeds SLC to advise government and places land reform on the agenda as never before.

We can probe the SLC activities by recalling the big asks by respondents to the Scottish Government consultation on the Land Reform Bill in late 2014 and early 2015; they were diversity, transparency and supportive land tax.

Diversity was promoted in part by community land purchases that were mostly aided by the Scottish Land Fund. This continues apace. Five hundred and ninety assets were in community hands as of December 2019, an increase of twenty-eight since the previous year. Four hundred and eighteen groups owned these assets which amounted to 191,290 hectares.[330]

Three times as much land is owned by communities compared to 2000AD. Recently, the size of purchases has dropped to include more buildings and their grounds. The target of one million acres set in 2012 by Alex Salmond has changed. It was unlikely to repeat the huge land areas transferred in the Western Isles and Highland.

Since 2016 three areas in south Scotland came into play. The land purchase of the moor at Newcastleton, the Wanlockhead bid and the Langholm Moor bid. All evolved due to the huge Buccleuch Estates shedding land surplus to their business plans.[331]

An outstanding case, the imminent sale of the island of Ulva, a hundred metres off the coast of Mull, prompted an emergency bid lodged in 2017 as the last resident of the Howard family who owned the island since the 1940s sought to sell. The bid was led by the North West

---

329. https://landcommission.gov.scot/downloads/5f5a028e118e2_2017-20%20Summary%20Our%20Progress%20So%20Far.pdf

330. https://www.gov.scot/publications/community-ownership-scotland-2019/

331. https://www.itv.com/news/border/2020-09-15/newcastleton-secures-milestone-community-buyout-from-buccleuch

Mull Community Woodland Company and like a latter-day Assynt attracted widespread publicity, support and some criticism.

First Minister, Nicola Sturgeon, announced at the SNP autumn conference in 2017 that the bid was receiving favourable treatment to much applause from delegates. Mr Howard, the owner, described the bid as a political stunt as the valuation was below his asking price. In the event, a sale backed by the Scottish Land Fund for £4.4 million was agreed and the handover effected in June 2018.

This purchase drew two strands of comment. Firstly, could the resident population of Ulva of five people justify this public investment of 95% of the purchase price? Secondly, should the public purse continue to line the pockets of private sellers to such large sums?

Eighteen months on, hundreds applied to live and work on the island in answer to a survey. Development of the housing potential, restoring and revisioning Ulva House and other sustainable economic proposals for the island have been approved by Argyll & Bute Council and other agencies.[332] Ulva is larger than community-owned Gigha but a little smaller than community-owned Eigg. These two are thriving and re-populating successfully. Ulva's topography is similar to that of Eigg but its east coast closest to mainland Mull is more sheltered from Atlantic storms than either Gigha or Eigg.

Transparency on Scottish land ownership moves too slowly. As I write in November 2020 around 42% of Scotland is now contained in the map register, the majority still in written form in the venerable Register of Sasines. 5 Most public land is now map registered while large estates, which have often remained in the same ownership for centuries, are not. Other registers such as that containing those with a controlling interest in land gather pace. Like many other countries the rate of modern registration takes far longer than most of us would wish. The considerable staff and cash resources required for registration were stretched before and added to during the covid-19 lockdown. The cost of map registration for private owners who may be land rich but cash poor is an issue. House sales trigger map registration but cover small plots in the total.

---

332. https://portal360.argyll-bute.gov.uk/civica/Resource/Civica/Handler.ashx/Doc/pagestream?cd=inline&pdf=true&docno=22239323

As to a 'supportive land tax', this has been studied in-depth by SLC. Its report in December 2018 used consultants to scope international evidence of the application of land value tax (LVT). SLC offers strong support for LVT to deliver Scotland's land reform objectives. It also indicates a range of practical issues that require resolution before a land tax is introduced such as, the role of the planning system, the land register and coordination with existing land and property taxes so as to avoid clashes with 'development viability and wider public policy goals'.[333]

A Scottish Government initiative to take early legislative steps to introduce LVT would be a bold signal of change. This could be done by making existing policy structures LVT ready and completing the land register quickly by enhanced procedures and inducements.

Ironically, the return of shooting rates to deer and grouse businesses saw the vast majority of shooting estates claiming small business bonus, successfully, to defray these non-domestic rates. From the income collected, however, over £2m was added to the Scottish Land Fund coffers.[334] I question how billionaire landowners can classify shooting businesses to meet the income criteria for rebates. This requires early attention.

Turning to the role of the Tenant Farming Commissioner (TFC), his work covers many strands of farming life. Various codes of practice have encouraged tenants, landlords and land agents into dialogue and compromise. Guidance on a range of practical matter has helped the parties concerned reach more beneficial decisions. Mediation to help resolve longstanding disputes and building confidence to use alternative dispute resolution has begun to steer tenants and landlords away from the Land Court and appeals in the expensive civil courts route.

An example of the TFC's work gave David and Allison Telfer, whose lease terminated in February 2018, use of the low ground on their shared partnership holding till November 2019 giving them time to arrange their affairs before Buccleuch estates sold their farm as part of a £19m

333. https://landcommission.gov.scot/news-events/news-blog/
report-examines-merits-of-land-value-tax-in-scotland
334. https://theferret.scot/9-of-10-shooting-properties-exempt-business-rates/

portfolio of land in the area to inflate Buccleuch estate income. The TFC Bob McIntosh helped broker a deal after 10,000 signed a petition supporting the Telfer family.[335]

One of the biggest bugbears of MSPs during the parliamentary stages of the 2016 Bill was the behaviour of land agents. RACCE wanted a statutory code of conduct. Since then the TFC has surveyed the operation of land agents involved in tenant farming matters and made recommendations to Ministers after consulting professional bodies. Guidance in professional standard and associated complaints system has resulted. Its effectiveness will be judged and reviewed in the coming SLC three-year plan.

Lord Gill spoke in March 2019 of his view that Section 10 failed to deal with a modern adaptation of farm tenancy law in the 2016 Act. Addressing the Scottish Agricultural Arbiters and Valuers Association's AGM, he called for a full review of the legislation. He acknowledged that Government and MSPs had recognised the cause of attrition in the sector but had dealt with the effects rather than the root causes.[336]

We should recall that Lord Gill's Court of Session judgement in 2011 in the Salvesen v Riddell case invoked ECHR on behalf of the landlord and set MSPs and the Scottish Government huge problems from the fallout over shared partnership tenancies which had produced a spate of writs of eviction in 2002. Gill's call for an investigation of alternatives to traditional tenancies suggests that he sees landlord and tenant relations improving by embracing contract and share farming agreements.[337] These entrench the landowner's powers.

Private landed rights as presently understood are far from progressive. Any further dilution of tenant rights would put more pressure on the farm partner not the landowning partner. Such matters will no doubt exercise the Tenant Farming Commissioner. His land matching

---

335. https://www.snpdumfries.org/
buccleuch-put-on-notice-at-snp-conference/2018-10/

336. https://www.fwi.co.uk/business/business-management/tenancies-rents/
scottish-tenant-eviction-battle-resolved

337. https://www.thecourier.co.uk/fp/business/farming/farming-news/848628/
law-lord-calls-for-review-of-2016-land-reform-act/

services seeking new entrant farmers and tenants' amnesties for agreeing improvements to their holdings address daily aggravations in the sector.

To tackle the extreme concentration of land ownership in Scotland, the SLC has identified three areas for legislation: a public interest test for significant land transfers, a requirement for land management plans for each large holding, and weighing these against the statutory Land Rights and Responsibilities Review. As yet there is no example of take up arising from the final piece of secondary legislation that became active in April 2020 which defines the legal route to transfer land for acute community needs.

Detailed work has been undertaken by Land Commissioners to normalise community ownership so as to become routinely and proactively planned-for. Scoping urban land reform via the neglected and abandoned land powers has triggered some early examples. Portobello and Kinning Park are in the lead.

Community Land Scotland, the lobby voice of the movement celebrated its 10th birthday in September 2020. It has guided a growing band of community groups to have their cases heard and their ideas shared in the debates on land ownership and use. They have successfully gained the ear of agencies, MSPs and government. They are invited to give evidence in the Parliament's committees and offer a running commentary on the progress of this sector. Its members are managing some 560,000 acres of land, home to some 25,000 people.[338]

Housing is still the most pressing aspect of land use, whether in remote scattered communities or in cities. The delivery of housing by the Scottish Government is under fire. Efforts since devolution in 1999 to deliver affordable, secure homes have fallen short of demand. Looked at in 2020 we can see flaws and successes. We see a commitment to end homelessness. We note the massive retrofit programme of insulation slowly progressed. We see acute problems stemming from depopulation in remote rural and island communities as in old industrial areas especially on the west coast. Covid-19 has pinpointed new pressures. The flight from inner cities to seek houses where home working can become the norm puts price pressures on desirable areas.

338. https://www.communitylandscotland.org.uk/

Young people are being priced out of the market in communities where they grew up or wish to live and work.

A snapshot of the current housing achievements since 2007 when the SNP took charge was offered by Housing Minister Kevin Stewart in response to a particular rural housing shortfall. However, it indicates the general trend.

> We recognise that good-quality, affordable housing is essential to help attract and retain people in Scotland's rural and island communities.
>
> The Rural and Islands Housing Funds were introduced to complement our Affordable Housing Supply Programme, which is delivering the majority of housing projects for rent or purchase in rural and island areas.
>
> Latest Scottish Government quarterly affordable housing supply statistics show that since the beginning of this parliamentary period we have delivered 34,791 affordable homes, over 23,000 of which were for social rent.
>
> These are part of the over 95,000 affordable homes delivered since 2007, over 66,000 of which were for social rent.
>
> Of these, more than 4,800 homes were delivered in rural and island locations. This includes the 68 homes delivered through the Rural and Islands Housing Funds, which form part of the wider Affordable Housing Supply Programme.
>
> We are also working to ensure those who aspire to home ownership are able to achieve it, with over 35,000 households supported by our existing shared equity schemes since 2007.[339]

---

339. https://www.thecourier.co.uk/fp/news/politics/scottish-politics/1547932/talking-big-but-failing-to-deliver-rural-housing-schemes-produce-just-68-homes-in-four-years/

Before I retired from Holyrood, I helped scrutiny of the Land Reform Scotland Bill in 2015/6. Our RACCE committee raised unanimous concerns in our Stage One report in December 2015 on affordable homes (see paragraphs 565 to 575). The Rural Housing Fund was the ministerial response.

In May 2018 on a visit to Mull, Iona and Ulva I held discussions with community activists there which centred on the difficulty of delivering community empowerment in both local clean energy production and housing.[340] These matters were strongly reinforced by research and policy development spearheaded by SLC and captured in their commissioned research in 2020 by land agents, Savills.[341]

The report sums up many of the means to coordinate delivery. Building affordable homes in scattered communities has been expensive and too slow. Clearly because targets are often set on high, the advice, support and preparatory work needed takes much longer to put in place than expected. To make projects shovel-ready to meet the demand in places people wish to live is clearly a work in progress.

While Savills saw 'land availability as just one of many pieces in a complex jigsaw' this gets to the heart of urban and rural delivery. It is widely recognised that volume house builders are not a solution for small communities. But the land banking activities of 'land promoters' is a major clue to the prominence of private housing provision that dominates the market. The Scottish Rural University College (SRUC) has assessed international initiatives to ensure repopulation go hand in hand with thorough analysis of more integrated housing policies when seen as a system.[342]

Ultimately, the story of land reform is a long march. Too lengthy for some. But in practice more focused research, analysis and proposals has been delivered to ministers than ever before. These must always

---

340. https://bellacaledonia.org.uk/2018/06/14/
community-proofing-land-reform/
341. https://landcommission.gov.scot/news-events/news-blog/
new-approach-needed-to-deliver-houses-for-rural-scotland
342. https://www.sruc.ac.uk/news/article/2698/
integrated_approach_to_repopulating_remote_areas

be set against Robin Callander's assessment of the components of land reform from his book *How Scotland is Owned*. Published in 1998, it delineates property law, administrative law and regulations and incentives.[343]

At the time I was drawing these conclusions on the priorities for land reform today, I read in a new book *Scoraig* by James MacGregor a history of the Wester Ross peninsula till 1963 when the last native crofters left the land. There are many reasons why they abandoned generations of life there. These include the crofting laws and prevailing view that such places should be allowed to depopulate. But an interesting shaft from 1948 was the attempt by members of Clann Albainn society to occupy derelict and abandoned croft land. This was unsuccessful, not because potential settlers lacked determination but because the sympathetic landlord was fearful that he might be due compensation payments to new tenants for their improvements to their holdings. Such had been decreed by the Land Court when an absentee crofter decided to claim his rights. Fewer worked crofts had allowed those still active to graze more unused croft land. Would-be settlers would disturb this loose arrangement. Additionally Clann members gave aid to the Knoydart land raiders at that time.[344]

As ever, the fundamentals of Scottish land ownership and its peculiarly concentrated pattern under our property law must be challenged by meaningful reform. This could be potentially costly and controversial in cash and legal terms, yet human rights, defined on United Nations covenants, could be the catalyst. A route map is on the table thanks to the Scottish Land Commission and to Scottish voters' stated demands.

I believe that we are closer to reclaiming our land than ever before. Political will based on a wide consensus for change is now in play.

– *Rob Gibson October 2020*

---

343. Callander, *How Scotland is Owned*, p 19
344. J MacGregor, *Scoraig, a peninsula and its people*, JRM Publishing, 2020

List of abbreviations

AHLRG	Agriculture Holdings Legislative Review Group
DMG	Deer Management Group
DMP	Deer Management Plan
ECHR	European Charter of Human Rights
HIE	Highlands & Islands Enterprise
ICESCR	International Covenant on Economic, Social and Cultural Rights
Lib Dem	Liberal Democratic Party
LRPG	Land Reform Policy Group 1998
LRRG	Land Reform Review Group 2012
NFUS	National Farmers Union Scotland
NNR	National Nature Reserve
RACCE	Rural Affairs, Climate Change & Environment Committee 2011–16
RAE	Rural Affairs and Environment Committee 2007–11
RICS	Royal Chartered Institute of Surveyors
SAc	Scottish Affairs committee

SAC	Special Area of Conservation
SLaE	Scottish Land & Estates
SNH	Scottish Natural Heritage
SNP	Scottish National Party
SSI	Scottish Statutory Instrument
SSSI	Site of Special Scientific Interest
STFA	Scottish Tenant Farming Association
UNCESCR	UN Convention on Economic, Social and Cultural Rights
VGGT	UN Voluntary Guidelines on the Responsible Governance of Tenure of Land, Forests and Fisheries
VGRGTLFF	UN Food & Agriculture Organisation's Voluntary Guidelines on Responsible Governance of Tenure of Land, Forests and Fisheries

Index

Lightning Source UK Ltd.
Milton Keynes UK
UKHW020058311220
375870UK00005B/37